Contents

Understanding Mentally Disordered Offenders

A multi-agency perspective

ANTHONY COLOMBO
Institute of Criminology
University of Cambridge

Ashgate

Aldershot • Brookfied USA • Singapore • Sydney

Published by
Ashgate Publishing Ltd
Gower House
Croft Road
Aldershot
Hants GU11 3HR
England

Ashgate Publishing Company
Old Post Road
Brookfield
Vermont 05036
USA

British Library Cataloguing in Publication Data

Colombo, Anthony
    Understanding mentally disordered offenders : a
    multi-agency perspective
    1. Criminals - Mental health 2. Insane, Criminal and
    dangerous 3. Criminal psychology
    I. Title
    364.3'8

Library of Congress Catalog Card Number: 97-72079

ISBN 1 85972 689 5

Printed and bound by Athenaeum Press, Ltd.,
Gateshead, Tyne & Wear.

Tables and figures

Preface

The purpose of this study is to understand and clarify the nature of implicit theories currently held about distinct types of psychopathological and criminal behaviour by respondents who represent a range of agencies: the general lay population (students and politicians), Criminal Justice (police), Mental Health (mental health practitioners) and Social Services (social workers and probation officers).

The study is in the form of a factorial experimental survey design employing the mail questionnaire data gathering technique. Semi-structured interviews were also carried out in order to provide supplementary qualitative data.

Of the four case vignettes used in the experimental design, two described the key symptomalogical behaviour underlying the condition of paranoid schizophrenia and two referred to the behavioural symptoms commonly associated with depressive psychosis. Each of these vignettes were further manipulated through the inclusion or otherwise of a criminal offence condition. The survey's measuring instrument, which was answered after reading a single case vignette, examined the three main scientific theories used to explain various psychopathological states (medical (organic), moral (cognitive-behavioural) and psychosocial) along several dimensions (aetiology, behaviour, treatment, function of the hospital, prognosis, rights and duties of both the patient and society) and was constructed specifically for the study.

Factor analysis, performed on the questionnaire data obtained from the overall sample of 961 respondents, revealed three underlying principal components: 'sick' role, medical-control and social-treatment. Using these implicit paradigms as a baseline, a multi-way analysis of variance demonstrated highly significant differences ($p<0.01$) in perception across the study's main treatment (type of mental disorder, type of criminal offence) and socio-demographic variables (age, gender, group surveyed and previous experience of the mentally ill).

The results are discussed in terms of each multi-agency group's approach towards the various treatment conditions as well as the theoretical and practical implications these findings may have at both a criminological and clinical level. Directions for future research are also considered.

The success of this research depended a great deal on the co-operation and help of several organisations and individuals. In particular, I would like to thank the Cambridgeshire Police Constabulary, Cambridgeshire Probation Service, Addenbrooke's NHS Trust and Peterborough District Hospital. Within these organisations, special thanks should go to Chief Inspector Terry Early and Sergeant Andy Gallichan (Police Constabulary, Parkside Division); Andy Smith and Mark Richards (Cambridge Probation Service); Graham Badger (Health Team Area Manager, Addenbrooke's NHS Trust) and Laurie Fentimen (Health Team Area Manager, Peterborough District Hospital); Linda Davies, Mary Coburn, Paul Smartt, Bennie Darky and Mary Donoghue (Clinical Staff Line Managers at Addenbrooke's District and Fulbourn Psychiatric Hospitals), and Maureen Fry (Secretary at the Department of Forensic Psychiatry, Addenbrooke's Hospital).

With regard to the production of the actual book, I would like to thank Dr. Adrian Grounds (Honorary Consultant in Forensic Psychiatry) who, despite heavy work commitments, found the time to offer many helpful suggestions throughout the course of this research; Dr. Trevor Bennett and Dr. Jackie Scott, for listening to my ideas on how to structure and make sense of both the methodological and data analyses, and for offering helpful advice on possible approaches.

I would also like to place on record a very special debt of gratitude to Tisha Hugg whose administrative skills and general help were invaluable all the way through the production of this book. Finally, a big thanks to my wife Jitka for her constant help and support.

Introduction

Lay and scientific theories

In an attempt to make sense of the social and physical world around us, so that it appears relatively stable, orderly, understandable and safe, people tend to develop theories or common sense explanations for phenomena salient to the society in which they live (Lerner, 1980). Very little is currently known about the origin of these lay theories - or belief systems - though it has been suggested that they develop through particular socialisation experiences such as observation, specific encounters or the acceptance of information from authoritative or persuasive others such as the mass media (Stacey, 1985, 1978; Sarbin et al, 1960). The function or purpose of these common sense theories is probably to make it possible for individuals to establish cause and effect relationships between phenomena, which in turn allows for the logical interpretation of events in terms of apportioning blame, praise or responsibility (Lerner, 1980; Gans, 1972).

These lay theories are often different from the sort of theories one is likely to find within academic disciplines such as the physical or social sciences, partly because they fulfil different functions. It is argued that academics such as social scientists hold particular patterns of beliefs for simply rational, dispassionate and objective reasons, their theories existing simply for the purpose of logically explaining particular behavioural phenomena such as the causes of delinquency, poverty, mental illness, etc. In these terms, lay theories appear to primarily serve a psychologically based function while scientific theories seem to have a more logical purpose (Furnham, 1988).

In fact, according to Valentine (1982) there exist a number of criteria along which the nature of lay and scientific theories may differ. The most prominent differences apparently being that scientific - or academic theories - are often formally expressed in a logical, internally coherent and consistent manner while, in contrast, common sense theories consist largely of belief systems that are often implicit and seldom formal, therefore, frequently ambiguous, incoherent and contradictory.

Of course, one could quite reasonably argue that this distinction between lay and scientific theories is by no means clear. For example, several authors have observed that many so called scientific theories do not satisfy Valentine's criteria, while many lay theories do (Chalmers, 1986; Jaspars, 1983). Furthermore, there are enormous individual differences in both the quality and quantity of theories people hold. A person may be a 'scientist' with regard to a theory relating to one particular issue but have a 'lay person's' beliefs about certain other matters. "Thus, one may be at once both naïve and sophisticated, complex and simple" (Furnham, 1988:20).

An unusual advantage available to many of the social science disciplines such as sociology, psychology and criminology is that they are able to offer an "explicit, formal, scientific explanation for certain behavioural phenomena" as well as an interest in the study of a person's personal "implicit, informal, non-scientific explanations" (Furnham, 1988:1) for that particular behaviour. This unique fact implies that it must, therefore, be possible to conduct research into the similarities and differences between both common sense and scientific theories as they relate to a particular issue of concern to social scientists, for example, the mentally ill.

Aims of the current research

The aim of this research is to try and utilise this particular advantage available to the social scientist in an attempt to answer certain criminological and clinical questions about persons whose behaviour is psychopathologically and criminally deviant in accordance with the social arrangements of our society.

Our intention is to obtain, understand and clarify common sense theories currently held about the mentally ill by professionals who work within the Criminal Justice, Mental Health and Social Services. In addition, there are compelling reasons why we must consider the views of the public, and so various segments of the general population shall also be included in the research.

These common sense, informal, non-scientific theories will be investigated by measuring to what extent each of the various multi-agency groups involved in the study is willing to accept/agree with the three most prominent scientific theories currently put forward to try and explain various psychopathological disorders, namely, the medical (organic), moral (cognitive-behavioural)[1] and psychosocial models.

A terminological note

Terminology is often the cause of many difficulties and this is especially so in the case of imperfectly understood areas such as beliefs about mental illness where there is often little or no agreement about basic terms. For this reason, it is necessary at the outset to pay some attention to the interpretation of certain concepts.

During the course of our everyday lives we are constantly, although most probably unwittingly, making distinctions between our opinions, feelings, attitudes and beliefs about a particular phenomena. For example, in one instant we may offer an opinion, 'I think it is going to rain' and in the next breath present an attitude, 'I hate it when it rains'. Yet, despite these apparently different conceptualisations, social scientists have found it extraordinarily difficult to pin down in clear and precise terms an exact taxonomy of these cognitive states. As a result, theories on the inter-relationship between such terms and on their association with actual behaviour are often diverse, in some cases incredibly complex and rarely, if ever, universally acceptable. It is not surprising, therefore, that most research intent on measuring attitudes either makes no comment on the issue or side steps the problem altogether with generalist statements such as "the terms 'attitude', 'opinion', and 'belief' are not well differentiated from one another" (Sudman and Bradburn, 1983:120).

As a result of these difficulties the terms 'attitude' and 'belief' have been used interchangeably throughout the first part of the literature review. However, in an attempt to overcome these limitations, a clear and specific approach will be adopted during the course of critically discussing the relationship between such concepts and actual behaviour. More specifically, we will explain that the central concept to be examined is 'beliefs' and that this concept will be defined in accordance with the specific theoretical approach offered by Farina and Fisher (1982).

Throughout this research a number of terms have been used rather generally and, frequently, interchangeably in order to discuss both 'non-scientific' and 'scientific' theories. With regard to the former position alternative terms including 'beliefs', 'belief systems' and 'non-scientific theories' have been employed. While the latter approach has been referred to through the use of terms such as 'scientific theory', 'academic theory', 'model', 'paradigm' and 'ideal type'. This difficulty over terminology has arisen largely due to the problem of trying to conceptualise exactly what constitutes a theory.

Attempts to clarify the nature of a truly scientific theory have been made on numerous occasions (Eysenck, 1981; Kuhn, 1970; Hull, 1943). Unfortunately, no satisfactory consensus has been arrived at and so epistemological terms such as model, paradigm and theory continue to be used interchangeably in order to represent whatever conceptual matter a particular author is trying to explain.

Thus for the purposes of the current research labels such as scientific and academic will be used as a prefix to the conceptual terms: theory, model and paradigm in order to represent the three working conceptualisations - medical (organic), moral (cognitive-behavioural) and psychosocial - which formally, logically and coherently try to explain the nature of psychopathological behaviour.

A variety of conceptual problems have also arisen with regard to lay theories. According to several authors the concepts used by lay people in order to make sense of an observation do not contain the properties of consistency, stability or rationality implicitly required by the term 'theory'. In particular, Fitzpatrick (1984) has objected to the term lay theory in preference for lay beliefs arguing that most people obtain their information from a variety of disparate sources, which results in a set of beliefs which are often highly idiosyncratic in nature. Norman (1980), however, considers the term belief system to be more accurately able to define lay views as it identifies both a knowledge component and the influence of cognitive states such as memory and perception. Thus for Norman (1980) the term system implies the integration of both beliefs and attitudes.

Again, in the absence of any clear academic distinctions about the nature of lay theories several terms will be applied generically throughout this research. In terms of content, these labels will represent isolated groups of beliefs. Thus phrases such as lay, non-scientific and multi-agency will prefix concepts such as belief, belief system and theory when referring to the informal, implicit and potentially incoherent set of beliefs (as defined earlier) held by both public and professional groups about the nature of psychopathological behaviour.

The term 'mental illness' is also often open to question and some would go so far as to suggest that it is a myth (Szasz, 1985, 1961). In general, those authors who oppose the organic model would argue that the use of any other synonym such as mental disorder and psychiatric disturbance are equally objectionable on the grounds that they, too, imply that the mind can be ill or diseased. A further problem that arises through the use of such labels is the implicit assumption that mental illness exists as a single uniform category or phenomena.

Probably no author is ever entirely satisfied with these terms, they continue to be used, all-be-it hesitantly, simply because no other appears to be more acceptable or convenient in the circumstances. Thus as one term is as bad or as good as another (depending on the author's perspective) they will be collectively used throughout this research. Unfortunately, this is as much as can be expected as the difficulties are inherent in the nature of the subject itself (Bean, 1985:XVI).

One particular term that is prominently used throughout this book is that of psychopathology. Of course, linguistically, the term still expresses the dominance of the medical paradigm and all that it implies, however, conceptually, phrases such as psychopathological behaviour seem to be marginally better at denoting the existence of more than one type of mental illness. This suggestion is probably implicitly derived from the fact that the term 'psychopathology' refers to the scientific study, in terms of cause and nature, of all psychiatric conditions (Reber, 1987).

Finally, definitions of the 'mentally ill offender' are even more complex and encompass many legal and clinical criteria (Nuehring and Raybin, 1986). For present purposes, generic terms such as the 'mentally ill offender' will refer to those persons who (1) have committed a criminal offence that has led to their arrest or detainment by the criminal justice authorities, and (2) are suspected of having a mental disorder of such severity as to question the equitableness of subjecting them to the criminal justice system.

Rationale

Initiatives within the field of mental health are presently affording increased prominence to programmes directed at deinstitutionalising the mentally ill in favour of establishing community based psychiatric care (Thompson, 1994; Pilgrim and Rogers, 1993). Alongside this process has been the emergence of a policy orientated towards diverting mentally ill offenders away from the criminal justice system and into care by health and social services (Home Office, 1990).

However, both politically and professionally it has been expressly stated that the implementation of such policies and the effective utilisation of scarce resources will only succeed through the development of satisfactory working relationships based upon the qualities of understanding and communication among the key agencies identified with these minorities, namely, the Criminal Justice, Mental Health and Social Services (Taylor and Taylor, 1989).

More recently, it has been recognised that in order for this high degree of inter-agency co-operation to exist in a functionally meaningful way, the individual professional groups within each respective agency must be able to identify with one another in terms of their beliefs, evaluations and actions. They should all have similar views in order to promote consistency of purpose (Department of Health/Home Office, 1992; Home Office, 1990).

Despite these requirements, no systematic research has been conducted which attempts to measure the extent to which this consensus between the various professions exists. Furthermore, in a pluralistic society such as ours it is very doubtful that all types of psychopathologically and criminally deviant behaviour will be viewed in the same way.

Thus, the primary significance of the current research is that it attempts to comprehensively address these and other concerns through the use of a sophisticated experimental survey approach, designed to simultaneously deal with a wide range of propositions.

On a more practical level, it is hoped that the research findings will contribute significantly towards elucidating some of the conflicting assumptions that generate misunderstandings between agency professionals, which in turn may provide us with a more realistic insight into a wide range of problems associated with managing both the mentally ill and mentally ill offenders.

Finally, the amount of recent academic research in the important area of mentally ill offenders is very limited and out of proportion to the degree of social and political attention the matter has received during the last decade or so (Watson and Grounds, 1993). Thus in conclusion, this current research takes an initiative in an area otherwise overlooked.

Note

1 Here the traditional moral model has been redefined so as to include the more contemporary practices associated with both behavioural and cognitive psychology. The nature of this paradigm will be discussed in detail later (see Chapter One, 'Models of mental illness').

1 A review of the literature

Introduction

Since the late 1940s, when the first attitudinal studies were designed, popular conceptions of mental illness have become a subject of great concern and research effort (Bhugra, 1989). In North America, Canada and to a more modest extent Britain a voluminous literature has appeared, scattered among a variety of different journals and which includes material from such wide-ranging sources as anthropology (Westbrook et al, 1993; Haldipur, 1984), history (Prins, 1984; Kroll and Backrach, 1982), sociology (Scheff, 1966), psychiatry (Szasz, 1985, 1961) and social-psychology (Furnham and Bower, 1992).

The central focus of this chapter will be directed towards reviewing this wealth of literature within the context of a fairly narrow framework. Thus no attempt has been made to cite every study or to deal with broader issues such as historiographical and anthropological accounts of attitudinal differentiation and change, nor will any attempt be made to review and unravel the chains of controversy surrounding the labelling perspective's qualitative analysis of popular reaction towards the mentally ill.[1]

Instead, attention will be directed towards a review of those studies which have been specifically concerned with the delineation of attitudes held by the public, various professional groups and the socio-demographic characteristics of respondents which are understood to influence attitudinal variation.[2] Furthermore, within the context of these studies, a broad overview of the attitude 'object' will be taken, focusing on opinion towards the mental patient and the former mental patient, mental health facilities, the mentally ill offender and for completeness the normal offender. It should perhaps also be pointed out that as many of the major studies in this area were conducted during the 1950s, the literature to be reviewed will span a period covering more than four decades. The selection of such a broad time parameter may further be justified on the grounds that reference to such a continuity of findings will enable us to highlight and discuss the progressive development of a number of key themes at both an ideological and methodological level which are vital to our understanding of the nature and purpose of the current research.

Having outlined the basic parameters of the literature review, it remains to describe how this chapter will be organised. The aim of section one will be to review the most commonly cited studies which have examined public attitudes towards the mentally ill. In particular, we will focus on the debate in the literature surrounding the ideological controversy between the protagonists of the social deviance paradigm and those who support a more medically orientated approach towards the mentally disordered.

In section two we will review the literature which has been concerned with certain professional groups. The professions that will be considered span three major service systems: Criminal Justice, Social Welfare and Mental Health Services. In general, the volume of research in this area appears to be small and the objectives of those studies that do exist seem to be highly fragmented and independent of each other. Our aim will, therefore, be to try and draw some of this research together and make sense of it within the context of determining the degree of similarity in attitudinal orientation amongst each of the key multi-agency professions involved with the mentally ill and mentally ill offenders.

As the main focus of this research is the mentally ill offender, the review will be broadened to include this minority. Section three will, therefore, consider research which is useful to our understanding of the perceptions of different study populations relating to both psychopathological and criminal deviance.

The aim of section four will be to consider some of the factors that may possibly influence both public and professional opinion. In particular, attention will centre around certain socio-demographic variables such as age, gender, education, socio-economic status and previous experience of the mentally ill.

The main purpose of section five will be to critically review the aforementioned literature on attitudes towards the mentally ill. After each of the theoretical and methodological limitations of these studies have been considered, possible directions for future research in this area will be discussed.

One of the most important methodological criticisms to be discussed in section five centres around the assertion that popular perceptions are being measured in relation to the mentally ill in general, instead of a particular psychopathological disorder. The aim of section six will be to consider this point further, and to discuss some of the more recent research which has investigated beliefs towards the separate disorders of schizophrenia and depression.

Section seven is more concerned with theory and serves as an introduction to the structure of the current research. In this section the three most important scientific theories or models of mental illness - medical (organic), moral (cognitive-behaviour) and psychosocial - will be considered in detail.

Finally, in section eight the purpose and structure of the current research will be briefly discussed in terms of the propositions to be tested and the overall research design to be employed.

Public attitudes towards the mentally ill

During the 1950s, when the major studies in this field were conducted, a number of authors convincingly demonstrated that society holds a 'traditional' perspective concerning the mentally ill which characterises such persons as unpredictable (Cummings, 1957), potentially violent (Joint Commission on Mental Illness and Health, 1961) and generally threatening and fear provoking (Star, 1955). Such a perspective is learned during early socialisation, apparently maintained in interaction with others (Scheff, 1966) and reinforced via the mass media's indiscriminate application of the 'mentally disturbed' referent to all child molesters, mass murderers and rapists (Scheff, 1966; Nunnally, 1961). Troubled by these early findings, the mental health profession launched intensive educational campaigns at both a local and national level in an attempt to re-educate the public in terms of the medical model of mental illness (Rabkin, 1974).[3]

Invariably, the studies on public attitudes carried out after 1960 were designed with the explicit or implicit purpose of assessing the success of the mental health movement's educational campaigns (Sarbin and Mancuso, 1972, 1970). The findings from these studies appear to fall into two categories: those that were 'optimistic' about the success of the educational programmes, and those that led investigators to a more pessimistic conclusion about the extent and direction of attitudinal change (Brockington et al, 1979; Rabkin, 1974). Furthermore, it would appear that there existed a direct correlation between an interpretation of the findings and the 'underlying ideology' (Rabkin, 1974, 1972) or 'premise and perspective' (Crocetti et al, 1974, 1972, 1971) of the researcher.

Thus investigators supporting the medical perspective (mainly medical personnel of the mental health profession) were encouraged by their findings which showed that respondents are able to identify certain signs and symptoms as indicating mental illness and that such persons are increasingly being offered "all the consideration due to suffering humanity" (Flew, 1985:115)[4] such as greater care and understanding, accompanied by less stigma and rejection (Crocetti et al, 1974). Those who subscribe to the opposing social deviance model, however, generally regard mental patients merely as persons who become involved in certain types of deviant behaviour.[5] These investigators tended to view any attempt at re-educating the pubic in terms of the medical paradigm as nothing more than an objectionable 'moral crusade' on the part of mental health professionals (Sarbin and Mancuso, 1970) which ultimately will do very little to alleviate the problems caused by those defined as mentally ill, as the implications arising from such a conceptual framework are disturbing. Evidence in support of their claim shows that the public remains fearful and ignorant of such persons, and as a result continues to strongly stigmatise and reject those who are labelled mentally ill (Sarbin and Mancuso, 1972).

After reviewing the major studies that were conducted during the 1950s, which assessed the quality and degree of public reaction towards the mentally ill, the work of the 'optimists' and the 'pessimists' - or psychiatrically orientated and sociologically orientated investigators of the 1960s onwards - will be discussed.[6]

Research before 1960

One of the first studies to examine popular thinking about the mentally ill was a nationwide survey conducted in 1950 by Dr Shirley Star of the National Opinion Research Centre (NORC), University of Chicago. Star (1952) found that her subjects strongly rejected the mentally ill and admitted only extreme psychosis, accompanied by threatening violent behaviour, into their working definition of mental illness. Overall Star concluded that the reaction of the general public was dominated by:

> "fear, distrust, suspicion and apprehension derived primarily from the assumption that the person could not really be cured" (Star, 1952:23).

This survey is also often commented upon for its important methodological influence. Star (1955, 1952) formulated six case history descriptions, often referred to as case vignettes, each describing a different pattern of psychopathological behaviour. These case vignettes, which were to be used as attitude 'objects' prior to the questioning of respondents, included a paranoid schizophrenic, a simple schizophrenic, a person suffering from depressive neurosis, an alcoholic, a compulsive phobic and a child behaviour disorder.[7]

A rather different approach to the study of attitudes and beliefs towards the mentally ill was carried out a year later in two small Canadian towns. In their book 'Closed Ranks' (1957) John and Elaine Cumming describe how they tried to change public opinion towards the mentally ill through the use of an educational programme designed to promote greater acceptance of mental illness. They conducted a field experiment in which the people in one town pseudo-named 'Blackfoot' were exposed to films and group discussion about mental health issues while the other town served as a control group. The researchers tried to promote three propositions: (1) That the range of normal behaviour is wider than often believed; (2) that deviant behaviour has a specific cause and so can be treated; and (3) that normal and abnormal behaviour fall along a single continuum and are not qualitatively different from each other.

The evidence from the survey, conducted after the six months educational programme, led the researchers to observe that the first statement was readily received by the townspeople of 'Blackfoot'. In fact, the impression to emerged from the findings was that:

"the definition of mental illness is much narrower in the minds of the lay public than in the minds of psychiatrists and professional mental health workers ... Our interviewers were shocked at the respondents' denial of pathological conditions in the case histories, because they assumed that lay people could accept less behaviour as normal. But a very wide spectrum of behaviour appears to be tolerated by the laity - at least verbally - as reasonably close to normal ... " (Cumming and Cumming, 1957:100-101).

The Cummings concluded that the sample strongly feared mental illness and so as a sort of defence mechanism they would deny its manifestation in all but the most extreme cases. The second statement of the curriculum was also acceptable as it justified the segregation through hospitalisation of those who were clearly mentally ill. Justification was based upon the notion that treatment would benefit both the patient and the community. The third proposition was, however, extremely unpopular, so much so in fact that the community rejected the entire education programme. The notion that illness and health lay along a single continuum appeared not to be accepted as it implied that anyone could become mentally ill under certain circumstances. According to the Cummings (1957), rejection was based upon the traditionally negative belief of the community that those who become mentally ill were pretty worthless and weak to begin with. Overall, this study demonstrates that particular communities may have their own system of opinions towards the mentally ill which are not easily atoneable to change and that in the particular case of 'blackfoot' their views may be negatively interpreted as a pattern of 'denial, isolation and insulation of mental illness' (Cummings, 1957:119).

At about the same time as the Cummings' (1957) study was being published in America, the first major piece of research on attitudes towards the mentally ill was being conducted in England (Carstairs and Wing, 1958). In January 1957 the BBC broadcast a series of five television programmes under the general title of the 'Hurt Mind' which dealt with various issues associated with mental illness such as aetiology, nature and treatment. Questionnaires were given to a representative sample of the viewing public of Greater London and a content analysis was carried out on 1,276 letters written to the BBC in response to the programmes. The authors concluded that while there existed a degree of constructivism and good will surrounding the mentally ill, the general impression was that such persons are perceived primarily in terms of the traditional 'madman' who was unpredictable, deluded and withdrawn. Overall, the researchers were of the opinion that the whole subject of mental illness generated a considerable degree of anxiety and fear among their naïve respondents.

Probably the most important study to be carried out on what the general public knew and felt about mental illness and its treatment was a 6-year survey conducted in America during the period 1954-59 (Nunnally, 1961). A nationally representative sample completed a 180 opinion statement questionnaire and a semantic differential attitudinal scale designed to measure their knowledge and feelings about mental illness. The knowledge scale was factor analysed to reveal ten interpretable factors which were labelled: look and act different; will power; sex distinction; avoidance of morbid thoughts; guidance and support; hopelessness; external cause versus personality; non-seriousness; age function; and organic causes. In summarising the results obtained from the semantic differential scale, it was claimed that compared to the normal person the mentally ill are regarded as relatively worthless, dirty, dangerous, cold, unpredictable and insincere. Overall, the rather negative findings produced by all the measures used in the survey led Nunnally (1961) to conclude that:

"as is commonly suspected, the mentally ill are regarded with fear, distrust and dislike. A strong negative halo surrounds all mentally ill, they are considered, unselectively, as being all things bad" (Nunnally, 1961:51).

Interestingly, in trying to account for this 'negative halo' Nunnally (1961) suggests that views were held not because the public were misinformed, perhaps generated through sensationalist media coverage, but because they were uninformed about current thinking in mental illness. Furthermore, it was observed that regardless of the level of knowledge about mental illness held by the respondents their attitudes were still markedly negative.

In order to measure public 'tolerance' towards discharged mental patients, Whatley (1959) devised a social distance scale which, although conceptually similar to the scale devised by Bogardus (1933) in order to measure society's response to ethnic groups, is original in content and refers specifically to the formally mentally ill. The scale consists of several statements which hypothesise a relationship between the respondent and the former psychiatric patient ranging from a minimal degree of contact - it is best not to associate with people who have been in mental hospitals - to a level of intimate social involvement - I would hire a woman as a baby-sitter if I knew she had seen a psychiatrist. Only 20% of respondents agreed that one should avoid the minimal degree of contact, however, only 15% would hire a former patient as a baby-sitter.

The importance of this study is in both its method and content. Whatley's social distance scale has introduced a major dimension in the analysis of attitudinal rejection towards the mentally ill by incorporating the variable of social intimacy into the social distance scale. Whatley (1959) defines this factor as 'ego-involvement'. This refers to the respondents' willingness to show sympathy and acceptance of former psychiatric patients in some situations rather than others. Whatley (1959) showed that the closer the social relationship with a former patient, the greater involvement of ego or self values and hence, an increased tendency to avoid social contacts with them. For example, more people are likely to accept a former mental patient as someone to 'sponsor in a club' than they are as someone 'for your children to marry'. In fact, the evidence seems to suggest that whenever this type of social distance scale is used, all the findings show such a pattern of ego-involvement (Brockman et al, 1979). The author interpreted his results as indicating the existence of "socially unhealthy environments" (Whatley, 1959:319). Unhealthy in the sense that the still recovering mental patient appears only to be tolerated in relatively impersonal situations, ie, on a secondary group level. The pattern of avoidance revealed in more intimate situations suggests that patients risk a certain degree of social isolation by being denied the opportunity for interaction at the primary group level.

A number of other smaller studies carried out prior to 1960 came to the similar conclusion that the mentally ill were feared, stigmatised and shunned (Bingham, 1951; Allen, 1943). The Joint Commission on Mental Illness and Health, established in America in 1955 and comprising of 36 national and public organisations, published its report, 'Action for Mental Health', in 1961. Influenced by the major studies of the time the report paints a gloomy picture of rejection and a punitive social response towards the mentally ill. People tended to deny behaviour psychiatrists viewed as pathological and showed clear signs of anxiety and discomfort when the label was authoritatively assigned. The report concluded that there existed at this time "a pervasive defeatism" concerning the mentally ill which had gained both intellectual and academic acceptance.

Research after 1960

Research since 1960 has resulted in divergent findings. This divergence invariably centres on researchers' qualitative interpretation of their empirical results, categorising them in either 'optimistic' or 'pessimistic' terms. The 'pessimistic' or 'negative' standard was established by the major studies conducted during the 1950s, in particular, the research carried out by both Star (1955) and the Cummings (1957). Subsequent researchers have frequently used these studies as a baseline on which to formulate substantive hypotheses of attitudinal differentiation and change. Thus if researchers offer a 'negative' evaluation of their findings, then by implication this suggests that they have found either some unacceptable level of sympathy, understanding or tolerance of the mentally ill, or a lack of significant improvement in attitude scores over earlier studies. Conversely, an 'optimistic' or 'positive' interpretation implicitly reflects a more acceptable level of public sympathy and awareness or a significant increase in favourable attitudes over earlier findings (Brockman et al, 1979).

Optimistic findings Probably the most vocal 'optimists' during the period after 1960 were Crocetti, Lemkau and their colleagues (Crocetti et al, 1974, 1972, 1971; Lemkau and Crocetti, 1963; Crocetti and Lemkau, 1962). In most of their work they used similar measures to those employed in previous surveys. These included the use of three case vignettes representing a paranoid schizophrenic, a simple schizophrenic and an alcoholic, an amended version of Whatley's social distance scale and several additional questions designed to extract overall opinions about the mental illness in general and the mentally ill in particular.

In their 1960 study of Baltimore City the authors tried to determine the degree of public acceptance of a home care plan for psychiatric patients. Their findings led them to suggest that the sample population was 'fairly well informed' and that they showed 'understanding and tolerance for the mentally ill'. A majority identified all three vignettes as mentally ill and felt that each should be referred to a physician who should offer treatment within a community setting rather than a secure mental hospital. Lemkau and Crocetti (1962) concluded that they had arrived at 'startling results' which were markedly inconsistent with the earlier findings of 'denial, rejection and isolation'.

The same research group conducted another large survey in Baltimore approximately a decade later (Crocetti, Spiro and Siassi, 1971). In this study the sample was drawn from a population of blue-collar workers, most were white and middle aged. Again social distance scales were administered in addition to questions about the effect of treatment and the appropriate help source. Ninety-nine per cent felt that a doctor's help was just as appropriate for the mentally as for the physically ill and 89% were optimistic about the prospects of a full recovery. Furthermore, they found no evidence of extreme rejection of the mentally ill. The authors reached the overall conclusion that there now exists sufficient evidence to prove:

> "that for at least a decade the public has accepted mental illness as an illness ... we must move away from assumptions based on studies of two decades ago. The time may have come to write a belated epitaph to the long-vanished 'closed ranks'" (Crocetti et al, 1971:46).

In fact, during the 1960s a number of studies replicating the work of Crocetti and Lemkau obtained evidence which confirmed the Baltimore findings. In Meyer's (1964) study, additional opinion items were included such as, 'Almost all patients who have a mental illness are dangerous'. The author concluded by stating that the public had become more tolerant, probably because they were less worried about the mentally ill being dangerous.

In 1963 the New York City Community Mental Health Board in conjunction with Columbia University carried out the most extensive research of the decade. Their aim was to assess the feelings of New Yorkers about current mental health facilities and services, and to explore public conceptions of mental illness and the mentally ill (Elinson et al, 1967). The format and scope of the study was similar to that carried out by Nunnally (1961) during the 1950s. Of the 2,610 respondents interviewed an overwhelming majority expressed the belief that mental illness was an illness just like any other, that there are many different kinds of mental illness and that they are treatable. There was also evidence to suggest that candid rejection of the mentally ill was no longer socially acceptable to confess and that the medical model is becoming more commonly known and accepted. In summarising their results Elinson et al (1967) suggest that there now exists sufficient evidence to dismiss the idea, that the mentally ill are systematically stigmatised and then rejected, as a highly simplistic and outmoded notion.

In fact, a subsequent study carried out by the Cummings (1965) adds further support to this view. They interviewed 22 people after discharge from a mental hospital and found that the stigma associated with being a former patient may be either real or simply perceived by the patient due to feelings of shame and a sense of being inferior. They also noted that the level of stigma depended upon the type of illness suffered and the roles adopted by the former patient upon their return from hospital. On the basis of these findings the authors concluded that in general, the stigma associated with hospitalisation for mental illness may be viewed as a form of ego damage which through time is reversible.

Rootman and Lafave (1969) hypothesised that the optimistic findings obtained by Crocetti and associates were due predominantly to disparities in sampling between studies. The Cummings' (1957) research had been carried out on an agricultural population in Canada whereas the Lemkau and Crocetti (1962) sample were drawn from an urban American City. Rootman and Lafave (1969) tested this hypothesis by selecting another rural Canadian town within the province of Saskatchewan (pseudo-named 'Saltwater') and compared their attitudes towards the mentally ill with those reported by the Cummings (1957). Overall, the authors found that their 'saltwater' sample had access to more information and were less willing to reject the mentally ill.

In 1970 a comparable study was carried out using 1,400 low-income, semiskilled respondents from a predominantly rural area of America (Bentz and Edgerton, 1971). The authors' aim was to determine whether or not respondents who identified someone as a mental patient would prefer to maintain greater social distance from the mentally ill than those who did not make such an identification. They found that there was no difference in the levels of social distance each group wished to maintain and that the mean scores should be interpreted in terms of acceptance rather than rejection.

In short, the cumulative impact of these various studies, which have used similar designs and measures but differing samples, clearly demonstrates that considerable progress has been made in changing public attitudes towards the mentally ill. According to Crocetti et al (1972), the overwhelming impression created by a review of the literature since 1960 is that the public have learned to identify mental illness as an illness just like any other and that the public no longer places a sizable social distance between itself and those labelled 'mentally ill'.

Pessimistic findings Since 1960, however, there has been a dissenting faction of researchers who claim that there is still a considerable stigma attached to being mentally ill and that when people encounter such labels they respond with the same level of dislike, fear and rejection traditionally displayed towards those who suffer from some form of psychiatric problem.

A particularly persuasive advocate of this perspective is the sociologist D L Phillips. During the 1960s he published a series of studies using several modified case vignettes and a social distance scale. The methodological and statistical techniques employed in his research were considerably more sophisticated than many of the earlier studies. Associated with each description was a help source referent, these were varied so that, overall, respondents saw each description as well as information about whether the person in the vignette had seen a psychiatrist, a clergyman, etc. A geo-latin square analysis was performed in order to measure the influence of both variables - behaviour deviation and help source - on rejection. Phillips' first study was reported in 1963 and showed that an individual in a case study was increasingly rejected as they were described as having consulted a clergyman, a physician, a psychiatrist or had received treatment in a mental hospital. This significant relationship between rejection and selection of help source led Phillips (1963) to conclude that seeking psychiatric help still has a stigmatising effect which is accompanied by rejection of both the mental patient and those who treat them.

In a subsequent study Phillips (1964) found similar evidence of rejection, however, on this occasion he attributes the variance in levels of social distance to how visible the behavioural deviations are from customary role expectations. In this study it was shown that by altering the gender of the case vignettes, males were tolerated less than females as their behaviour was seen as being potentially more disruptive.

Bord (1971) repeated and extended the research design used by Phillips (1963) on a sample of 350 college students. His findings were fairly similar, though Bord (1971) offered an alternative explanation to try and account for the observed levels of rejection and the general responses given to the help source.

Bord's interpretation is based on the amount of information that is available to the respondent about the seriousness of the case vignettes and the extent to which the behaviour seems unpredictable and dangerous. He suggests that Phillips observed an association between rejection and help source not because of the added stigma from associated labels such as clergyman, physician, psychiatrist, etc, but because Phillips (1963) used respondents (housewives) who were psychiatrically naïve and who relied on the help source as an additional source of information regarding the seriousness and offensiveness of the behaviour in the case descriptions. This point appears to be substantiated by the fact that other studies which used more sophisticated respondents such as psychiatric nurses and college students, found the help source to be less significant in its effect (Kirk, 1974; Schroder and Ehrlich, 1968). Bord also disagrees with Phillips' (1964) assertion that the crucial variable determining rejection is the visibility of the deviant behaviour. Instead Board (1971) suggests that the degree of unpredictability and the threat implied by the behaviour is far more influential on rejection. Thus the nature of the deviation is considered to be a more important factor than the actual visible degree of deviation from accepted normative behaviour.

The key point to this debate is that while it was still considered reasonable to conclude that the respondents level of tolerance towards the mentally ill had not changed dramatically since the 1950s, theories attempting to explain popular attitudes had. As support for the labelling theory began to decline, it became increasingly apparent that other social identities and situational factors relating to the 'deviant' are equally vital to an understanding of popular social reaction.

In fact, the idea of manipulating salient non-deviant identities with reference to the attitude 'object' appears to have gained support amongst a number of more recent studies. Nieradzik and Cochrane (1985) systematically altered the nature of their case vignettes through the inclusion of social roles such as 'bank clerk', 'gifted painter' and several psychiatric labels. The authors found that the level of rejection was decreased by the availability of an alternative non-deviant role associated with the behaviour. It was also observed that the labels indicating mental illness were much stronger determinants of rejection than the actual behaviour per se.[8] Eker (1985) examined the effect of 'type of cause' on attitudes. His findings demonstrated some rather interesting trends, in particular, the tendency:

" ... to perceive mental illness more and to desire more social distance in organic cases (ie, where the 'type of cause' is described as organic) than in the psychosocial cases" (Eker, 1985:246).

While the work of Phillips was the most sustained programme of research which offered an alternative view to the 'optimists' of the 1960s, other researchers, using a variety of alternative methodological strategies, also found evidence in support of his observations (D'Arcy and Brockman, 1977, 1976; Olmstead and Durham, 1976; MacLean, 1969).

A study on community attitudes in Edinburgh was carried out in 1966 on a sample of 500 respondents. The measuring instrument consisted of a 47 item questionnaire designed to gage attitudes and opinions about the mentally ill. On the basis of her findings MacLean (1969) concluded that clear signs of the traditional stereotypes still remained, in particular, the persistent tendency to regard mental patients as potentially unpredictable and violent. Furthermore, there still existed the belief that mental illness was contagious and that hospitalisation was necessary for their segregation, thus suggesting that respondents viewed the function of mental hospitals in terms of custodialism rather than for the purpose of administering care and therapy.

In an attempt to determine whether or not this generally negative attitude persisted over time, Olmstead and Durham (1976) carried out a longitudinal study on two comparable sets of college students. A semantic differential consisting of eight concepts and twelve scales was administered to the first sample in 1962 and then to the second sample in 1971. They summarised their findings by stating that contrary to expectations attitudes were remarkable similar for the two samples, thus:

"on the basis of [our] data it does not seem reasonable to hypothesise that popular mental health attitudes have discernably changed [since the 1950s]" (Olmstead and Durham, 1976:42).

In an attempt to look more closely at the extent of change in attitudes towards the mentally ill, several authors re-examined the Cummings' (1957) 'closed ranks' study community of 'Blackfoot' using essentially the same research instruments and tactics (Brockman et al, 1979; D'Arcy and Brockman, 1977, 1976). In terms of the public's recognition of various psychiatric symptoms only relatively minor changes were observed. There was an increase in the number identifying the child behaviour disorder as mental illness though a decrease in the case of the depressive neurotic. In terms of social distance attitudes, some change was observed in the direction of increased public acceptance of the mentally ill though the authors generally felt that the magnitude of any change was far less than that which one would reasonable expect from reading the literature. In fact, their overall conclusion was that they found no evidence to support post-1960 claims of a more enlightened populous.

"The findings show no dramatic change. Indeed, the 1974 results were more like the original Cummings' results than most other studies" (D'Arcy and Brockman, 1977:68).

Summary

Despite certain theoretical and methodological limitations with the early research on attitudes towards the mentally ill, there does appear to exist a fine line of plausible fact.[9] Regardless of one's ideological point of view, people overall are better informed about mental illness. Questions found in research such as Ramsey and Siepp (1948a, 1948b) - 'insanity is God's punishment for some sin' - are conspicuous by their absence from the more recent studies. The concepts of psychopathology prevalent among mental health professionals during the 1960s appear to have become widely accepted (Crocetti et al, 1974). However, as Sarbin and Mancuso (1972) point out, the public still remains unconvinced about the value of this conceptual framework. Indeed, a vociferous minority were still able to produce evidence clearly demonstrating that the lay population continues to be frightened of the mentally ill (Phillips, 1967).

Furthermore, it is clear from the findings and the ideological discussions that have taken place in many of the more recent surveys carried out since the 1970s that the research is still, to some extent, caught up in the old controversies surrounding a positive/negative dichotomy of perceptions about the mentally ill. Consequently, while the methodologies adopted by these studies have become more refined, their findings and implications remain narrow and inconclusive. One issue that cannot be disputed from the evidence, however, is the fact that public attitudes are far more diverse than the earlier research would have us believe (Eker, 1985).[10]

Professionals' attitudes towards the mentally ill

While the opinions of particular professions has been fairly extensively investigated with regard to certain issues,[11] relatively few studies have examined the relationship between occupational frame of reference and expressed attitudes about mental illness (Roskin et al, 1988; Halpert, 1969). One of the main goals of the current research is to obtain information on various professional agency's beliefs about the mentally ill and mentally ill offenders. This section will, therefore, consider the previous research which has been carried out on the major professional groups providing a service to such persons. These professions span three large service systems: Criminal Justice, Mental Health and Social Services. The research relating to these groups will be reviewed in chronological order, the central aim being to try and make sense of the findings in terms of any real differences that may exist between each profession's attitudinal orientation towards the mentally ill.[12]

One of the earliest studies to consider professional attitudes towards the mentally ill was Woodward's (1951) survey of Louisville. Included in the author's population cross-section was a random sample of lawyers, doctors, teachers and members of the clergy. While a number of large differences were observed between the groups, the most clear-cut conclusion drawn was that lawyers were by far the most conservative and least 'enlightened' in terms of mental health. Via the use of case vignettes similar to those developed by Star (1955), it was observed that only 27% of the lawyer sample (N=108) favoured sending a juvenile delinquent to a psychiatrist. This figure is comparable with that of the lay population where only 25% considered a psychiatrist as appropriate. Meanwhile, as high as 54% of the teachers (N=135) and 49% of the physicians (N=123) believed this action to be appropriate. With regard to the case vignette describing a paranoid schizophrenic, only 8% of the lawyers thought that hospital care was appropriate while 15% believed that a priest may be able to help. Thirty-one percent believed that mental hospitals treat patients badly and 68% felt that there was a stigma attached to issues of mental illness. Woodward (1951) concluded from this evidence that lawyers present a minor stronghold of reaction against the modern scientific ideas of the mental health profession.

A decade later 87 community leaders of a chosen health district in New York City were surveyed on their attitudes towards the mentally ill (Dohrenwend et al, 1962). In general, the leaders were quite able to identify each of the six case vignettes used as symptomatic of mental illness. Furthermore, the findings seem to suggest that a majority of the community leaders refused to put very much social distance between themselves and former mental patients. The community leaders which are of particular relevance to the present study are those within the fields labelled 'politics and legal affairs'. The specific occupations included under this heading were: state senators, city council men, judges, and police captains. Overall 56% of this group managed to recognise mental illness in five out of the six case vignettes and 70% recommended mental health care in at least four cases, however, only 44% of this occupational subsample defined more than three of the case descriptions as serious, therefore, 56% would not extend their definition of seriousness beyond the three types of disorder - paranoid schizophrenic, alcoholic and juvenile character disorder - which appear to threaten others. Dohrenwend and his co-researchers suggested that their legal background may have led them to perceive the psychiatric disorders more in terms of harm to others than to the actual patients themselves.

During the 1960s a number of studies considering the attitudes of mental health workers towards mental illness were conducted. The most extensive series of these surveys were carried out by Cohen and Struening (1965, 1964, 1963, 1962). The 19 occupations studied within the Veterans Administration Psychiatric Hospital were empirically grouped into four clusters as determined by the Opinion about Mental Illness (OMI) questionnaire. One of the clusters contained personnel such as psychologists and social workers. This cluster was found to be low in authoritarianism and social restrictiveness while strongly supporting on the mental hygiene ideology and interpersonal aetiology dimensions. Psychiatrists were found not to fit neatly into any cluster, though they tended to be similar to social workers.[13]

Ehrlich and Sabshin (1964), using a 28 page questionnaire dealing predominantly with issues associated with psychiatric hospitalisation, discovered that psychiatrists could be grouped into three independent ideological orientations: psychotherapeutic, somatotherapeutic and sociotherapeutic. The psychotherapeutic position is supported largely by psychoanalysts and accepts the mental hygiene movement's goals, though within their analytical framework. The somatotherapeutic point of view advocates aetiological explanations within chemical and physiological terms, and the sociotherapeutic position is concerned largely with the patients' social environment. This latter position is probably endorsed by the same people who would obtain high scores on Baker and Schulberg's (1967) Community Mental Health Ideology (CMHI) scale. This 38 item questionnaire was developed in order to measure attitudes towards the new ideology of therapeutic care within a community context. Psychologists obtained the highest scores, followed by occupational therapists and then a random sample of psychiatrists. The group who were least orientated towards accepting the ideology of community mental health were respondents from the American Psycho-analytic Association.

Of considerable relevance to the present author's research is a recent study carried out by Nuehring and Raybin (1986). Their aim was to examine the attitude of service providers towards community based care for mentally ill offenders. Criminal justice professionals (N=36), mental health and forensic professionals (N=38), and a variety of social service agency members (N=21) were surveyed.[14] The evidence obtained suggested that a majority of the respondents (at least 64%) believed that mentally ill offenders can be treated in the community in a similar way to other psychiatric clients. However, despite this fact, a number of diverse responses to certain survey items were evident. With regard to assessments of dangerousness and unpredictability, criminal justice professionals more frequently believed mentally ill offenders to be dangerous if not under medication[15] and generally more unpredictable than other clients.[16] Various agencies also showed concern over the fact that mentally ill offenders may frighten other clients - social service professionals showed the strongest level of agreement with this view at 62%. Nuehring and Raybin (1986) make a rather interesting observation regarding this result, that is, because it is not clear how other clients would obtain knowledge of the criminal histories of such offenders, this question may in fact have identified the true attitude of the social service respondents though projected into other clients.

Regarding the issue as to whether mentally ill offenders should be able to live independently in the community, both criminal justice and social service respondents (61% and 62% respectively) believed that supervised residential treatment was essential once such offenders were discharged from institutions, while only 31% of the mental health professionals agreed with the idea of community supervision. Generally, however:

> "the concept of community based care for this client group [mentally ill offenders] is regarded positively, given the limitations of jails, prisons and mental hospitals to deal with their needs" (Nuehring and Raybin, 1986:19).

Some information was also obtained on attitudes towards greater co-operation among agencies. In response to open-ended questions, 32% of all respondents commented on the need for a bridge between in-patient and community services. Furthermore, when the respondents were asked to suggest a suitable scheme for the delivery of services within the community a majority favoured:

> "a collaborative service delivery model, with services co-operatively provided by the forensic hospital and community agencies" (Nuehring and Raybin, 1986:31).

Roskin et al (1988), commenting upon previous studies dealing with professional attitudes towards mental patients, noted that:

> "these studies were done some years ago and current research in attitudes towards patients has been limited. A major problem has been the difficulty in developing measuring instruments of appropriate scope, reliability and contemporary relevance" (Roskin et al, 1988:188).

Roskin and his co-workers developed a questionnaire which measured attitudes towards mental patients in addition to beliefs about the aetiology and treatment of mental illness. A comparative analysis was performed between groups of psychiatrists, psychologists, psychiatric social workers, and nurses. One-way analyses of variance revealed highly significant differences among the groups. Psychiatrists were found to be more psychodynamic in terms of their approach to the aetiology and treatment of mental illness than all other groups. In terms of a biological orientation towards the aetiology and treatment of psychiatric disorders, nurses scored the highest. Psychiatrists were found to be the most authoritarian with patients, and psychologists were found to show less distance-detachment from patients than social workers, psychiatrists or nurses. The authors concluded that most of their findings could be accounted for by individual personality characteristics on one hand, and training, exposure, and clinical experience within the given discipline on the other. Furthermore, the authors believe that the notion of certain disciplines attracting a particular type of person does not seem to be supported by the evidence.

Finally, the most recent study of professional attitudes towards the mentally ill offender available to the writer is Jackson's (1988) survey of professional perceptions of dangerousness and other forensic issues. Samples of psychiatrists, forensic social workers, psychiatric nurses and lawyers watched videos of accused subjects and answered questions relating to their degree of dangerousness, level of mental illness, treatability and criminal responsibility. On a general level similar responses were found for all groups, though lawyers and psychiatrists were more confident about their answers. However, significant differences were found. lawyers tended to see mental patients as more dangerous and they were also more willing to label the accused subject as mentally ill. In terms of treatability lay persons, lawyers and nurses similarly viewed the patients as relatively untreatable. Social workers were in fact shown to be more optimistic than psychiatrists, though the difference was not significant.[17]

Summary

The research reviewed in this section covers a broad time period of around thirty years. The nature of these studies as well as their findings clearly show that the various professional groups considered have, to a certain extent, adapted and changed their views in order to more readily accommodate contemporary approaches towards dealing with both the mentally ill and mentally ill offenders. Unfortunately, a degree of caution surrounds such an optimistic comment as the evidence suggests that distinct attitudinal patterns between the various agencies still remain. In particular, respondents within the criminal justice profession appear less 'enlightened' than mental health practitioners in their overall approach towards psychopathological behaviour, while some social service personnel tend to have ambivalent views, especially when dealing with mentally ill offenders (Nuehring and Raybin, 1986).

The attitudinal relationship between mental illness and criminality

Until now, the primary concern of this paper has been to review previous social-psychological literature examining popular attitudes towards the mentally ill in general. A central concern of the current research, however, is to describe public and professional beliefs about persons whose behaviour represents both psychopathological and criminal deviance. It would, therefore, seem appropriate to consider some of the research which has examined attitudes specifically towards both the normal offender and the mentally ill offender.

There is some evidence to suggest that the public assumes a relationship between mental illness and criminality (Joint Commission on Mental Illness and Health, 1961). The aim of this section will be to consider whether or not there exists a generally negative attitudinal orientation towards both the mentally ill and the normal offender. This will be achieved by reviewing the previous research in terms of the answers it provides to the following three question: (1) Are the mentally ill so negatively evaluated that they are seen as more like the criminal rather than the physically ill? (2) How negative are attitudes towards the normal offender? and (3) Are those who engage in criminal behaviour more negatively evaluated if they also show signs of mental disorder?[18]

Perceptions of the mentally ill: offender or patient

There are some indications from empirical research that the mentally ill are strongly stigmatised and that a propensity for violent, bizarre and dangerous behaviour forms a fundamental part of this stereotyped image (Nunnally, 1961). In fact, evidence from a minority of these studies seems to suggest that the public's image of the mentally disordered may be more like that of the normal offender.

A study by Swarte (1969) which was carried out in the Netherlands observed that respondents not only saw mental patients as dangerous but also strongly believed that the incidence of rape would be reduced if they were more securely confined. Furthermore, a majority felt that young girls must take particular care around such persons. Thus it would appear that there is a tendency to associate mental patients with certain types of crime, in particular, sexual offences, crimes against children and crimes of violence against the person in general rather than property offences.

A further study by Tringo (1970) offered additional support to these observations. The aim of the research was to obtain a hierarchy of lay preferences for various groups of deviance, including the disabled, sick, and those with general social problems. A social distance scale similar to that developed by Bogardus (1933, 1925) was used, of which the extreme responses were 'would marry' and 'would put to death'. First preference was given to the physically disabled, while the four deviant groups that were ranked the lowest included: ex-prisoners, the mentally retarded, alcoholics with the mentally ill in last place.

More recently, it has been shown that the public considers the mentally ill to be dangerous and believes that they are likely to act violently and commit horrific crimes (Appleby and Wessely, 1988), particularly offences of a sexual nature (Levey and Howells, 1995).

Thus it would appear that lay evaluations of the mentally ill are more in line with their view of the normal offender rather than the physically sick. Despite this assertion, however, there are some indications that the situation may be changing. Other researchers who have considered their respondents' perceptions of crime and mental illness have interpreted their results as showing no definite association. For example, evidence obtained from the studies on public attitudes carried out during the 1960s demonstrated that at least 50% of their samples agreed with the statement, that people who have been in a state mental hospital are no more likely to commit crimes than others in normal state hospitals (Crocetti et al, 1974).

Another more recent study (Skinner et al, 1995) has shown that while the stigma associated with the ex-mental patient continues, attitudes towards this deviant social role have evolved in a more positive direction over the past 25 years. In this research, Skinner et al (1995) re-examined a survey by Lamy (1966) which looked at the generalisability of stigma across different forms of deviant behaviour. In the present study a 'deep-level' attitudinal scale including items on issues such as aetiology, treatment and psychological and social functioning was administered in response to the labels 'ex-mental patient', 'ex-convict' and 'ex-drug addict'. The results showed an attitudinal hierarchy with the ex-drug addict receiving the lowest amount of negative evaluation and the ex-convict eliciting the most.

Perceptions of the normal offender

A large number of studies surveying public opinion regarding important topics such as crime, criminal justice, sentencing and other related areas are widely available (Cohn et al, 1991). Within this sphere of law and order, however, little systematic research has directed its attention towards gaining a better understanding of public beliefs about normal offenders. With the exception of those surveys which have been interested in the public's theories of crime causation,[19] the protagonist of the criminal arena appears to have largely been ignored as a legitimate topic for concern. Those who have reviewed some of this vast amount of literature may perhaps feel that the neglect within this area is perfectly justifiable. For example, a great deal of the evidence suggests that crime is feared by a number of strata within society and for a number of reasons (Last and Jackson, 1989; Kennedy and Silverman, 1985; Hough and Mayhew, 1985), that criminal justice agencies should 'get much tougher with criminals (Hindelang, 1974), and that overall custodial sentences should be far more severe (Walker and Hough, 1988). Thus judging from the available research, it would seem difficult to assume anything other than that normal offenders are evaluated in highly negative terms. The meagre evidence available on the stigma of offending does, however, seem to suggest that such an assumption may be misplaced.

The few studies that are available to the present author were conducted in North America and deal exclusively with the degree of stigma attached to ex-offenders. Furthermore, most studies have measured the extent of negative attitudes by examining either the effect of conviction on employment, or the willingness of the American public to re-instate certain civil rights.

Reed and Nance (1972) stated that simply changing the law, so that certain civil disabilities were either modified or eliminated (Cohen and Rivkin, 1971), was not enough. They argued that such extra sanctions, like the criminal law in general, are based upon a morality that equates crime with sin and everything bad. Thus the only way to restore their former status would be to convert the public away from the view that ex-offenders are eternally damned. In order to determine whether such sanctions reflect an out-moulded morality, Reed (1979) examined the attitudes of teachers, farmers, maintenance men and students towards the 'civil disabilities' applied to ex-offenders ie, had respondents' attitudes changed to the extent that they would be willing to reinstate certain rights? The author found an overall reluctance to restore important civil rights for both imprisoned offenders (such as the right to privacy, unlimited mail, etc) and ex-offenders (such as the right to qualify for jury service, apply for certain jobs, etc).

"What is significant is that the research ... demonstrates that a conviction has lasting consequences. People do not 'want to forgive or forget'. They carry moralistic ... attitudes that socially incapacitate offenders for the rest of their lives" (Reed, 1979:226).

Since Cohen and Rivkin's (1971) conclusion that the present law regarding 'civil disabilities' had serious consequences on ex-offenders' efforts to re-acquire their normal status, most states have developed some procedure for the restoration of rights. As a result of this new policy, there appears to have been a marked change in attitudes since the findings of Reed (1979). For example, it has been noted that:

"many jurisdictions today interested in a total rehabilitation program are eliminating such civil disabilities and treating ex-offenders as fully fledged citizens" (Senna and Siegel, 1978:448).

With regard to employment opportunities available to ex-offenders, a number of the earlier studies did in fact observe that there was a strong negative attitude associated with conviction (Rubin, 1958). Though probably the most often quoted is the research carried out by Schwartz and Skolnick (1962). Their 100 respondents, who were potential employers, were divided into four treatment groups (N=25), then to each group of employers one of four personnel folders was shown. Unknown to the employers the applications were fictitious. These four folders differed only in the applicants' record of criminal court involvement. folder one, stated that the applicant had been 'convicted and sentenced for assault', in folder two, he had been 'tried for assault and acquitted', folder three was the same as folder two but a letter from the presiding judge was also included 'reaffirming the legal presumption of innocence'. In folder four there was no mention of a criminal record.

The results showed a clear relationship between an offer of employment and the presence/absence of a criminal history. The convicted offender was only accepted by 1 out of the 25 employers, clearly demonstrating that:

> "conviction constitutes a powerful form of status degradation which continues to operate after ... the individual's 'debt' has been paid" (Schwartz and Skolnick, 1962:136).

In the 'acquitted without letter' folder, 3 out of 25 employers showed an interest while in the folder which included a letter from the judge, 6 employers were interested. Nine employers, however, responded positively to the applicant with no record. This study thus clearly demonstrates that even those acquitted of a crime carry a stigma.

Such a negative image of ex-offenders does not appear, however, to have been confirmed by the more recent studies. Baker (1966) surveyed a sample of inmates 6 months after their release and observed that only 23% reported problems in securing employment primarily due to their prison record. Furthermore, there is some evidence to suggest that ex-offender status does not specifically cause failure to re-integrate within society (Gibbons, 1975).

The most recent study dealing with the stigma associated with offending follows the lead of Schwartz and Skolnick (1962). Homant and Kennedy (1982) compared student responses to a management-employee conflict in order to obtain discriminatory attitudes towards ex-offenders. The conflict situation involved an employee who had written to the owner of a shoe store chain requesting re-employment after having been fired by the personnel manager. In one of the questionnaires the employee was described as an ex-offender and in the other no such identifying information was given. Scores on the questionnaires ranged from 7 to 42, a high-score equalling pro-employee. The mean score of the offender questionnaire was 28.81 while the mean score of the control questionnaire was 28.62. Attitudinal differences were, therefore, minimal though directionally slightly more supportive towards the ex-offender.

In order to test this conclusion further a second experiment was conducted. This time the control letter was replaced by two additional letters, one describing the employee as having a previous mental problem and the other describing the employee as obese. Respondents were students whose subjects placed them into one of four occupational groups - criminal justice, businessmen, scientists and the helping professions. The different questionnaires were then randomly allocated to each group. The authors found that overall, ex-offenders are not the object of negative attitudes, except from criminal justice personnel. "Viewing the groups as a whole there is little if any evidence of any blanket discrimination" (Homant and Kennedy, 1982:391). In fact, the obese employee scored low ie, was more stigmatised than both the ex-offender and the mental patient.

There are only two systematic studies known to the present author that have produced empirical evidence directly related to the degree of stigma associated with mentally ill offenders.[20] The first of these was carried out in North America by Steadman and Cocozza (1978). They found that 29% of their sample (N=413) felt that people in general feared former mental patients 'a lot', while 61% felt that people feared former criminally insane patients 'a lot'. The strength of this negative attitude was also clearly shown when their sample applied semantic differential scales to the three concepts: 'normal person', 'the criminally insane' and 'a mental patient'. The authors concluded from the results that:

"public conceptions of the criminally insane are dominated by fear of the extreme danger they are seen as possessing, and this danger is substantially greater than that posed by former mental patients who have been shown in previous studies to be highly rejected and feared individuals themselves" (Steadman and Cocozza, 1978:527).

It could be argued that the conclusions arrived at by Steadman and Cocozza (1978) provide firm evidence in support of the claim that both the mentally ill and the normal offender are negatively evaluated. Mentally ill offenders have a double deviant identity; they share with mental patients their abnormality and its accompanying stigma, in addition to the stigma associated with being a criminal. Thus the fact that mentally ill offenders are rated in very negative terms, particularly as more dangerous, violent, harmful and unpredictable than the mental patient, is quite unsurprising.

Perhaps a more relevant comparison would be between the normal offender and the mentally ill offender. For if a strongly negative attitude is in fact attributed to both the mental patient and normal offender then again it would be reasonable to expect the mentally ill offender to be more highly stigmatised. The important question is thus: Is the stigma associated with a person who has engaged in criminal behaviour increased by the additional knowledge of mental illness? The level of stigma on the one hand may increase due to the negative evaluation of a double deviant identity. On the other hand, however, the mentally ill offender may be less stigmatised if knowledge of the mental abnormality is more positively perceived, perhaps as an illness just like any other. In such a situation the abnormality will be considered as a mitigating factor.

Howells (1984) attempted to resolve this issue using a more sophisticated methodological approach. Case vignettes were used in two pilot studies each with four different experimental conditions, each altering both the type of disorder and the types of offence committed. Thus study one included a description of a man who had committed a murder or robbery whilst suffering from schizophrenia, and another man who had been charged with murder or robbery while showing no psychiatric problems. In study two, the disorder was altered to depression and the offences used were grievous bodily harm and criminal damage. On the basis of these two studies Howells (1984) concluded:

> "the subjects did indeed make allowances for mental illness, seeing the mentally ill offender as less responsible and less blameworthy for the offence committed [and more appropriate for treatment rather than punishment]. In general, this held equally for both serious and less serious offenses. [Furthermore] ... there is no support in the present results for the hypothesis that the mentally ill offender will be perceived as more dangerous and will be more likely to be socially rejected" (Howells (1984:157).

Summary

In both the older and more contemporary research on attitudes, there appears to be very little empirical information relating directly to the popular image of the mentally ill offender. Much more attention seems to have been directed towards investigating attitudes towards the mentally ill in general. Furthermore, an additional area for which there appears to be a gap in the literature concerns public perceptions of the normal offender. From the research presented in this section, it would seem reasonable to conclude that in situations where the two forms of social deviance clash, either through respondents making an association between mental illness and crime or through the actual commission of crimes by the mentally disordered, very little evidence can be found to support the over-simplified double deviance identity hypothesis.

Sources of variation influencing attitudes

It has become increasingly apparent throughout this review of the literature that both public and professional attitudes are determined, to some extent, by the personal attributes of the patient. Similarly, a large amount of research has indicated that certain characteristics of the respondents themselves may also influence attitudes towards the mentally ill. Respondents can be differentiated on the basis of both demographic and psychographic variables. Knowledge of such variables is important for a number of reasons: Firstly, they will help to identify the particular social environments in which patients who are or have been mentally ill will most effectively interact. Secondly, the relevance of making comparisons between studies may be substantially reduced if information were readily available on such variables. Finally, the differences between respondents may help explain why no clear overall trend in the results has been established.

The central concern of this section will, therefore, be to discuss the findings in terms of some of the main sources of variation among the different populations' attitudes towards the mentally ill, namely: age, gender, education, socio-economic status, race and ethnicity, and previous experience with the mentally ill. For completeness some attention will also be paid to certain characteristics of the social context which may influence public attitudes, in particular, the effect of establishing psychiatric services within the community.

Attitudes: the influence of age, gender education and socio-economic status

Ramsey and Seipp's (1948a, 1948b) principal finding was that enlightened attitudes were positively correlated with a person's educational level and negatively correlated with age. Such observations have in fact been confirmed in several later studies which considered prejudice in general (Clark and Binks, 1966; Lawton, 1964) and the rejection of the mentally ill in particular (Phillips, 1966; Phillips, 1964; Freeman, 1961; Whatley, 1959). It has also been observed that respondents from both high and low socio-economic status differ in terms of their perception of the mentally ill. Surveying the relatives of mental patients Hollingshead and Redlich (1958) noted that the lower the status the greater the level of fear and resentment, while those respondents who occupied the higher socio-economic groups had higher levels of shame and guilt. Similarly, Dohrenwend and Chin-Shong (1967) found that the higher status groups were more likely to recognise descriptions of psychopathological behaviour as signs of mental illness. Furthermore, with particular regard to the influence of gender on attitudes it would appear that no difference in approach has been found between male and female respondents (Phillips, 1963; Whatley, 1959).

A more recent study on attitudes towards the mentally ill, carried out in Ireland during the early 1990s, shows a considerable degree of support for these earlier findings (Murphy et al, 1993). In general, this study revealed four underlying factors: fear; lack of sympathy; perceived community rejection and personal rejection, from which only factor 2, was significantly associated with the study's main socio-demographic variables. Overall, lack of sympathy correlated with old age, low educational level and low socio-economic status. Notably, the respondent's gender had no influence on any of the study's four principal components.

With regard to this lack of a gender effect on attitudes, a recent series of articles (Wolff et al, 1996a, 1996b, 1996c), reporting on the findings of a baseline study about community perceptions of the mentally ill, reached the same conclusion (Wolff et al, 1996b). A factor analysis of their results revealed three implicit components: fear and exclusion; social control and goodwill. The main determinants of more social control were low social class and increased age with high education showing the strongest independent effect on goodwill towards the mentally ill (Wolff et al, 1996b).

It has been suggested that the attitudinal differences generated by these variables may be due to a number of inter-relating factors. Traditionally, unsympathetic attitudes are acquired during early socialisation and they are only modified as one moves through the formal education system and becomes more aware of the psychiatric perspective (Bord, 1971; Scheff, 1966). Thus the attenuation of formal education, largely amongst the lower status groups, will limit their opportunity to become familiar with the 'enlightened' ideology. Instead, the traditional view is re-enforced via the media (Matas et al, 1985). The frequent portrayal of the mentally disturbed in films, on television, and theatre drama, etc, probably misinforms people about psychiatric problems as much as it informs via educational documentaries, etc.[21] However, such an explanation does not satisfactorily account for the strong relationship found between age and generally optimistic attitudes. With regard to this fact it has also been suggested that there exists a common factor running through all three variables.

"As to what this factor might be, it is likely that some form of culturally generated liberalism is responsible ... " (Whatley, 1959:316).

Thus traces of the 'traditional' perspective remain among the older respondents carried over from an earlier generation, while the younger persons' more favourable attitude is the product of a more liberal and humanitarian society.[22] By implication, this suggests that younger respondents are more liberal in their approach because their socialisation experiences are more directly related to the mentally ill via increased information and contact in the community. A view confirmed by Wolff et al (1996c) who showed that those who were more willing to socially control the mentally ill, namely, those over the age of 50 years old, had less knowledge about the mentally ill. In fact, when knowledge was regressed out of the equation, the age variable no longer demonstrated an effect.

Whatever the reason, it would appear that young, well educated, middle class individuals are less likely to cling to the traditionally negative stereotypes, are more likely to recommend professional treatment, and are more optimistic about the outcome of treatment. Furthermore, one could infer from these findings that patients interacting within such groups are more likely to encounter social environments conducive to their needs, which in turn will help during the course of their re-adjustment to the community (Murphy et al, 1993; Alder et al, 1952).

Unfortunately, there exists a fair amount of evidence which challenges this generally accepted viewpoint. With regard to the relationship between these variables and the interpretation of psychopathological behaviour, D'Arcy and Brockman (1976) argue that the reported findings are either limited or show no real pattern. Ambiguities have also been found within studies which have considered the relationship between demographic variables and prejudice. Nunnally (1961) showed that the negative attitude held towards the mentally ill was very general:

"old people and young people, highly educated people and people with little formal training - all tend to regard the mentally ill as relatively dangerous, dirty, unpredictable and worthless" (Nunnally, 1961:51).

To obscure the issue still further, some studies have observed a positive change in attitudes among samples which are predominantly of a lower socio-economic status and less educated (Crocetti et al, 1971; Lemkau and Crocetti, 1962). Furthermore, earlier assumptions have recently been made even more equivocal. Howells (1984) concluded that age and education have little effect on the overall positive public image of the mentally ill offender. Finally, in terms of attitudinal social distance Eker (1985) and others have suggested that the characteristics of patients themselves are more important than other factors. While with regard to socio-economic status in particular, Dohrenwend and Chin-Shong (1967) noted that when a pattern of behaviour is defined as mentally ill by both high and low status groups, the latter are more rejecting than the former. Their research partly dispels the notion that lower status groups accept more deviant behaviour due to their unwillingness or inability to identify the case vignettes as mentally ill.

"Lower status groups are predisposed to greater intolerance of the kinds of deviance that both they and higher status groups define as serious mental illness. Their definition of serious mental illness is narrower than that of higher status groups, giving the appearance of greater tolerance of deviance from the vantage point of the higher status groups, including the mental health professionals" (Dohrenwend and Chin-Shong, 1967:321).

Freeman (1961) also challenges the strong relationship found by Hollingshead and Redlich (1958) by stating that their findings may be accounted for by the inclusion of education as a factor in their social class index. Freeman (1961) concluded that:

"enlightened attitudes towards mental illness can be more parsimoniously accounted for on the basis of differential verbal ability [measured by a multiple choice vocabulary test] than on the basis of differences in 'style of life'" (Freeman, 1961:65).

Attitudes: the influence of race and ethnicity

Because the variables of race and ethnicity are nearly always confounded with socio-economic status, age and education, it is almost impossible to determine whether or not it has a specific influential effect on attitudes. Some evidence suggests that blacks tend to adopt a traditionally unsympathetic and authoritarian approach (Fournet, 1967) while others have shown that middle class blacks are no more rejecting than their white counterparts (Ring and Schein, 1970). More recently, Hall and Tucker (1985) found significant differences in both blacks' and whites' understanding of mental illness. Blacks were more likely to believe that the mentally ill look and act differently from most people and that such disturbances could be controlled by the avoidance of morbid thoughts. Furthermore, Wolff et al (1996b) noted that one of the most striking findings to be revealed by their research was the influence of ethnic origin (Asians, Caribbeans and Africans) on increased social control. Thus there appears to exist some additional support for Edgerton and Karno's (1971) implicit claim that beliefs could be culturally specific. One possible criticism of the studies which have considered the attitudes of various race and ethnic groups is the researchers' neglect to contextualise those minorities being studied. Most of the surveys have been carried out in America so we can deduce that the respondents were American blacks (Tucker, 1979). However, in order to conclude that attitudes are culturally specific a great deal more information is required as to the type of communities from which these samples were drawn, for example, was mental health education available and how ethnically mixed were these communities?

Attitudes: the influence of previous experience with the mentally ill

With regard to previous contact with the mentally ill, Link and Cullen (1986) tested the conceptual scheme developed by Jones et al (1984). Briefly, this theory states that contact with mentally disturbed persons will to a certain extent influence opinions.

> "Thus contact between 'marked' and 'unmarked' persons will modify the preconceptions each has about the stigmatised condition" (Link and Cullen, 1986:289).

If this is in fact the case, then activities which bring the mentally ill and the public together, such as community integration, will encourage more positive attitudes towards the mentally ill. However, although Link and Cullen (1986) have recently found a statistically significant inverse association between contact and perceptions of dangerousness, earlier and more recent research has produced evidence which is not so clear.

In evaluating the impact of contact on attitudes, different approaches have been used. Most studies have involved college student participation in volunteer programmes or psychiatric nurses who have completed their training, though another main approach used has been to measure the effect that personal acquaintance with the mentally ill has on attitudes towards this minority. In the former type of study, a pre-post test experimental design was implemented, the intervening condition being contact with mental patients. Improvements in attitudes via the use of this technique have been noted on many occasions (Malla and Shaw, 1987; Chinsky and Rappaport, 1970; Smith, 1969). Such studies, however, may be strongly criticised on methodological grounds as the subjects were probably not 'naïve' during the course of the experiment.

"It seems unlikely that they could have failed to receive the message, implicitly or explicitly, that they were supposed to adopt more humanistic views towards mental patients" (Rabkin, 1974:23).

Holmes (1968), using a sample which was much less motivated towards a sympathetic understanding of mental patients and a design which included behavioural as well as attitudinal measures, concluded that contact alone is not enough to provoke change in attitudes. Johannsen (1969) suggested that the environment in which these experiments are conducted may be responsible for the lack of change. Institutional tours, like tours of zoos may provoke certain immediate emotions such as pity and sadness but are not likely to stimulate a sense of respect for mental patients.

With regard to the other main approach - personal acquaintance - Phillips (1963) noted that the level of social distance was reduced between respondents and patients as their relationship moved from 'no acquaintance' to 'friend' and to 'family'. Swingle (1965), however, appears to have found an inverse relationship ie, visitors who were 'related' to hospitalised mental patients were more rejecting than 'non related' visitors.

More recently, it has been suggested that knowing someone who has suffered from a mental disorder is not sufficient per se to reduce the need to exercise a degree of social control (Wolff et al, 1996b) nor to produce a generally more positive perception (Murphy et al, 1993). These findings actually conflict with other evidence which has shown that previous experience of the mentally ill is associated with a generally more tolerant approach (Brockington et al, 1993; Taylor and Dear, 1981).

Attitudes: the influence of professional groups' demographic variables

In section two, studies regarding the attitudes of various professional groups towards mental patients were considered. Of these groups, investigators only appear to have reported on the sources of variation among attitudinal difference held by personnel engaged in the areas of social welfare and mental health - psychiatrists, psychologists, social workers, nurses and assistants. While a general review of the literature on professional groups led us to conclude that each occupational category within each field appeared to have an independent attitudinal orientation, a few studies have suggested that these attitudes are also influenced by the demographic variables age, education and social status, just as choice of occupation is sometimes determined by these variables.

Middleton (1953) and Lawton (1965, 1964) both found that prejudice in general and authoritarianism and social restrictiveness in particular were positively related to age and years of service. Baker and Schulberg (1967) also found that age was related to a positive view of community mental health. Cohen and Struening (1962) failed to reach a similar conclusion with regard to age, though the authors did manage to find a negative correlation between education and authoritarianism, and a positive correlation between education and factors concerning mental hygiene ideology and interpersonal aetiology.

Recently, Moore and Kuipers (1992) examined the behavioural correlates of the psychographic variable expressed emotion on mental health staff's interactive relations with long-standing mentally ill patients. The authors found that staff with high levels of expressed emotion generally tended to be more negative about the patient and more authoritarian during the course of interaction.

Attitudes: the influence of the social context

In the interest of completeness a brief mention should perhaps also be made of the very limited amount of research which has considered certain contextual features that may shape public attitudes towards the mentally ill. Probably the most important variable within the social context that may influence attitudes is the geographical proximity of psychiatric facilities. It seems reasonable to suggest that, in areas where there exists a variety of treatment modalities such as day hospitals, crisis centres, etc, less stigma and rejection will be shown towards the mental patient than in communities where such facilities do not exist. The findings on this issue, however, appear inconclusive. Smith (1981) found that people who lived near a community mental hospital showed greater acceptance of those who were described as seriously mentally ill than those who lived further afield. However, Hall et al (1979) reached the opposite conclusion on the basis of their earlier evidence ie, greater distance was correlated with greater attitudinal tolerance. Of course, it could be argued that while such facilities may have initially encouraged greater public acceptance, the increasing presence of chronically disturbed individuals in the community may ultimately have a negative impact. As Rabkin (1980a) has pointed out, improvements in community attitudes may have reached a 'plateau' with current trends in deinstitutionalisation threatening a decline in general acceptance. Smith (1981) has suggested that the overall effect of distance is small or acts as a surrogate for other variables. Segal and Aviram (1978) offer support to this view by suggesting that successful reintegration and positive attitudes towards the mentally ill are linked to a number of characteristics such as the type of host community, for example, low or high social cohesion and the type of facility and its residents to be placed within the community.

Two more recent studies concluded that while the respondents of Bromsgrove, an area served by a traditional mental hospital, were slightly more tolerant than respondents in Malvern, an area with a community based service, their (Bromsgrove's) interpretation of mental illness was much narrower. When the members of the Malvern community were presented with case vignettes of mentally ill persons, however, their attitude seems to have become more positive and tolerant (Brockington et al, 1993; Hall et al, 1993).

Wolff et al (1996a) found that while 82% of their sample had heard about the policy of community based care for the mentally ill, only 29% were aware that such psychiatric services for the long-term mentally ill were about to be set up in their street. A majority of the respondents (66%) were opposed to the idea of closing psychiatric hospitals and while accepting the need for some form of community based care, at least one-in-five felt that such facilities would have a bad effect on the community.[23]

Summary

Judging from the evidence it would appear, perhaps with the exception of gender, that certain socio-demographic variables clearly have an impact on the nature of respondents' perceptional orientation towards the mentally ill. However, the picture relating to which particular characteristics have the greatest level of influence on a specific attitudinal trait remains unclear. The findings which point to an association between negative evaluations of the mentally ill by respondents of a lower educational level, increased age and limited experience, appear to be more pronounced particularly amongst the more recent studies. However, while these results may implicitly increase our confidence about such associations, there still remains a sufficient degree of inconsistency within the research findings to justify the equivocal conclusion that:

"major demographic determinants of attitudes toward mental illness are as yet unidentified" (Freeman, 1961:66).

A critical review of the research on attitudes towards the mentally ill

The central aim of the debate in the literature and the analyses performed on researchers' quantitative findings was to try and persuade the observer to interpret the variance within the research results in accordance with a particular ideological position. Approximately twenty years has gone by since the last major study in this area was published, however, (D'Arcy and Brockman, 1976) and these then so important discussions between the supporters of the medical paradigm and those who favoured a social deviance view, seem to have somehow lost their impetus within contemporary mental health epistemologies. It no longer seems appropriate or even enough to simply carry out another study and thus provide yet more evidence for or against either the medical or social deviance paradigm. Instead, perhaps the time has come to step back for a moment and engage in a more critical examination of the way researchers have studied attitudes towards the mentally ill.

An era in attitudinal surveys 1950s - 1970s

What seems most striking from an analysis of the literature is the time frame in which these studies were carried out. Enthusiasm for research in this area was initially set alight in a small Canadian town pseudo-named 'Blackfoot' during the 1950s (Cummings, 1957). Coincidentally, 'Blackfoot' was also the town which marked the end of an era, for after its re-survey in 1974 only a smouldering interest in the debate between the psychiatrically and sociologically orientated approaches to the subject of attitudinal differentiation and change remained. However, within the twenty years or so that this ideological conflict reigned, scores of studies were carried out on attitudes towards the mentally ill, covering dozens of geographical areas in both North America and Canada. Moreover, within the epistemological context of the time each research programme often had quite specific aims: some were concerned primarily with attitudes towards former mental patients (Whatley, 1959), while others investigated attitudes to mental health and illness in general (Nunnally, 1961). Some studies considered change over time (Olmstead and Durham, 1976), while others wished to concentrate upon the variance within specific demographic variables (Freeman, 1961). Still others were more concerned with verifying the psychometric properties of a particular measuring instrument (Jegede, 1976).

So why did this particular ideological approach to the study of attitudes towards the mentally ill burn out after only two decades? The answer probably has something to do with the underlying purpose of these surveys which was to examine the influence, if any, that the intensive mental health educational campaigns of the late 1950s and early 1960s had upon attitudes. The central objective of the mental health movement was to enhance the general public's understanding of the medical model ie, to regard mental illness with the same non-rejecting valuations as somatic illness. In more practical terms, it was hoped that a higher degree of understanding of mental health issues amongst the public would help them to become more tolerant of the emergency clinics and home care services that were being established within communities during this period (Lemkau and Crocetti, 1962).

By the 1970s, no clear conclusions had been reached as to the success of these educational programmes. Disillusioned by this fact, a number of researchers began to seriously question the theoretical and methodological framework in which these studies were being carried out. The primary purpose of such a critical analysis was to determine whether or not these inconclusive results were more artifact than real. Although ultimately, the collective effect of each of the problem factors considered probably explains why the continued pursuance of such research fell out of favour with most investigators.

In the remainder of this section these theoretical and methodological criticisms will be reviewed within the context of contemporary academic thought. During the course of considering these issues, an attempt will be made to develop some alternative structural and procedural measures - an essential prerequisite to the task of clarifying our understanding as to how the study of attitudes towards the mentally ill has started to be reshaped since the 1980s.

The narrow interpretation of models

Probably the main reason for the abandonment of this research framework was the growing realisation among researchers that a chasm had emerged between survey rhetoric, which still attempted to measure the effects of the mental health education programmes, and the reality of contemporary psychiatric thought. It is clear from the discussion that has taken place throughout this review that the research is based primarily upon two diametrically opposed ideologies, namely, the medical model and the social deviance model.[24] The irony of the 1970s was that the surveys still measured the influence of campaigns which taught the public about the medical model of mental illness at a time when an increasing number of professionals were extending their conceptualisation of the mental disorders to include a psychosocial paradigm.

Furthermore, there appears to have been some murmuring of discontent for the social deviant model. Authors such as Sarbin and Mancuso (1972, 1970) have a psychosocial conception of mental illness, yet in actual fact what their research in support of this view does, is object to the whole notion of mental illness. The research thus supports a social deviance/conspiratorial model (Szasz, 1987) and not a psychosocial model, as the surveys do nothing more than produce evidence which questions the view that the public has become more aware of the concept mental illness, and show that those persons who have been identified as mentally disturbed are treated unfavourably. Crocetti et al (1972), writing about those studies which have dismissed the medical model, states that:

> "their assertions suggest an underlying premise: that there is no such thing as mental illness, but that there is simply deviant behaviour" (Crocetti et al, 1972:4).

It can be seen that within this social deviance model there are clear signs of influence from the then dominant labelling or social reaction theorists (Scheff, 1966; Goffman, 1961) and those who were critical of psychiatry itself (Szasz, 1961; Laing, 1961). The fact that discontent with this model arose at a time when both the labelling and anti-psychiatry perspectives were losing respect during the early 1970s is probably more than just coincidental (Gove, 1975).

Today the psychosocial model stands as an accepted positive ideological framework. There is a clear need to identify vulnerable populations at risk in the community so that early intervention and treatment can be provided. This model had in fact been clearly identified in the 1960s (Siegler and Osmond, 1966). Unfortunately, while the opportunity was there, no one was prepared to apply it to the study of public attitudes.

> "Alternative formulations of a psychosocial nature offer greater explanatory value. Concepts developed within this latter framework today seem more important to communicate to the public, but prevailing educational efforts still follow the older, traditional format (of a medical model). It would seem ... that Sarbin and his colleagues would be best justified in criticising Crocetti, and other workers who hold similar views, on this basis" (Rabkin, 1974:29).

Future considerations A wide array of evidence regarding various forms of psychopathological behaviour is now available. In a pluralist society such as ours data may be obtained from such diverse sources as anthropology and existential epistemology; physiological and behavioural psychology; psychopharmacology and sociology; psychoanalysis and organic psychiatry. Future research on attitudes towards the mentally ill must, therefore, avoid becoming tied to the consideration of any one specific model, for no matter how methodologically sound it may be, it will only serve to provide a very limited and probably distorted picture.

The influence of epistemology upon objectivity

Conflicting results in the area of attitudes towards the mentally ill may be partly explained via a consideration of the underlying epistemological differences that existed between those who supported a medical model of mental illness and those who promoted the social deviance paradigm.

> "[Their] divergent evaluations of current public attitudes seems at least partly due to differences in underlying ideologies and research strategies that lead to differences in expectation regarding the amount and direction of attitude change regarded as necessary and desirable" (Rabkin, 1974:13).

Thus of fundamental importance to the maintenance of scientific objectivity is the nature of the researchers' underlying epistemology, for although the validity of most researchers' qualitative interpretation of their quantitative findings should possibly not be considered as a factor influencing attitudinal variance, people's ability to conform with scientific canons when they take up causes probably should (Nettler, 1970). For example, personnel in the medical profession are interested in providing mental health care services within the community. Furthermore, they also represent the impetus behind the public education campaigns. Ironically, these personnel are also the researchers who design and carry out the studies, thus as their findings may partly affect policy decisions regarding services, they have little incentive to remain impartial.

Moreover, the research strategy adopted by the supporters of either paradigm has a tendency to produce different results. For example, an analysis of the research techniques used in 17 surveys showed that 8 out of the 12 studies using structured interviews observed positive findings, while the findings from all 5 self-response questionnaire studies were negative. Interestingly, those adhering to a medical model tended to use the structured interview technique in 10 out of 12 cases (Brockman et al, 1979).

Future considerations The aim has been to show the role ideological perspectives may have upon determining methodological considerations. If future researchers wish to remain under the auspice of academic objectivity, rather than merely following a research path which would result in the most suitable outcome for their profession/discipline, then they must remain conscious of the potential bias that may exist within the exclusive use of any one particular data-gathering technique. The employment of alternative data collection strategies within a single study should be seriously considered and researchers should also be prepared to justify their choice of methodology (Creswell, 1994).

Psychometric properties of the key attitudinal measuring instruments

The failure of the overall findings to show a linear progression may be partly explained in terms of the adequacy of a particular measuring instruments' psychometric and other properties. The most commonly employed (either partly or wholly) instruments include: Nunnally's (1961) questionnaire, Gilbert and Levinson's (1957) Custodial Mental Illness Ideology Scale (CMI), Cohen and Struening's (1962) Opinions about Mental Illness Scale (OMI), Osgood, Suci and Tannenbaum's (1957) Semantic Differential Scale (SDT) and Whatley's Social Distance Scale.

Nunnally's (1961) questionnaire was structured around ten factors which were found to identify the content of public knowledge and attitude towards mental illness. These factors, however, are statistically very weak as few correlations reached a score higher than 0.40. Thus the scale's poor inter-item consistency (Ahmed and Vishwanathon, 1984), in addition to the fact that the 10 factors represented only 25% of the total item variance originally used to derive the factors, suggests that this instrument may not in fact be accurately reporting on all the mental health components that it is assumed to represent.

Gilbert and Levinson's (1957) CMI scale was designed to extract information on the ideological beliefs of respondents. Ideology was measured by the respondents' overall position on a continuum, each polar end representing humanism or custodialism. While this scale has not been criticised regarding its psychometric validity, it has been challenged on the basis of its underlying assumption that attitudes about mental illness fall within a single dimension. Respondents may well be humanistic in their outlook, however, in terms of therapy, for example, we do not know whether they favour medical or sociotherapeutic forms of care.

Cohen and Struening's (1962) OMI questionnaire was not subject to this criticism as it was a multidimensional scale. The five dimensions represented were authoritarianism; benevolence; mental hygiene ideology; social restrictiveness and interpersonal aetiology. It is a popular measure among researchers and its psychometric properties appear to be strong (Struening and Cohen, 1963). However, it has been criticised as being too complex (Lawton, 1964). This suggests that information derived from the scale may be inaccurately interpreted or lost during the analysis phase.

The SDT scale, originally developed by Osgood and his colleagues in 1957, has found an important place in attitude research and is often used in the field of mental health. The meaning of a concept such as 'mental illness' is determined by rating a series of adjective scales which are polar opposites such as good - bad, dangerous - safe, etc. The scale is normally coded from 1 through to 7. It has been criticised on the grounds that it is never clear whether the whole domain of a concept has been covered by the scales used, and so only certain aspects of the attitude parameter towards a particular concept are being examined. Olmstead and Durham (1976) were probably aware of this when they observed that:

"failure to detect a change may not mean that it has not occurred but only that the instrument used did not detect it" (Olmstead and Durham, 1976:42).

Whatley's (1959) social distance scale has been used quite extensively as a means of determining society's level of rejection/acceptance of the mentally ill. Yet, such standard instruments have a fairly limited potential. This scale offers the implicit assumption that reactions to a Guttman-type scale of social distance items is sufficient in itself to characterise the essence of the relationship between 'them' and 'us'. The scale, however, is limited to the extent that it excludes the more complex possibility that rejection may co-exist or indeed interact with feelings of sympathy, understanding and compassion (Doll et al, 1976).

Another problem contributing to the limitation of scales in general is a statistical one regarding the size and significance of an effect. In stating that respondents can recognise psychopathological behaviour, what percentage of the sample must label the cases and how many of these must they label? Furthermore, what amount of social distance constitutes rejection? For example, Phillips (1964) observed a mean scale score of 4.73, but what does this signify? Does this mark public rejection or not? The figure only appears to become significant during a comparative analysis with other similarly designed studies - independently each study appears to offer very little.

More generally, a number of studies, particularly those carried out during the 1950s and early 1960s, have used measures whose psychometric properties in terms of reliability or validity have never been tested (Ramsey and Siepp, 1948a, 1948b) or have proved controversial (Bord, 1971). Furthermore, their data analyses were either non-existent or unsophisticated (Freeman, 1961; Carstairs and Wing, 1958). Such factors must bring into serious doubt the significance of their findings.

Future considerations It is evident from the above discussion that the measurement of attitudes is beset with problems and difficulties. As a result, the task of formulating the questions and extensively pretesting the final measuring instrument can be time consuming. For this reason replication within attitudinal studies is greatly encouraged (Sudman and Bradburn, 1983), always assuming, of course, that one uses good quality questions which do in actual fact measure the attitude that is intended to be studied.

Furthermore, not only should subsequent research include a wider array of models of mental illness as discussed earlier, but one must ensure that the wide array of dimensions that are present within a given ideological framework are also measured by the survey instrument. Thus a multidimensional measure similar to that offered by Cohen and Struening's (1962) OMI scale would be more appropriate than other unidimensional scales.

With regard to the quantitative analyses of future studies, it is clear that more sophisticated statistical models such as principal component analysis and other multivariate techniques should be applied, in order to gain a more accurate understanding of the underlying structure and differentiation of popular views.

Characteristics of the referent

A considerable number of the studies reviewed, surveyed social responses to the mentally ill in general through the use of questions simply referring to 'someone who has been mentally ill' or 'a person in a mental hospital'. Methodologically, it is assumed that the use of such referents as 'mental illness' or 'mental patient' will remove any experiences or biases that the respondents may have. However, there is no evidence in support of such an assumption (Siassi et al, 1973). In fact, the available data seems to suggest that the use of such blanket terms increases the likelihood of bias. Elinson et al (1967) found that 76% of their respondents would have answered the social distance questions they were initially asked somewhat differently, had they known in advance what kind of mental illness the person had. The type of bias attached to labels such as 'mental illness' has been extensively documented within the literature of the social reaction theorists (Scheff, 1966; Goffman, 1961; Lemert, 1951). On the basis of this evidence it is hardly surprising that measurement techniques such as the semantic differential only ever produce generally negative results (Olmstead and Durham, 1976; Fracchia et al, 1976; Nunnally, 1961).

A number of studies did, however, use Star's (1955) case vignettes in their questions instead of merely a label. These descriptions succeeded in presenting this minority group in a much more realistic light, by making the respondent alert to the fact that there were various kinds of mental illness whose pathology differed from each other to extreme degrees. Unfortunately, one of the first questions that was asked about these case vignettes was 'Do you think that the person in the case description is mentally ill?' As with the single label referent, the true nature of the response is being smothered by the cultural stereotype associated with such labels.

Future considerations Even with the added depth provided by the case vignette approach, a unidimensional picture is still being presented to the respondent as no other identities, apart from the deviant behaviour held by the actor, are being evaluated. Future researchers would do well to remember that our image of others is not made within a vacuum, on the contrary, it is contingent upon other types of information.

"The 'mentally ill' are not simply isolated entities in social space but are composites of intersecting relationships ... the meaning and definition of any given act, is dependant upon social characteristics of the actor other than those indicating deviancy" (Bord, 1971:498).

The homogeneous or heterogeneous nature of attitudes

Because both Star (1955) and the Cummings (1957) obtained very similar results, despite large differences in the nature of their study samples, most of the following research has tended to assume a homogeneity of attitudes at a national or even a continental level. This fact is quite evident from the literature which clearly shows the authors' enthusiasm for comparing methodologically similar studies. In such situations, evaluations are made by indiscriminately comparing one study with another, or by making sweeping generalisations about public attitudes on the basis of a very restricted piece of research. The possibility that such assumptions may be erroneous due to the wide disparity in study sample characteristics has never been fully considered (Brockman et al, 1979).

With regard to the population samples used in the studies, not only do they differ dramatically in size but there are also large variations in the nature of each sample. Star (1955) carried out the only nationwide study (N=3,500), whereas the Cummings (1957) sample was based upon a small Canadian town 'Blackfoot' (N=100). Moreover, the studies carried out during the 1960s were largely based on towns in North America.

Even in North America there were great variations between their samples. For example, Lemkau and Crocetti's (1962) study - which was the first to observe any real change in attitudes - stated that the "population that comprised our sample was not a highly educated, well-to-do group" (Lemkau and Crocetti, 1962:694).

Forty-one per cent of the sample was black which was not even representative of the USA as a whole, whereas the Cummings' (1957) study town of 'Blackfoot' consisted largely of white British settlers who were fairly well educated and predominantly middle class. Furthermore, Dohrenwend and Chin-Shong's (1967) study sample was ethnically mixed including: Jews, Irish and Puerto Rican respondents, while two thirds of Bentz and Edgerton's (1969) sample were poorly educated Baptists. Thus on the basis of the evidence pertaining to the unique nature of each of these studies, it would not be unreasonable for us to seriously question the validity of performing such comparative analyses.

Justification for the homogeneity approach appears to derive from the fact that a modest proportion of the studies carried out since the 1960s do not replicate the earlier findings. This is true whether the study area is urban or rural, in the United States, Canada or Britain. For example, Rootman and Lafave's (1969) Canadian survey results are very similar to the North American study of Lemkau and Crocetti (1962). Sydiaha (1971), however, who was concerned with ethnic factors in relation to community attitudes towards the mentally ill, used Rootman and Lafave's (1969) survey community 'Saltwater' as one of four study areas and concluded that:

"every community had its own sort of conception about mental illness and its own way of dealing with it, and it really was not very sensible to try to generalise across communities in terms of social parameters" (Sydiaha, 1971:389).

Placing these comments within the context of 20 previous studies on attitudes towards the mentally ill, it has been observed that 17 different geographical areas have been considered. Furthermore, several of the studies have samples drawn from specialist groups. On the basis of this evidence Brockman et al (1979) argue that collating these studies for the purpose of comparing, evaluating or generalising is clearly in danger of overlooking the possible heterogeneous nature of attitudes. Hence, what so many authors interpret as a positive or negative directional flow in attitudes could in fact be the discovery of individual group norms and attitudes which have always existed.[25] If this is in fact the case, then the only way to truly measure directional change is by controlling for the population sample, thus re-surveys appear essential (Brockman et al, 1979).

Future considerations Prospective researchers must be aware of the dangers involved in making general statements on the basis of results obtained from populations with narrowly defined parameters. In order to measure attitude change via replication, a study needs to be very specific about the geographical areas surveyed, the types of samples used, the variations within samples, etc. Furthermore, most of the studies were carried out with the sole purpose of being able to compare their findings with earlier work. Thus as we mentioned earlier, the value of each survey per se is probably fairly limited. It is important, therefore, that subsequent researchers ensure that the design of each survey is such that the information it provides can be used independently for both theoretical and practical purposes.

Attitudinal theory and its relationship to behaviour

A common misconception held by most investigators of attitudes towards the mentally ill is that "attitudes are precursors or determinants of overt behaviour (Rabkin, 1974:24).

The empirical evidence, claiming that such a view is misconceived, is extensive. A review of the literature in the area conducted by Wicker (1969) found that 'words' and 'deeds' are typically unrelated or only slightly related, with correlations rarely rising above 0.30. In fact, some studies have shown marked discrepancies between these two categories of information (Deutscher, 1966).[26]

Such findings, however, are hardly surprising in view of the large number of factors that may influence their actions. For example, factors such as other attitudes, values and beliefs held, our social and cognitive characteristics, the influence of others and the range of possible alternative behaviours available may all influence our actions. Other sources of discrepancy are methodological, for example, it is much easier to express prejudice to a mail questionnaire than in an interview situation (Bord, 1971). Furthermore, the use of labels within questions, such as 'mental patient', provoke a culturally defined stereotype which is seldom apparent in a face-to-face situation with such an individual.

Despite these facts, a link between attitudes and behaviour regarding mental illness has on occasion been demonstrated. Cohen and Struening (1965, 1964) carried out a series of studies assessing the effect of hospital atmosphere on length of patient stay. The OMI questionnaire was administered to the staff members of twelve neuropsychiatric hospitals. Their findings showed that patients in hospitals with a strong authoritarian-restrictive atmosphere were admitted for longer periods of time, thus a relationship was found between attitudes and the discharge timing of mental patients.[27]

Throughout this review the terms 'attitude' and 'belief' have been used interchangeably, the assumption being that each concept is acting merely as a synonym for the purpose of describing an individuals cognitive state towards the phenomenon of mental illness. With regard to their relation to behaviour, however, some authors have made quite specific distinctions between these terms. In particular, Farina and Fisher (1982) have differentiated between 'attitudes' and 'beliefs' by stating that the latter refers to "assertions which are objectively verifiable" (Farina and Fisher 1982:49). For example, an answer to the question: 'Are more men than women diagnosed as mentally ill?' expresses a belief, for in principle we can confirm whether the answer is true or not through an examination of medical records. 'Attitudes' on the other hand are individual subjective feelings or values towards an object. For example, a semantic differential scale asking about whether the mentally ill are good or bad, provokes a response which expresses an 'attitude' - a point of view which cannot be empirically verified. To put it another way an 'attitude' is a psychological state which is unverifiable except by the individual reporting it.

In fact, in terms of this conceptual distinction both 'attitudes' and 'beliefs' about the mentally ill appear to have quite different properties. According to Nunnally (1961) beliefs are influenced by demographic variables such as age and education while attitudes remained constantly negative. Furthermore, over time beliefs seem to change continuously while attitudes remain fairly stable (Farina, 1983). Though probably the main distinction that can be made between attitudes and beliefs towards the mentally ill is their contribution to our understanding of actual behaviour. Previous evidence suggests that there is a very tenuous link and complex relationship between an individual's attitudes and his or her ultimate actions (Wicker, 1969). However, the relationship between beliefs about mental disorders and actual behaviour towards those who occupy this minority group, seems to be much more comprehensible, useful and promising (Furnham and Bower, 1992; Furnham, 1988b; Farina and Fischer, 1982).

Future considerations Thus to enhance the theoretical and in particular practical utility of a survey study, current thought seems to favour the use of a measuring instrument which obtains information and knowledge about objectively verifiable phenomena. An important point to note is that such an approach does not imply that we should only measure views towards those issues that can currently be 'proven' in a tangible sense, such as beliefs about the proportion of women to men clinically diagnosed with depression in a single year. Rather, the notion may also apply to ideas which have yet to be conclusively verified, such as the possible existence of an organic basis to the schizophrenias.

Summary

The central aim of this section has been to critically consider the main theoretical and methodological limitations of the research on attitudes towards the mentally ill. From this analysis it has been possible to briefly identify certain structural and procedural measures which may usefully be considered in future studies.

It would appear that the major task facing research workers in this area today is to develop a research instrument incorporating not only traditional and contemporary psychiatric ideologies, but which also has sufficient scope to account for the complex layers of theories that can be found within each paradigm, and which additionally uses a more socially realistic referent. The items of the questionnaire itself should be directed towards obtaining information on beliefs rather than attitudes, and the data analysis should be more sophisticated than the mere presentation of percentages. Finally, careful consideration should be given to the way in which the survey is designed and administered.

Distinct psychopathological disorders

Probably the most important methodological criticism discussed in the last section centred around the claim that many of the studies, either explicitly or implicitly, measured popular perceptions about mental illness in general, instead of a particular psychopathological disorder. Within this context, however, the referent 'mental illness' is unclear, as only mental illnesses which qualitatively differ from one another exist. Indeed, it is extremely improbable that beliefs about distinct psychopathological disorders such as neurosis or depression would be highly homogeneous (Elinson et al, 1967). More recently, some researchers have started to address this issue by considering attitudes and beliefs towards a single type of mental disorder. Thus the aim of this section will be to review a number of these studies. In particular, attention will be directed towards those surveys which have been concerned with the psychopathological states referred to as schizophrenia and depression.

These individual psychiatric conditions have been chosen as the central concern of the current research for two primary reasons: firstly, because both schizophrenia and depression may be considered as the most commonly recognised forms of psychiatric morbidity (Arkar and Eker, 1994; Rix, 1987), and secondly, because the association between crime and these types of psychopathological disorder have been well documented (Hodgins, 1993; Lindqvist and Allebeck, 1990; Spry, 1984; Lawson, 1984).

Explanations of schizophrenia

Furnham and Rees (1988) set out to examine the structure of lay beliefs with regard to the causes and characteristics of the mental disorder 'schizophrenia'. Two questionnaires were administered to a sample (N=120) of the population. The first questionnaire dealt with 'common beliefs' and the second with the 'causes of schizophrenia'. Factor analysis of the former instrument's results showed that the public still regarded those who suffered from schizophrenia as potentially dangerous. This factor accounted for 25% of the variance and such a view was also shown to be linked to lay perceptions of the unpredictable nature of the condition. The remaining three factors referred to the amorality (untrustworthiness); egocentric (only considering themselves) and vagrant nature of the schizophrenic. The authors also found that most of the public adhered to a strong misconception about what the disease actually represents. The item which obtained the highest mean value described the schizophrenic as possessing a 'split personality', thus such individuals are viewed as modern day 'Jekyll and Hyde' characters.[28]

Factor analytic results of the questionnaire dealing with the causes of schizophrenia revealed lay beliefs which demonstrated a link between "explicit academic and implicit lay theories" (Furnham and Rees, 1988:218). The main principal components to emerge as causal explanations of schizophrenia included: psychological stress and pressure; biological and genetic; low intelligence and brain damage. Thus it would appear that while there exists some degree of support for the contributory role of psychosocial factors to the onset of schizophrenia, by far the most common explanations seem to centre around aetiologies of an organic nature as postulated by the medical model.

The aforementioned study was limited to the extent that it only investigated lay beliefs in terms of the medical and psychosocial paradigms of schizophrenia.

Acknowledging this weakness, Furnham and Bower (1992) set out to extend this previous work by considering the public's acceptance of the full range of current scientific theories as described by Siegler and Osmond (1966).[29] A questionnaire was developed, containing items describing the following five models - medical, moral-behavioural, psychoanalytic, social and conspiratorial - along eight dimensions - aetiology, behaviour, treatment, function of the hospital and the rights and duties of both the patient and society. Over a hundred respondents completed the questionnaire (N=106), the results of which showed that overall:

"the lay model appears to defy reduction or classification into any one of the five main academic models" (Furnham and Bower, 1992:207).

The factor analytic results do, however, appear to provide a useful insight into the type of lay model most favoured. In terms of aetiology, factor one, which accounted for 11.6% of the variance, revealed that stress, either in childhood development, interpersonal relations or social life generally, was viewed as an important causal agent. Factor two dealt with the schizophrenic's right to the 'sick' role and implicitly suggested that there was a strong degree of support for the belief that schizophrenia and somatic disorders should be treated in a similar way. Another main principal component to emerge, factor three, showed that the public were in favour of schizophrenics being accorded basic human rights and freedoms.

The finding that the general public tends to perceive people with schizophrenia as dangerous (Furnham and Rees, 1988) re-affirms the implicit view of earlier studies. In particular, Nunnally (1961), using global categories on a sematic differential scale, found that both lay and professional respondents believed that 'psychotics' were more dangerous and unpredictable than 'neurotic' patients. Furthermore, given the suggestion that perceived predictability diminishes as the severity of behavioural symptoms increase (Socall and Holtgraves, 1992), we might reasonably expect the schizophrenic to be generally viewed as more unpredictable. This point may be additionally substantiated by the wealth of research which shows that the mental illness concept is strongly stigmatised and feared (Bhugra, 1989; Miles, 1987), while contemporaneously the behavioural patterns associated with the schizophrenic constitute the most widely recognised form of mental illness (Arkar and Eker, 1994).[30] More recently, it has been shown that while schizophrenics are perceived as highly unpredictable and generally feared, they are not considered dangerous (Levey and Howells, 1995). Furthermore, probably as a consequence of the public's generally negative reaction, people with schizophrenia are typically rejected more in terms of social distance than other forms of psychopathology (Levey and Howells, 1995; Hall et al, 1993) and are also perceived as qualitatively different from 'normal' people (Levey and Howells, 1995). This differentness is possibly being characterised by the quintessentially alien nature of the schizophrenic condition which has been described as: "strange, puzzling, sinister and frightening" (Porter, 1987:21).

Explanations of depression

In contrast to the voluminous literature on mental illness in general, there are surprisingly few studies which have investigated popular attitudes and beliefs towards the psychopathological state of depression (McKeon and Carrick, 1991).

Research on lay theories of depression has been dominated largely by the explanatory and descriptive work of Rippere (1981, 1977). These studies consistently demonstrated that there is a great deal of understanding and agreement as to the causes and treatment of depression. It would also appear that this information and a general preparation for the experience of depression are learnt through socialisation, though it is still not clear:

> "what people learn, from whom, how, where, and how, having learnt, they apply their knowledge in their daily lives" (Rippere, 1977:62).

Rippere has also attempted a cross-cultural replication of her work by comparing British and Spanish answers to the question 'what's the thing to do when you're feeling depressed?' Overall, both groups' ideas of depression are similar. A later study by Caro et al (1983) found 12 consensually held solutions for depression. Generally, these included the belief that there was a definite cause which could be controlled as long as one had social and moral support and kept busy by engaging in distracting recreations.

Miralles et al (1983) asked the same cross-cultural sample "when you're feeling depressed what sort of things can make you feel worse?" Overall, both subsamples believed that isolation, being reminded of the issue causing the depression, more problems or a generally worsening situation, would all contribute towards making the respondent feel more depressed.

What is interesting about all these studies is the paradoxical nature of the findings. Certain opposites may have a similar effect, for example, rejection and sympathy, isolation and social contact may all contribute towards making the situation of the depressive person better or worse:

> " ... so many of the situations mentioned as making people feel worse when they are feeling depressed are variants of the same situations which subjects of the previous studies mentioned as being 'the thing to do when you are feeling depressed': seeking social support and sympathy, crawling away on one's own, scrutinising and analysing the reasons for one's depression, working hard, [etc]" (Miralles et al, 1983:490).

A recent survey conducted in Ireland on a nationally representative sample (McKeon and Carrick, 1991) investigated attitudes towards the sufferers of depression and their beliefs as to the condition's aetiology, its susceptibility to treatment and the most appropriate treatment methods. Overall, 65% of the respondents agreed with the statement, 'people who suffer from depression are not mentally ill'. Furthermore, the majority felt that depression was not the product of a weak will or of feeling sorry for oneself. With regard to the issues most frequently supported as the primary cause of depression: stress, in the form of family or work pressures, (61% agreeing), followed by bereavement (24%) and hereditary factors (13%) received the highest ratings.

Almost three-quarters of the sample (73%) felt that depression could be successfully treated and approximately 50% felt that the best form of therapy would be via the use of 'verbal' treatments such as counselling or talking their problems over with friends. Twenty-three percent of the sample thought that medication would help. Overall, there was a clear willingness to sustain a close degree of contact with those who had suffered from depression and generally it was felt that the respondents:

> "expressed positive attitudes to the depressed ... [furthermore] their concepts of causes and possible treatments of mood disorders generally concurred with those currently used in clinical practice" (McKeon and Carrick, 1991:119).

In a more recent study, which is of particular relevance to the current research, Arkar and Eker (1994) investigated the influence of specific psychiatric labels (paranoid schizophrenia and anxiety neurosis/depression) and the behavioural symptoms associated with each type of psychopathology, on various attitudes and beliefs (recognition of mental illness, social distance, expected burden, prognosis and treatment). The results obtained from a two-way ANOVA showed that both treatment effects ie, type of label and type of psychopathology had a significant effect on public perceptions.

Emphasising the results obtained from the ANOVA main effects in relation to the type of psychopathology per se, it was shown that the paranoid schizophrenic was significantly more likely to be recognised as mentally ill, as a physical burden, as less likely to recover from their illness and as less likely to benefit from counselling therapies than the anxiety neurotic/depressive.

Summary

The focus of this section has been on reviewing those studies which have considered lay attitudes and beliefs towards various psychopathological disorders, namely, schizophrenia and depression. Overall, the research suggests that the structure of implicit lay theories appears to be broadly similar to expressed academic models. Though within the context of these lay theories, beliefs about each type of mental disorder appear to be markedly different.

In general, it has been shown that the schizophrenic is primarily viewed as representing all that is typically associated with the term mentally ill. Thus such patients are perceived as dangerous, violent and unpredictable, feelings which in turn generate a degree of fear and intolerance (Trute et al, 1989). The aetiology of schizophrenia is generally viewed in terms of organic factors which are not susceptible to psychotherapeutically based treatments such as counselling, furthermore, respondents are pessimistic about the prospects of recovery. Almost in direct contrast, the depressive patient is not feared and is clearly accepted by society. The cause is understood primarily in terms of psychosocial explanations and the prognosis is generally optimistic.

Models of mental illness

The aim of this section will be to consider three of Siegler and Osmond's (1974) 'models of madness' - medical (organic), moral (cognitive-behaviour) and psychosocial - in some detail,[31] using only the dimensions (derived from the medical model) most appropriate to the study of popular theories about the mentally ill. We will start by considering the origin and nature of these models before preceding toward a detailed discussion of how the key dimensions of each model (aetiology, behaviour and treatment) are shaped and extended by contemporary academic theory and practice. Finally, it should be kept in mind that the models will be presented as ideal types, thus the impression will be given that each is mutually exclusive. In practice, however, programmes designed for the treatment and care of mental patients do not always adhere to a single paradigm.

Models of mental illness: origin and nature

The territory of most mental disorders is controversial. This point was made very clear to one of the authors (Siegler) during the course of researching her paper 'Attitudes Towards Naming the Illness'. Astonished at the "frequent and often acerbic differences of opinion which arose between staff members", she related her confusion to the other author (Osmond), who replied "why, that's because they are using different models" (Siegler and Osmond, 1974:1). Since that occurrence in 1964 both Siegler and Osmond have worked closely in the study of what they refer to as 'models of madness'.

The authors likened the confusion that existed in psychiatry at the time to the infamous Tower of Babel only worse as:

"each person uses a hodgepodge of bits and pieces of ideas, theories, notions and ideologies in order to engage in a supposedly common enterprise with others similarly confused" (Siegler and Osmond, 1974:11).

In an attempt to both explain and alleviate this confusion, they set about constructing a classification system using material gained from observations in the mental Health Centre "where this problem [had] forced itself unexpectantly upon [their] attention" (Siegler and Osmond, 1974:13).

With additional material from a survey of the then current psychiatric literature they had by 1974 succeeded in sorting the plethora of competing, complementary and sometimes contradictory perspectives into various models.

In particular, these models deal with questions about what sort of thing madness is, what should be done about it and how those involved - the patient, family and society in general - should behave. In fact, it is these common elements that furnish the dimensions of their models. As a result of this achievement, it is now possible to provide not only a summary of modern scientific theories within the field of mental illness, but also a means by which they may be compared.

This idea of using models is not new, however, it does re-awaken particular psychiatric issues which appear to have been long forgotten. As Osmond (1961) observes:

"although the idea of using models of madness in psychiatry is at least a century old, it has not been greatly used until the last decade or so" (Osmond, 1961:221).

In fact, since the original publication of their paper on 'Models of Madness' in 1966 very little attempt has been made to expand upon their work. It is true that a rival set of models were developed by Williams, (1971), however, while they in part derive from the authors models they seem to do so in a rather "truncated and distorted way" (Siegler and Osmond, 1974:7), thus they are viewed as having very little to offer.

The medical model

The principles of this model dominate our understanding of all physical illnesses such as pneumonia, measles, coronary disease, etc. The model's authority in the treatment of mental illnesses is also the most strongly held at the present time[32] although this fact is less obvious.

Aetiology According to Hunter (1973)[33] abnormal mental states and the associated symptoms are not illnesses in themselves, but are the 'epiphenomena' of underlying physical and chemical disturbances primarily in the brain. To date, the aetiology of most mental disturbances including the two most well known psychiatric conditions - schizophrenia and depressive psychosis - is at best unclear. For the time being these two disorders are viewed as functional (rather than organic) due to a failure to find any physical pathology. Despite this fact, however, there are clear grounds for optimism as the:

"list of conditions in which psychological disturbances appear to be symptomatic of underlying physical pathology continues to expand" (Clare, 1980:45).

According to Clare (1980) this list includes: certain dementing conditions which could be caused due to the affect that arteriosclerosis has on the blood vessels of the brain, acute toxic psychosis resulting from substance abuse (alcohol, amphetamines and LSD), and other general psychological problems caused by a variety of physiological disorders such as epileptogenic lesions, brain tumours, etc. Furthermore, it is only recently that biochemists and physiologists have been able to examine the brain in some detail with the help of sophisticated equipment such as computerised tomography and positron emission tomography (PET), in addition to other brain-image techniques such as regional cerebral blood flow (rCBF) (Granville-Grossman, 1985). Recently, biochemists have shown that excess quantities of a neurotransmitter 'dopamine' which regulates levels of arousal, may cause schizophrenic symptoms (McKenna, 1987). Finally, there is some evidence to suggest that genetic factors may also be responsible in some of the schizophrenias (Shields and Slater, 1975; Heston, 1972).

Behaviour Within contemporary psychiatry deviant behaviour is the physician's most reliable tool for making a diagnosis of the type and severity of mental disorders.

"The symptoms and signs [behaviour] are said to be explained by the disease condition ... so if symptom X and sign Y exist then disease Z exists" (Bean, 1985:75).

Within the medical paradigm, however, behaviour is viewed as epiphenomenological ie, it incidentally accompanies some other physio-chemical processes and nothing more. Thus its importance will most certainly decline as more sophisticated techniques such as "electrophoresis, chromosomal analysis and electron microscopy" are developed, which improve clinicians understanding of the patients inner state by "producing yet further concepts of disease expressed in terms of deranged biophysical structures, genes and molecules" (Kendell, 1975:19).

Treatment Within contemporary psychiatry a very large number of psychotropic drugs are readily available for the treatment of mental patients and their use clearly dominates over all other therapeutic methods. In a recent study by Rogers (1993) 98% of her sample of psychiatric patients were given a form of physical treatment compared to only 60% who gained access to other forms of therapy. In general, these psychotropic drugs may be categorised under three broad headings: 'sedatives and tranquillisers', 'hypnotics' and 'antidepressants' (Taylor and Taylor, 1989).

The other major treatments that may be used within this model include surgical (psychosurgery) and electric shock (electroconvulsive therapy) techniques. Their use has, however, declined substantially during the last decade or so as more effective medical drugs became available (Minto, 1985).

The moral (cognitive-behavioural) model

The moral model per se portrays psychopathological behaviour in terms of deviant behaviour, and the mentally ill as autonomous, self-willed individuals who are responsible for their anti-social activities (Clare, 1980). When psychiatrically disturbed, a person may engage in behaviour which others find generally unacceptable. Those members of society, normally friends and relatives, who attempt to bring the behaviour within more tolerable limits are in effect using a moral model of madness. There are a variety of moral models, though overall each utilises the same repertoire of positive and negative sanctions, varying only in degree.

In addition to this "amateur version of the moral model" (Siegler and Osmond, 1974:28), there are those who have a professional knowledge in the techniques of behaviour modification. Essentially, the methods and aims of behaviour therapists are the same as the 'amateurs', the only difference appears to be that the effectiveness of the positive and negative reinforcement schedules used by behaviourists have been demonstrated experimentally, rather than on the basis of conventional wisdom.

Since Siegler and Osmond's formulation of the moral-behavioural model, the discipline of behaviour therapy has grown and diversified out of all recognition.

"It is no longer the monolithic entity it once was, and certainly it is not tied by an 'all-sustaining' behaviouralistic umbilical cord" (Herbert, 1985:247).

Fundamentalist or radical behaviourists are conspicuous by their absence. Nowadays, most embrace a cognitivist conceptualisation of behaviour. This new cognitive approach to psychopathology and the associated principles of cognitive therapy have a great deal in common with the goals of behaviourists, namely, to alleviate overt symptoms of disruptive behaviour directly (Beck, 1989). The central premise underlying the two schools of thought differs, however. The aim of cognitive psychotherapeutic treatment is to alter maladaptive thinking in order to re-modify behaviour, whereas the behaviour therapists use techniques that are directed towards changing the overt behaviour itself.

It should not, however, be assumed that these two treatment approaches are mutually exclusive and that changes in cognitions are brought about exclusively through the use of cognitive psychotherapy. Frequently, behavioural techniques are also employed and often constitute an essential element in cognitive therapy (Gelder, 1986). In fact, it is for this reason that a number of authors (Hawton et al, 1989; Beck, 1989) prefer to conceptualise an inter-related cognitive-behaviour discipline.

Thus the approach which is to be the concern of this section may be termed the moral (cognitive-behavioural) model. The continued inclusion of a moral model element is important for two reasons: Firstly, as discussed earlier, the moral model has some link with the traditional behavioural model and although its usefulness may now be considered as largely historical, its inclusion ensures that the full array of dimensions contained within each model remain comprehensive and complete, as Siegler and Osmond (1966) originally intended. Secondly, the traditional moral element probably still has a great deal of relevance in terms of the central concern of this paper, namely, mentally ill offenders.

The psychotherapeutic techniques associated with the moral (cognitive-behavioural) model have been developed and successfully applied to an increasingly wide range of psychiatric disorders, including: anxiety states, phobic and obsessive disorders, drug abusers, depression, eating disorders and the psychological distress caused by serious sematic illness (Scott, 1989).

Aetiology An important approach towards understanding the aetiology of psychopathological behaviour is in terms of learning theory. Generally, abnormal behaviour is conceptualised as a problem in living (Jehu, 1985), a learned response to the stresses of a complex social environment. Today, however, this learning theory cannon is not restricted to the laws of conditioning but draws upon other principles such as the sufferer's distorted cognitive perceptions (Kazdin, 1978). Aetiological knowledge is, however, of little significance to the central aim of changing the actual behavioural state.

> *Behaviour* "Behaviour therapy is based on a theory which maintains that there is no neurosis underlying the symptom but merely the symptom itself" (Eysenck, 1963:12).

Historically, cognitive-behavioural principles appear to have developed almost as a compromise between behaviourism which denied the importance of the patient's thoughts and perceptions, and psychoanalysis which concentrated exclusively on the patient's unconscious processes thus ignoring any current visible problems (Karasu, 1990). Thus the general focus of moral (cognitive-behaviouralists) is on the conscious (rather than unconscious) process of behaviour which requires evaluation rather than interpretation. Consideration is given not only to the symptoms of that consciousness ie, the maladaptive behaviour (as in Eysenck's interpretation of behaviour therapy), but also the abnormal states of thought which are believed to be an underlying factor causing the dysfunction.

On clinical assessment, the behaviour and underlying thought processes are often evaluated as in breach of either moral or legal principles. Once the symptoms are understood in these terms, therapists can start to 'cure' the disorder.

Treatment This is the central and most important aspect of the model. Each type of cognitive-behavioural psychotherapy is directed towards helping the patient recognise and overcome patterns of distorted thinking and maladaptive behaviour. Essentially, the treatment which is offered within this model represents an educational process in the broadest sense, through focusing on the patient's opportunities for new adaptive learning.

A variety of treatments may be used to a greater or lesser degree, including: simple moral exhortation, applied behavioural analysis, neobehavioural stimulus-response approach (Eysenck, 1975) and pure cognitive therapy. Though probably the most used psychotherapeutic technique within contemporary clinical psychiatry is social learning theory (Jehu, 1985). Here the wide array of cognitive-behavioural treatments available are integrated into a comprehensive framework directed towards the control of the deviant behaviour. Within this approach particular emphasis is given to cognitive processes ie, distorted perceptions and irrational beliefs. Thus early behavioural techniques such as classical and operant conditions, shaping and systematic desensitisation are re-structured in order to account for those cognitions that are influential on certain aspects of behaviour.

The psychosocial model

All psychosocial models start from the premise that there are fundamental aetiological relationships between mental illness and a generally malfunctioning society (Rack, 1982; Clare, 1980). Mental illness is viewed as just another indication of a 'sick' society. Others include: the high rate of marital breakdowns, juvenile delinquency, the generally high crime rate, increased drug addiction, etc.

Aetiology The causal factors in mental illness are believed to result from the pressures of modern life, such as poverty, overcrowding, psychological stress, pollution and many other social, economic and familial pressures. For example, there are a number of epidemiological studies which show that it is often those who are impoverished and disadvantaged (Dohrenwend, 1975; Myers and Bean, 1968)[34] or belong to a certain migrant culture (Rack, 1982) in our society who suffer most from these types of mental illness. With particular regard to depressive disorders, it has been empirically shown that women are more prone to this type of illness than men (Weissman and Klerman, 1985, 1977), that a loose social network reduces the level of emotional support offered, thus increasing the risk of the depressive syndrome occurring (Caplan, 1981) and that the disturbance is more common among those who are unemployed (Warr, 1982; Finlay-Jones and Eckhardt, 1981). Evidence regarding the causal relationship between social factors and schizophrenia seems fairly limited, overall there appear to exist plenty of theories though very little definitive proof (Miller and Cooper, 1988). More recent studies have focused upon the influence of social factors with regard to the course and outcome as opposed to the cause of schizophrenia (Miller and Cooper, 1988). This research appears to be far more productive, for example, Leff and Vaughn (1985) have shown that strongly expressed-emotion among the care-giving relatives of a recovering schizophrenic is likely to cause the patient to relapse.

Behaviour The psychopathological behaviour that psychiatrists define as symptomatic of an underlying disease is generally viewed as an unfortunate consequence of the psychological and situational pressures of society.

Treatment It is society and not the individual that requires change according to those who adhere to the psychosocial conception of mental illness. The factors causing stress and conflict that exist within a community must be reduced. Towards this goal sociotherapy may be viewed as one possible approach.[35] Here mental illness is viewed as a social project which concerns not only the patient but:

> " ... his friends and relations, neighbours, work mates and employers. The local authority and the Department of Social Security and Health may be involved. If he goes to hospital, psychiatrists, nurses, social workers, psychologists, occupational therapists, and welfare organisations of various kinds all come into the situation" (Schoenberg, 1972:43).

Furthermore, if the patient commits a criminal offence, presumably criminal justice agencies would also have a part to play in assisting those who are mentally disturbed (Home Office, 1990).

Internal consistency of models

In general these models are internally coherent:

"the dimensions of any single model are not independent but inter-related, and are normally a direct consequence of the aetiological stance taken by the model's proponents" (Furnham and Bower, 1992:204).

For example, in the medical model the cause is considered to be organic, the behaviour is merely a symptom of this physical malfunction and both these factors indicate the need for some form of physical treatment. The patient's rights and duties are the same as those of the physically sick, and the rights of society are similar to the rights of someone suffering from a contagious organic disease ie, the right to isolate the patient from society. Whether the dimensions of the various multi-agency groups' implicit theories are this consistent is a moot point and one which this present research aims to examine.

Propositions and structure of the current research

The aim of this chapter so far has been to discuss the early major studies on attitudes towards the mentally ill, critically review them in terms of their key theoretical and methodological limitations, consider more recent studies which have examined attitudes and beliefs towards individual psychopathological disorders and establish the three scientific models which are to form the framework of the current research. In this final section of chapter one the main objectives of the present study will be introduced.

Propositions of the current research

The central purpose of the current research is to try and gain a clearer understanding of how our particular multi-agency groups perceive the mentally ill. This goal will be achieved by addressing several questions we believe to be pertinent to the issue in hand. Each question may be viewed as building upon earlier conclusions. Thus collectively they should provide information about the way in which multi-agency beliefs about the mentally ill change across a range of intuitively meaningful variables. The actual questions may be stated as follows:

1. How do multi-agency and scientific theories of the mentally ill in general compare?
2. How does behaviour defined as psychopathologically (depression/ schizophrenia) and/or criminally (presence/absence of an offence) deviant influence multi-agency thinking?
3. How do the socio-demographic factors (age, gender, group surveyed and experience of mental illness) influence multi-agency thinking towards the mentally ill in general?
4. How do the socio-demographic factors (age, gender, group surveyed and experience of mental illness) influence multi-agency thinking towards behaviour defined as psychopathologically or criminally deviant?

Structure of the current research

In order to gain a more comprehensive overview of the present study, its structure and several of the concepts mentioned in the aforementioned questions should perhaps be briefly defined.

In question one we aim to measure to what extent our multi-agency approach towards the mentally ill is consistent with any of the three scientific models - medical, moral and psychosocial - outlined in this research. The purpose of this question is essentially directed towards establishing a common basis to multi-agency thinking and may be viewed as formulating the dependent variable of the current study. Thus at this stage we are starting from the assumption that all null hypotheses are true by setting aside the possibility that differences may exist between the various treatment and socio-demographic variables included in the study.

Once an overall approach towards the mentally ill has been established there will exist a basis for making comparisons within and between various independent variables. It is within this context that the remaining questions will be addressed. Thus the primary concern of propositions two, three and four are to explore the possible influential effects that the various independent variables of interest to this study may have upon our dependent variable.

These remaining questions are designed to investigate the effects of six independent variables in total, of which five are in the form of two level factors - disorder, offence, age, gender and experience of mental illness - and one which comprises of six levels, namely, the six sample populations of the survey (Table 1.1). Thus we may describe the nature of the current research as formulating a 6×2^5 factorial design.

Table 1.1
The various levels within each
independent variable

Independent variable	Levels	
Disorder	(1) Depression	(2) Schizophrenia
Offence	(1) No-offence	(2) Offence
Group surveyed	(1) Students	
	(2) Members of a political party	
	(3) Police	
	(4) Social workers	
	(5) Probation officers	
	(6) Mental health practitioners	
Age	(1) 18 - 35	(2) => 36
Gender	(1) Male	(2) Female
Experience of the mentally ill	(1) Previous experience	(2) No experience

At this point, it is important to make a distinction between the various types of independent variable that make up the factorial experiment. Some of the variables, namely, disorder and offence have been purposely manipulated during the survey. They have been manipulated in the sense that respondents have been randomly assigned to specifically chosen levels within each factor As a result, these factors may also be referred to as purely independent variables or treatment variables, as their random nature ensures their higher degree of independence from other features of the experimental situation. The key treatment condition disorder is represented in the experiment by a description of a schizophrenic or a depressive person and the offence condition is varied by the presence or absence of a criminal offence associated with each mental disorder.

The other main variables of this research, however, have not been manipulated as they are properties of the subject and so cannot be separated from the individual who has them, and randomly assigned. These variables which include: age, gender, group surveyed and experience of mental illness are often referred to as organismic or subject variables. Conceptually, each of these subject variables may be viewed as elements from within our generic multi-agency group.

Summary

The aim in this section has been to briefly introduce the key elements contained within the current research. While these issues will be more thoroughly dealt with when we discuss the methodological approach of the research, it was felt that a basic understanding at this stage would help clarify the propositions to be investigated and assist in the transition from the purely conceptual to the operational nature of the research.

Concluding overview

It is evident from the literature reviewed in this chapter, that the study of attitudes and beliefs towards the mentally ill has been a subject of concern to researchers for a number of years. Within the context of these previous studies our intention has essentially been directed by two inter-related objectives: firstly, to gain a clear and detailed understanding of what we know about popular perceptions of the mentally ill, and secondly, to thoroughly consider the way in which the study of attitudes and beliefs in this field has developed since the 1950s.

With regard to our first objective, we have shown that recent research has started to become far more dynamic and focused in its approach towards the study of opinions about the mentally ill. Increasingly, consideration is being afforded to the analysis of unconsciously held belief systems identified in response to referents whose nature has become far more socially realistic and meaningful than the narrowly defined 'mental illness' concept frequently applied in earlier research (Osmond and Durham, 1976; Fracchia et al, 1976; Nunnally, 1961).

The intention of the second concern of this chapter has been to enhance our understanding as to how this generally more sophisticated approach towards the study of popular perceptions came about, through constructively highlighting the key ideological and methodological problems that limited many of these earlier studies.

Once a review of the literature was complete, our attention focused upon the development of the three models that are to form the basis of the current research. Within each of these paradigms we drew together an ideal type picture of the theories pertaining to the nature and management of the mentally ill.

Finally, we highlighted and discussed the main propositions of the current research. In general, each statement has been purposely designed to build upon another, the primary aim being to develop a sequence of findings which, it is hoped, will collectively come together into a clear and concise picture of popular beliefs, as they relate to a complex and diverse set of factors.

Notes

1 Those who wish to consider some of the issues raised by the labelling theorists with regard to the mentally ill should refer to the following: Miles (1987), Scheff (1966), Szasz (1985, 1961), Goffman (1961), Laing (1967, 1961), Lemert (1951) and for an empirical critique Gove (1975).

2 Attitudes held by other specific groups such as children (Spitzer and Cameron, 1995; Weiss, 1994, 1986, 1985), mental patients (Angermayer et al, 1987) and the general influence of the media (Williams and Dickinson, 1993; Appleby and Wessely, 1988; Matas et al, 1985) will not be discussed. However, individual studies which are of particular importance will be mentioned.

3 These educational campaigners were specific to both North America and Canada, particularly during the 1950s and 1960s.

4 Flew (1985) was quoting Philippe Pinel (1745-1826) on the impetus behind the medical model. "The mentally ill, far from being guilty persons who require punishment, are sick people whose miserable state deserves all the consideration due to suffering humanity".

5 It is important to note that this social deviance model is not the same as the more contemporary psychosocial model. This point will be fully discussed later in this chapter when we critically review the research.

6 During the course of reviewing the earlier research on attitudes towards the mentally ill, it is important that the reader remains alert to the fact that these findings were obtained during a period when the nature and configuration of mental health services were very different from today. Care in the community was only a blue-print, thus provisions were still very institutional by nature and there were few media scandals highlighting the serious crimes committed by some mentally ill patients. Ultimately, such a context may have influenced certain views.

7 The term 'simple schizophrenic' reflects the state of psychiatry at the time these studies were carried out. The term is seldom used today.

8 Indeed, the psychiatric label attached to the case vignette accounted for a significantly greater proportion of the variance ($F=138.19$) than the behaviour ($F=3.69$).

9 These limitations will be discussed in some detail at a later point in this chapter.

10 The research that has been carried out since the latter part of the 1980s has become increasingly more sophisticated at both an ideological and methodological level. The nature of these more recent studies is in many ways fundamentally different from the research we have just considered. To appreciate this fact, the more contemporary research will be discussed once we have critically analysed the key limitations of the earlier studies.

11 For example, a variety of studies dealing with professional groups have looked at whether attitudes may be changed via didactic training schemes (Drolen, 1993; Malla and Shaw, 1987), while others have focused their attention upon more specific issues such as the attitude of the medical profession towards the practice of psychiatry (Buchanan and Bhugra, 1992).

12 Due to the limited amount of information available on the subject of professional attitudes towards the mentally ill, no other method of systematically evaluating this research appears possible. From a chronological analysis, the reader should not assume that the studies form an influential continuum, on the contrary, due to the fact that few studies cite the earlier work, they should be considered as independent of one anther.

13 These findings were supported by a number of other studies including Wright and Klein (1966), Appleby et al (1961) and Williams and Williams (1961).

14 While this study's findings are interesting, we must treat them with some degree of caution due to the very small sample sizes that were used.

15 Criminal Justice 42%, Social Services 29% and Mental Health Staff 21%.

16 Criminal Justice 41%, Social Services 29% and the Mental Health Staff 31%.

17 As with the study by Nuehring and Raybin (1986), the sample sizes for each group were very small and were not selected on the basis of a probability sampling technique. Thus the generalisable nature of their findings are weak.

18 Clearly, there are a number of other important research areas peripheral to the fields of mental illness and crime such as the fear of crime (Last and Jackson, 1989), attitudes towards sentencing (Walker and Hough, 1988) and the relationship between mental disorder and dangerousness (Monahan, 1992). The focus of the current research, however, directly relates to perceptions of the deviant actor per se, and so we will construct our review of the literature around this particular issue. Those studies whose findings directly relate to certain aspects of our research will be mentioned where appropriate.

19 In particular, Furnham and Henderson (1983), Kidder and Cohen (1979), Erskine (1974).

20 Perceptions of the mentally ill offender and related issues are of course manifested in a whole variety of forms such as via media coverage (Williams and Dickinson, 1993; Appleby and Wessely, 1988) and through public enquiry reports (North East Thames and South East Thames Regional Health Authorities, 1994). As mentioned earlier, however, the parameters of this review are more specific.

21 Though the influence of the media in the long term has been questioned (Appleby and Wessely, 1988).

22 It could of course, also be argued, though dismissed by Whatley (1959), that attitudinal differences are due to psychological conservatism produced by aging which leads to a more unfavourable opinion of the mentally ill (Murphy et al, 1993).

23 It would appear that this study is ongoing as the researchers intend to evaluate: "the effects of an educational campaign on community attitudes and patients' social integration" (Wolff et al, 1996c:197).

24 It should be highlighted at this point that the research carried out during the period 1950s to the 1970s was conducted within an ideological vacuum centring around the medical and social deviance perspectives. Current psychiatric thought covers a much broader and more comprehensive range of ideological positions. Thus the tripartite set of models to be used in the current research are fundamentally different from the earlier approaches as we shall demonstrate later.

25 The fact that D'Arcy and Brockman's (1977) resurvey of 'Blackfoot' produced remarkably similar results to that of the Cummings' (1957) strongly suggests that attitudes may be specifically located.

26 Such discrepancies were first demonstrated by La Piere (1934). The author found that while restaurant owners were willing to accept a Chinese couple in a face-to-face situation, they refused them access when responding to a questionnaire.

27 Other studies showing a positive correlation between attitudes and behaviour include Ellsworth (1965) and Fischer (1971). A strong relationship is also evident from those studies which have reported a positive improvement in attitudes as compared with general social conditions. For example, there has been a substantial increase in the availability of community mental health facilities in both North America and Britain since the 1970s, while the civil rights of the mental patient via legislation have dramatically improved (Mental Health Act 1983).

28 Behaviour of this type would be described in psychiatric terms as multiple personality disorder (American Psychiatric Association DSM IV, 1994).

29 The current research was in fact partly influenced by the work of Furnham and Bower (1992).

30 This point is further emphasised by the fact that in the earlier research on attitudes towards the mentally ill, the most common case vignette to be labelled mentally ill was the paranoid schizophrenic (Rabkin, 1974).

31 There appear to be five major paradigms for dealing with the mentally ill (Furnham and Bower, 1992). However, due to the constraints of time and resources, this study will only investigate beliefs with regard to the three models stated in the text. Thus the psychoanalytic and conspiratorial models will not be considered. This decision may be justified on the grounds that in Britain most programmes for dealing with the mentally disordered are based primarily on either the medical (organic), moral (cognitive-behavioural) or psychosocial models (Taylor and Taylor, 1989).

32 This point is clearly illustrated by the fact that the terminology used is taken from this paradigm. The mentally 'ill' may enter a 'hospital' and be cared for by 'doctors' and 'nurses'. The 'patient' will be 'diagnosed', given 'treatment' and offered a 'prognosis'.

33 A psychiatrists formally working at the Institute of Neurology, London, who is an extreme exponent of the organic orientation. Reported in Clare (1980).

34 Dohrenwend (1975) carried out an extensive review of the research in this area and found that out of the 33 studies considered 28 of them had concluded that there existed a strong correlation between the onset of mental illness and low social class.

35 Other approaches may be on either a macro level such as improving the general social, economic and political conditions of the poor via urban redevelopment to reduce over-crowding and a generally higher standard of living, etc, or, on a micro level, through practices such as the development of stress management schemes for company employees.

2 Methodology

Introduction

The central purpose of this chapter will be to discuss in some detail the key methodological issues associated with the design and implementation of the current research.

Section one may be considered in two parts. At the outset, we will provide a general summary of our research design through briefly commenting upon the most important methodological decisions associated with the study. Our goal in the succeeding paragraphs of this section will be to elaborate upon each point, while at the same time attempting to justify the decisions that have been made, the primary aim at this stage being to present a defensible overview of the study's methodological 'forest' before moving on to a detailed consideration of the 'trees'. Thus in the remainder of this chapter we will be expanding upon the key elements of the research design by discussing the main procedures to be followed.

The primary concern of section two will centre around the sampling procedures used in order to obtain the study's pool of respondents. Each of the six sample populations will be discussed in turn with emphasis being placed on the following principal issues: the nature of the sample population, access to the organisation, the structure and content of the sampling frame and the sampling techniques employed. We will then move on to explain how our respondents were randomly assigned to each of the four experimental conditions of the survey's factorial design before finally, briefly considering the pattern of interviews conducted across the whole sample population.

In section three we will deal comprehensively with a whole range of issues surrounding the content, format and general operational nature of the study's measuring instrument. The discussion here will also focus, all-be-it briefly, on the pretests that were performed, as well as on how both the reliability and validity of the measuring instrument were examined.

Once our subjects have been identified and the measuring instrument constructed, the next stage is to make contact with the respondents in order to obtain the data. Thus section four will be concerned with a consideration of the main procedures associated with the two principal data gathering methods used in the present study, namely, the mail questionnaire and interview technique. Information will also be presented on how the data, once collected, was coded, edited and structured in preparation for the statistical analysis phase.

Within the social sciences, increasing prominence is being afforded to the ethical nature of the various procedures and techniques used in order to carry out a successful research project. The final section in this chapter, section five, will, therefore, be directed towards a discussion of the key ethical considerations that presented themselves throughout the course of conducting this research.

Research design

Overview of the research design

The current study is in the form of a factorial experimental survey design, employing the mail questionnaire data gathering technique. Semi-structured interviews were also carried out in order to provide supplementary qualitative data. The mail questionnaire measuring instrument consisted of a schedule which contained specific statements and structured response categories. Six lay and professional groups were used to represent the study's multi-agency population. The respondents within each organisation were selected through the use of either systematic probability sampling or a complete census. The quantitative data were analysed in two stages using principal component and multivariate statistics, while the study's qualitative material was structured through carrying out a thematic content analysis. The results were presented in a variety of ways including the use of correlational, cross-tabular and graphical formats.

Justification of the key methodological decisions

The factorial experimental survey design Empirical research within both the social and behavioural sciences tends to be carried out within a variety of settings and contexts. As a result, the social or behavioural phenomena being studied are usually interlaced with a plethora of variables who's nature is such that their identification, control and management is often difficult. The importance of these extraneous variables should never be understated, however, as their mere presence can act as a source of invalidity with the potential to open up any research findings to plausible, rival interpretations (Smith, 1975). Thus it would appear that, in order to increase the accuracy of our data with regard to any conclusions made about associational or causal path relationships among the key variables under study, we must be prepared to account for those variables which may act as a source of invalidity, within the context of our research design.

The factorial design A key feature in the overall design of the current research is the use of the factorial experiment. This method may take on a variety of forms though essentially it involves experimentally setting up every possible combination of two or more variables, normally in post-test only form.

Table, 2.1 illustrates how two independent variables or factors each containing two levels are arranged and analysed within a factorial experiment.

Table 2.1
A 2×2 factorial experimental design

Factor Y	Factor X		Effect of X
	Treatment X	Treatment No-X	
Treatment Y	(A) YX	(B) Y No-X	A - B
Treatment No-Y	(C) No-YX	(D) No-Y No-X	C - D
Effect of Y	A - C	B - D	A - D

It will be observed that the effect of each factor in the experimental design may be measured in two ways. We could examine the main effects of treatment X while controlling for Y, or we could look at the main effects of Y while controlling for X. Furthermore, under such a design we are also able to measure the combined effect of the two factors (A - D), thus enabling us to determine whether or not there exists a statistically interactive effect.

Significance of the factorial experimental survey design Science is predominantly concerned with the problem of causality. The main aim being both to predict and describe the effects that a particular independent variable has upon a predetermined dependent variable (Kidder et al, 1981). The experimental design is ideally suited to this task as it is arguably the only method that directly concerns itself with questions of a causal nature (Smith, 1975).

This statement is sometimes challenged on the basis that, due to improvements in statistical techniques and in survey designs generally, it is now possible for survey research to go beyond merely reporting on distributions and relationships, instead questions of a causal nature may now be explored (Hays, 1994). A detailed philosophic discussion of the complexities surrounding the topic of causality will not be attempted here, suffice is to say that a strategy for the logical examination of causal relationships within the context of a survey design has been developed and is referred to as the 'modes of elaboration' (Kendall and Lazarsfeld, 1974; Rosenberg, 1968).

However, despite the fact that the aims of survey research have been broadened, there still exists a considerable degree of evidence to suggest that the survey method is generally not very useful for testing causal propositions due to the design's weak level of internal validity (Cook, 1979).

To elaborate on this point. Because survey research tends to deal primarily with naturally occurring variables, it is impossible to manipulate or control their effect. Certain statistical techniques such as multiple regression analysis could be used in order to examine relationships through supposedly controlling potentially spurious variables, and indeed this approach is often used (Walsh, 1990; Cook, 1979). However, unless the conceptual model within a particular substantive area is strong, enabling the consideration of such confounding factors, the use of the survey method becomes problematic, as there will constantly exist a high degree of ambiguity about such issues as the direction of causal inference and the spurious nature of certain causal factors.

Within the context of true experiments, however, the problems surrounding manipulation of the relevant independent factors and control over the effects of extraneous variables that may contaminate the results can, within reason, be easily overcome (Edwards, 1969). In the specific case of the factorial design, the investigator is in a position to be able to plan ahead and purposefully manipulate subject's exposure to the experimental stimuli by varying the treatment conditions in a systematic manner. Any design which provides the opportunity for such a high degree of control over the introduction of various independent variables is extremely valuable as it: "allows for the isolation and precise specification of important differences" (Aronson and Carlsmith, 1968:9).

In addition to being able to manipulate those variables that we wish to study the effect of, experimentation can be used to control the influence of those variables that are extraneous to the purpose of the study (Bryman and Cramer, 1990). If, as we have already stated, manipulation of the variables is possible, then randomisation of the subjects under the various conditions of the experiment can also be employed. Such a strategy is based on chance probability procedures in which each subject has an equal chance of being selected for any study treatment. Thus extraneous variables are controlled through randomly assigning subjects to the various experimental conditions.

By using this procedure, we can be reasonably certain that any extraneous differences that exist between the respondents of each experimental condition can only be due to random chance fluctuations (Moser and Kalton, 1971). Thus by achieving pre-experimental equivalence via the randomisation of subjects to groups, we can be fairly confident in assuming that we have controlled for the key threats to the internal validity of our study.

In addition to the issue of causality, a further goal of science is to be able to generalise the findings to a wider population (Kidder et al, 1981). Unfortunately, a major drawback with experiments is the problem of external validity, ie, it is often impossible to determine how generalisable or representative the findings are within the context of a more natural environment. It has been suggested that there are three key issues that need to be addressed in order to improve the external validity of experiments: firstly, it has been argued that experiments are merely artificial tests of hypotheses and that this puts into doubt their relevance to the real world (Babbie, 1973). This point is based on the fact that most experiments are conducted in laboratories which set up highly controlled artificial conditions for testing a particular phenomena. Secondly, some authors have commented that the findings from experiments may not be generalisable to other segments of the population (Sedlack and Stanley, 1992; Smith, 1975). Often college students are used in an experiment and then these findings are generalised to a wider group.[1] However, for many social science questions the respondents must be more heterogeneous than college students, for example, socio-demographic factors such as ethnic, educational and also cultural backgrounds may be important. A third criticism of experiments is that they provide no useful descriptive data (Babbie, 1973). For example, if a study showed that 35% of the subjects within a treatment conditions agreed with a particular issue, then this would tell us nothing about how the wider population felt.

In an attempt to overcome the artificial nature of most experimental designs, we propose to conduct the factorial experiment within the context of a field setting as opposed to under laboratory conditions. This will be achieved by combining the main independent variables of interest into a factorial design and then writing brief descriptions (case vignettes) to represent each of the design's conditions. Finally, a single vignette will then be incorporated into each survey questionnaire which can then be given to representative samples of respondents who will be able to answer the questions in their natural surroundings and in their own time. Furthermore, as we mentioned in the previous chapter, the use of detailed case descriptions rather than simple labels such as 'the mentally ill' will help present mentally disorder patients within a more realistic social and situational context, which will hopefully elicit a more natural and genuine response.

The artificial nature of the experiment also extends to the fact that experimentation normally only concerns itself with one independent variable and one dependent variable, yet phenomena within both the social and behaviour sciences usually have multiple causes. The assumption in experimental research is that multiple causes of some events are additive, a situation which in real life is rarely found. The use of a factorial design, however, allows us to overcome this limitation by offering the flexibility to be able to consider multiple variables in terms of both their independent and interactive effects. Thus such an approach serves to strengthen our research's level of external validity as we can, to some degree, account for the possibility of variations in the way real world events occur.

As the factorial experiment is to be placed within a social context, we will also be able to overcome the second criticism relating to the fact that experimenters are forced to work with essentially localised homogeneous samples. Our survey experimental design will be extended to include six markedly heterogeneous sample populations, thus enabling us to generalise our findings to a wider target population while maintaining a high degree of experimental control.

The third limitation put forward to demonstrate the weak external validity of experiments refers to the representative level of the actual samples. A crucial question in every piece of research, including the present study, is whether the conclusions drawn from a set of data are representative of the population from which the immediate sample of survey subjects originated. This threat to the external validity of the research was overcome by incorporating, as an essential design element of the current research, the survey technique of probability sampling. Applying such methods to our research would enable us to systematically select representative samples from our study populations, which will in turn allow more generalised statements to be made about our research findings.

Summary The aim of this subsection has been to justify the use of the factorial experimental survey design. Basically, this approach may be viewed as an experiment embedded within a sample survey. The primary purpose of such a design centres around the need to maximise both internal and external validity within a single study. It is hoped that the justifications given clearly demonstrate that, although such complex designs are rare within the social sciences (Bryman and Cramer, 1990; Moser and Kalton, 1971), they nevertheless represent a feasible way of carrying out research.

The mail questionnaire data gathering technique The advantages of the mail questionnaire discussed in this section serve the purpose of justifying the predominant use of this data gathering technique over the other main survey design methods that could also have been utilised in this research, namely, variations on either the face-to-face or telephone interview.[2]

Economic considerations The sample populations to be considered in the present research are fairly large, often difficult to contact and to some degree geographically dispersed. Thus the practical decision to implement the mail questionnaire survey method was partly determined by economic considerations.

It would not be unreasonable to suggest that this technique has the potential to afford high benefits at a reasonable return in terms of cost, time and effort. To express this point rather more bluntly, "Questionnaires can be sent through the mail; interviewers cannot" (Moser and Kalton, 1971:257). Thus contacting the respondents within each sample population by mail, rather than through direct contact, avoids the high costs associated with paying interviewer salaries and field expenses such as meals, travel or telephone bills. Instead, a standard postal charge is normally all that is required.[3] The mail survey also consumes the least amount of time as the questionnaires are posted simultaneously to everyone involved in the study. Furthermore, the time consumed through 'call backs' due to the difficulties associated with contacting certain subjects are, to a large extent, eliminated as the questionnaire, once delivered, may be answered at the respondents' convenience. Finally, the effort involved in producing and distributing the questionnaire is minimal compared to other research methods; no interviewer training is involved and most of the delivery work is done by the appropriate postal services.

The nature of the study and its measuring instrument Justifying the use of this data gathering technique on the basis of simple economics is, however, not sufficient. The suitability of the actual study itself to the mail questionnaire approach must also be considered.

In the absence of an interviewer to offer assistance, numerous difficulties may arise during the course of answering the questions which may lead either to a complete refusal to participate in the study or the return of inaccurately completed questionnaires. It is essential, therefore, to ensure that complex sieve and filter questions are avoided, that words and statements are clear and that the schedule does not appear too tedious and boring. Fortunately, the nature of the current research is based upon a set of clearly defined objectives which, through a course of rigorous pretests, will facilitate the construction of a measuring instrument ideally suited to the mail survey method ie, one which is well structured, unambiguous, devoid of technical terminology and easy to answer.

Moreover, the nature of the research subject itself - beliefs about the mentally ill - may be viewed as a fairly sensitive issue. Respondents will be very aware of the chasm between what may be considered a humanistically desirable response and their personal view which may not be so acceptable. Faced with this dilemma, respondents are likely to forfeit their real views in place of a more socially desirable response during interview situations as their anonymity appears less safeguarded. Mail questionnaires, on the other hand, have shown themselves to elicit a more realistic response (Bord, 1971).

Sampling considerations The sample populations to be considered in the current research are each associated with an appropriate sampling frame. As a result, the mail questionnaire data gathering technique will make it possible for us to use far more sophisticated sampling methods. Thus sample designs such as systematic probability sampling can be used rather than the less precise cluster or quota sampling techniques normally associated with interview based surveys (Brockington et al, 1993; Moser and Kalton, 1971). A further advantage of employing the mail survey technique in the current research is that it makes it possible for the researcher to have a high degree of control over the administration of the study's experimental conditions. The absence of interviewers also enables a more standardised approach to be adopted, effectively eliminating the potential hazard of direct interactive bias which may seriously undermine the reliability and validity of the survey results (Rosenthal, 1966).

Response rates Unfortunately, the benefits of the mail questionnaire technique are often distorted by a number of potentially research destroying limitations. Though probably the most common problem plaguing researchers is the low response rate. Generally, the non-response rate is very much higher than it is for interview-based surveys. Apparently, it is not uncommon for inexperienced researchers to obtain a response rate of only 20% after a first mailing (Miller, 1977). In fact, the response rate problem is so fundamental that one may question whether any researcher can be confident about justifying this method, no matter what the other potential advantages may be, unless they are able to introduce a rigorous set of procedures which will ensure that this potential problem is minimised as much as is reasonably possible.

Although 20 years ago potentially high non-response may have caused a great deal of anxiety amongst researchers, the situation is somewhat different today. Their capabilities greatly exceed those that tradition has ascribed to them and although non-response still remains a serious problem which may create difficulties, it is now viewed as a limitation which is by no means insurmountable. The attainment of high response rates sufficient for social science research is now possible (Hagan, 1989; Rossi et al, 1983). High rates may be achieved by following a set of standardised mail survey procedures known as the Total Design Method (TDM) (Dillman, 1978).

Essentially, the TDM addresses two broad questions: (1) What factors effect response rates to mail questionnaires? and (2) What steps can be taken to increase the overall level of response?[4] Thus guided by a set design approach similar to that of the TDM, a reasonable response rate should be achievable.

Confidence in a satisfactory high return rate may also be reasonable to expect when one considers the nature of the actual sample populations to be studied. Each sample group included in the survey is well educated and most respondents will have a modest to high degree of professional interest in the subject being studied and so are ideally suited to this type of survey approach.

More generally, we may conclude by suggesting that those researchers who are willing to put in a little 'extra effort' during the course of designing their mail questionnaire data gathering technique are likely to gain substantial benefits.

"Indeed, if mail surveys reached their potential in practice, it is doubtful that many researchers would employ either face-to-face or telephone interviews" (Dillman, 1983:359).

Supplementary qualitative data   One important limitation of the mail survey approach is that it is fairly inflexible in the sense that the subject's initial response to a statement is final.   There exists no opportunity for the researcher to probe further into a particular issue in order to gain more background information on why a question was answered in a particular way.   In an attempt to overcome this problem, techniques for obtaining qualitatively based data were incorporated into the present study.

At the end of the questionnaire itself an open-ended question was presented, asking respondents for any general comments they may wish to make about any aspect of mental illness.   In addition, unstructured/semi-structured interviews were carried out with several subjects from each sample population, the aim simply being to give the subject the opportunity to express their general opinion about the mentally ill and other related issues.

The content of the qualitative responses obtained from both the end question and the interviews were thematically analysed, and the results were then used in order to help us elaborate on, and add a degree of substance to, certain aspects of the more general empirical findings.

Lay and professional groups   The mail questionnaire survey was sent to six different sample populations representing various organisations within the city of Cambridge.   These groups, which included two lay samples - post graduate students and members of a political party - and four professional agencies - police, probation officers, social workers and mental health practitioners, were selected as they all, to some extent, play a part in determining the career of both the mentally ill and mentally ill offenders.

In terms of the lay population, the initial aim was to obtain a representative sample of the general public.   However, due to a number of unforseen difficulties and the study's financial constraints, it soon became apparent that this option would not be tenable in practice.   The main obstacle to obtaining a sample of the general population was the inadequacy of the electoral register as a sampling frame.   The research was planned during a period when collection of the unpopular Poll Tax was still being vigorously enforced.   Coincidentally, a considerable minority or residents had avoided registering their names, which resulted in a fairly unrepresentative district register.   In fact, it was estimated that at the time, the register only contained about 69% of residents within Cambridge.[5]

As a result of these problems, it was considered more appropriate to examine the views of particular lay groups rather than the overall general public.   The study's two lay populations were initially selected because they were easily accessible to the researcher and because to some degree, they may be viewed as representing a fairly broad and socially useful public audience.

Post graduate students were chosen because it was felt that they would represent a more heterogeneous group in terms of age, academic interest and general 'life experience' backgrounds than undergraduates. Furthermore, if we accept the tentative conclusion that correlations between opinions and standard socio-demographic variables including education are non-existent or at best very small (Furnham and Bower, 1992; Nunnally, 1961) and also bare in mind the fact that being a student is only a temporary status, then we may assume that this group of respondents do in fact represent a key sector of the general public to which they will eventually return.

The second lay sample to be surveyed - members of a political group - may also be viewed as a useful sample population. The political party is typically associated with those who represent the less affluent end of the socio-economic scale (Seyd and Whitely, 1992), they also to some extent tend not to be well educated,[6] and are likely to be widely dispersed in terms of age.

Furthermore, those members who have received proportionately more formal education tend to represent a key segment of 'community leaders' within the city of Cambridge and include: councillors, magistrates, school and college governors and voluntary workers. Many, either directly or otherwise, are key influencers and situational definers within the community and are in a position to have a disproportionate effect on public attitudes, to the extent that their views will be highly influential on others and will be transmitted to a wider public than is normally accessible (Olmstead and Durham, 1976).

Thus overall, the inclusion of these lay populations may be reasonably justified on the grounds that the combined attributes of both samples are possibly representative of a fairly wide, socially diverse and generally useful sector of the general public.

The four professional sample populations included in this research were chosen due to the specific role each has with regard to the mentally ill in general and mentally ill offenders in particular. Each profession was chosen from in and around the city of Cambridge itself in order to maintain a degree of common experience between the groups.

While each group represents a distinct sample population in themselves, the way in which their day-to-day activities may inter-relate also ensures that they represent a substantial part of the city's multi-agency approach towards dealing with the mentally ill. Furthermore, it would also seem reasonable to include our two lay samples under this multi-agency umbrella as most committees, organisations, QUANGOs or working parties set up to 'manage' this minority tend to include lay representatives typically drawn from either the academic or political environment.

Thus in terms of how generalisable these sample populations are, it would seem justifiable to consider them as autonomous individual lay and professional groups, whose occasional involvement with the mentally ill or mentally ill offenders integrates them into a collective overall multi-agency population.

Systematic sampling and the census   The fundamental basis of probability sampling in general is that a sample's parameters will be representative of the whole population only if each element of the population has a known (non-zero) probability of being selected (Sedlack and Stanley, 1992). There are several types of basic probability design - simple, systematic, stratified and clustering - though the simple random sampling model is often seen as the classic procedure associated with the use of inferential statistics (Hays, 1994), and all other probability designs are simply variation on its key procedures which stipulate that each element of the population must have an equal opportunity of being selected and that each selection must be made independently. In practice, however, while one may start with a statistically random sample, the probability of ultimately concluding with such a sample distribution is substantially reduced due to issues pertaining to sampling and non-sampling error (Sedlack and Stanley, 1992). As a result, this sampling method is often considered more highly by authors than is actually merited, this point is evidenced by the fact that the simple random sampling design is less commonly used than one might expect (Smith, 1975).

In order to obtain the two lay samples included in the current research, a systematic probability sampling method was used. Before a systematic sample can be drawn, there must exist an accurate sampling frame of the sample population. If such a list is available, a systematic sample is generated when every nth element from the sampling frame is selected after a random start within the first sampling interval (Blalock, 1968).

In practical terms, systematic samples are often considered as "one of the simplest, most direct, and least expensive sampling methods" (Smith, 1975:121). Furthermore, this type of sampling design is often viewed as virtually identical to simple random sampling.

"If the ordering used in compiling the list can be considered to be essentially random with respect to the variables being measured, a systematic sample will be equivalent to a simple random sample" (Blalock, 1972:514).

In fact, some authors have argued that systematic samples can, on occasion, be slightly more accurate than simple random samples, as the former sampling method tends to produce a more even spread of the sample over the population list, whereas with simple random designs there always exist the statistical possible of clustering (Babbie, 1989).

One possible problem which may severely distort the representative nature of a systematic sample would be the presence of some degree of ordering within the sample frame. In such situations, every nth element may actually coincide with a particular periodic or cyclical trend existing in the list. In order to overcome this potential difficulty, the lists were thoroughly examined to ensure that they were not arranged in accordance with any feature or variable which was directly related to the subject matter of the survey.

With regard to the four professional sample groups that were included in the survey, a full population census was taken of each. This ensured that a sufficient number of respondents would be available for analysis in terms of the four experimental conditions contained within the survey's factorial design.

The measuring instrument The term 'structured schedule' refers to the nature of the measuring instrument and usually implies that it will contain specific items with a closed ended choice of responses. The use of specific items in the form of statements, as opposed to questions, are generally recommended as they are considered as more convenient:

> "we're not really sure why but the results seem to be easier to understand and interpret when one tries to measure attitudes using statements rather than questions" (Sedlack and Stanley, 1992:157).

Furthermore, there are numerous gains to be made from using likert-type response categories, for example, the nature of the closed-ended categories will enable us to obtain information not only on the direction of the respondents' evaluation of each particular belief statement, but also on the strength of their evaluations. Standardised responses are also ideally suited to the process of comparative analysis as they offer a high degree of uniformity within the results.

More generally, this type of structured schedule is most useful to research where the questions have been pre-determined and the mail survey method is being seriously considered as the main data gathering strategy. The schedule's straight forward nature strongly implies that it can be easily understood, not only by respondents, but also by those whose job it is to code and analysis the data. Finally, these advantages are not new, this type of structured schedule has been used successfully for some time in opinion surveys (Hagan, 1989) and it continues to be strongly recommended (Furnham and Bower, 1992).

Sampling design

As we mentioned earlier, the present study surveyed beliefs about the mentally ill held by six separate sample populations - two lay and four professional groups.

It is the intention of this section to describe the nature of each population and how they were attained.

The nature of the sample populations

Post graduate students The first sample to be contacted was a group of post graduate students from the University of Cambridge, a post graduate being defined as someone who has completed a first degree and has been enrolled for any type of higher degree course. To be a member of the University, each student must also be affiliated to one of the thirty-one associated Colleges. It would appear that each College includes a certain number of post graduate students on their roll, and so our target population would more accurately be defined as including all post graduate students attached to a University College.

Access to the target population Contacting all thirty-one Colleges would have been impossible given the amount of time and resources available and so it was decided to select only those Colleges which were predominantly or exclusively for post graduate students

Once the research had been approved by the University's Psychological Research Ethics Committee each of the College's Senior Tutors were approached requesting permission to carry out the survey.[7] Of the eight Colleges contacted. six agreed to participate in the research and consequently forwarded a list of post graduate students.

The sampling frame On recept, the sampling frames were no more than a few weeks old and contained each student's name and contact address. All six lists were entered onto a computer data base to form one large sampling frame for the purposes of the current research. Each College list remained intact and within each College sector the students' names were alphabetically ordered.[8]

Obtaining the sample Including all six sampling frames, the total number of sampling elements equalled 1,249. The size of the sample to be drawn was 400 students. This figure was determined on the basis of a number of considerations: firstly, it was very difficult to anticipate what the response rate may be, therefore, it was felt necessary to take a sample with the expectation of only a 50% response rate. Such a low rate of return would still leave a suitably large sample for analysis. Secondly, the research involves four experimental conditions, thus the sample would have to be divided into four subsamples at the very minimum which, with a 50% response, would give us 50 subjects per condition ($4 \times 50 = 200$) and it has been suggested that there should not be less than 20 elements within each subdivision for statistical purposes (Sudman, 1983).

The main step in drawing a systematic probability sample is to determine the sampling interval. This is obtained by dividing the desired sample size by the total number of elements in the sampling frame. Thus, if SI = sampling interval:

$$SI = \frac{\text{Total size of sampling frame}}{\text{Desired size of sample}} = \frac{1249}{400} = 3.37$$

we will have a sampling interval of 3, which means that, once a random start has been established, one element from every set of three elements will be selected in order to make up our sample of 400 elements.

Members of a political party The parameters of this sample population include every individual living in the city of Cambridge who was a fully paid up member of the political party during the year 1993-94.

Access to the target population Permission to conduct the research was given by the Local Party's Executive Committee and an appropriate sampling list was made available.

The sampling frame Fortunately, a complete computer listing of the name and address of all current members was available. The sampling frame was divided geographically in terms of the city's 14 Electorial Wards and the members' names were alphabetically listed within each Ward. The final listing was up-to-date and contained information on all current members, a total of 1,004 in all, representing around 1% of the resident population within the city of Cambridge.

Obtaining the sample As with the post graduate students, it was decided to select a systematic probability sample. In total, the frame contained 1,004 elements and it was decided to extract a sample of 200, thus our sampling interval would be:

$$SI = \frac{\text{Total size of sampling frame}}{\text{Desired size of sample}} = \frac{1004}{200} = 5.02$$

Again as with the student sample, once a random start has been established our sample of 200 respondents can be systematically obtained.

Police officers The police target population included all those officers who worked within the boundaries of the city of Cambridge, thus no attempt was made to consider those who operated in the rural divisions serving the necklace villages around the city itself in a region known as South Cambridgeshire.

Access to the target population Several meetings with senior officers of the Cambridge Division were necessary in order to fully discuss the nature of the research, what purpose the results would serve and how the survey could be best implemented in practice. Once agreement to participate had been finalised, a police sergeant was appointed as liaison for the purposes of conducting the research.

The sampling frame and the census The City Division sampling frame was up-to-date and consisted of 195 officers in total. The list was divided in terms of the officer beats, administrative posts and those attached to CID. The names of several civilian employees were also on the list, these were identified and excluded. The ordering would have been important if a systematic sample was to be selected, however, as the overall number of officers was fairly small, it was decided to take a complete population census, thus every sample element on the list was selected for inclusion in the survey.

Probation officers The initial aim was to survey all those probation officers who worked within the city of Cambridge itself. However, it soon became apparent that the sample size was too small for the purpose of the present research and so the limits of the target population were extended to include all probation officers working within Cambridgeshire.

Access to the target population After discussions with several senior probation officers, permission was granted to carry out the study on the condition that no direct access be given to lists of employees, It was, therefore, necessary for me to work closely with a local contact in the probation service in order to implement the study.

The sampling frame and census The co-ordinator was asked to obtain a list of officers in Cambridgeshire. Apparently such a list was available, alphabetically ordered, up to date and containing 120 sampling elements. As the numbers were again fairly small, a total population census was taken.

Mental health practitioners With regard to this target population, the aim was to survey mental health practitioners working at the two main hospitals servicing the city of Cambridge, namely, Addenbrooke's General Hospital and Fulbourn Psychiatric Hospital.

Access to the target population The first task was to try and obtain access in order to be able to do the research. This involved making an application to the District Health Authority's Ethics Committee. The Committee approved the research and suggested that the Personnel Manager of the Trust be contacted in order to obtain listings of staff at the hospitals. The Personnel contact was, however, only willing to provide a listing of Line Managers and suggested that each should be contacted and asked if they would consider participating in the survey.

The term mental health practitioner was, therefore, defined by those Line Managers who agreed to their staff being surveyed and were willing to provide a list of personnel within their departments. As a result, the sample population comprised largely of practitioners within the fields of: psychiatry, occupation therapy, rehabilitation and clinical nursing care.

The sampling frame and the census In total six lists were obtained. On inspection, it was noted that there were several duplications and so these were filtered out and removed to leave an overall sampling frame containing 222 elements from which a full census was taken.

Social workers With regard to defining precisely which social workers were to form the basis of our target population, a number of discussions were held with Senior Managers at the County's Social Services Department. Eventually, the decision was made to limit the scope of the research to those social workers who were attached to the two main hospitals, namely, Addenbrooke's and Fulbourn. This final selection process was predetermined largely by the fact that the procedures for gaining access to a more widely diverse group of members within the profession were extremely long and complex, as a detailed research application would have to be made to the Social Services Research Committee which was set up primarily to oversee national studies.

Access to the target population Access to both hospitals had already been established via approval from the District Ethics Committee so it was simply a case of approaching the Health Team Manager, informing him of the Ethics Committee's approval and asking for his consent to survey those personnel under his sphere of responsibility. Approval was granted and a list of social work personnel employed by both hospitals was made available. It soon became evident from the sampling lists, however, that the number of social workers at each hospital was not large enough for the purposes of the current research. As a result, it was felt necessary to extend our target population to include members of the social work profession attached to Peterborough District Hospital in Cambridgeshire. Agreement was sought from the appropriate department's Senior Manager and a list of staff members was requested.

The sampling frame and census The three lists were combined and entered into a data base in alphabetical order. Several elements were excluded as they were suspected of being administrative staff within the departments. The final sampling frame contained 103 elements from which a complete census was taken.

The experimental conditions

Once each sample had been selected, the next step was to randomly allocate/assign each respondent to one of the four experimental conditions included in the factorial design of the current research. The four conditions were numbered 1 to 4, written onto small square cards and placed into a box. Each sample subject was then assigned to an experimental condition by randomly picking a number out of the box with replacement. A random numbers table could also have been used for this procedure, however, as there were only four numbers involved it was decided that the box method was much simpler, quicker and just as accurate (Kidder et al, 1981).

The nature of the interviewee sample

It can be seen from Table 2.2 that, in general, the nineteen interviews were disproportionately spread across each of the study's various sample populations.

Table 2.2
Number of interviews conducted across
each sample population

Number of Inter-views	Group Surveyed						Row Total
	Stud-ents	Polit'l Party	Police	Social Work's	Prob'n Offic's	Mental H. Staff	
Inter-views	4	4	4	3	2	2	19

The original intention of the research was to obtain the qualitative material simply through each subject's response to the final open-ended question. However, during the course of conducting the survey, a considerable number of respondents accepted the introductory letters' invitation to make contact in order to discuss any questions that they wished to raise.

In an attempt to take advantage of these direct contacts, the decision was made to try and obtain more general information from each respondent. The interviews were, therefore, not based upon any form of random probability sampling, nor was the number of interviews conducted proportionate to the size of the sample. Overall, the respondents may be viewed as members of their population who were particularly interested in the area of mental illness and health, and had fairly definite views on the subject. Thus we cannot consider any definitively strong comments made by the interviewees as totally representative. Instead, the specific information they provide will be treated, where appropriate, as anecdotal to the empirical data obtained from the mail questionnaire.

There is a slight caveat to this line of thinking, however, as each of the respondents were initially selected through the use of either a random or representative technique. It would, therefore, be reasonable to conclude that their more general comments are merely supplementary to any written statement they would have made in response to the open-ended question. Hence, there exists some justification for analysing the thematic content of their responses along with the other written statements.

Operationalisation

Discussion of the factorial experimental design

The nature of the design The survey experiment used in the current research involved presenting subjects with a questionnaire and a case vignette. The actual experiment consisted of a complete 2×2 factorial design which included four case vignettes, each describing various levels of the study's two main experimental stimuli, namely, type of psychopathological behaviour (depression or schizophrenia) and criminal offence condition (presence or absence of an offence). The design is complete in the sense that collectively, the four case vignettes produced a matrices of all possible treatment combinations as shown in Figure 2.1:

Conditions	Depression	Schizophrenia
Offence	Depressive offender	Schizophrenic offender
No-offence	Depressive non-offender	Schizophrenic non-offender

Figure 2.1 A complete 2×2 factorial design matrix

Each of the respondents read only one of the case vignettes before completing the questionnaire, this is in contrast to a majority of the previous studies who tended to use between three and five descriptions for each subject (Phillips, 1964;

Cummings, 1957). The main advantage of randomly assigning only one case description is that the subject is kept naïve as to the real nature of the study, commenting upon several descriptions would enable subjects to measure or weigh up their responses relative to each description.

The case vignettes As we mentioned earlier, one of the main advantages of using case descriptions, as opposed to simple concepts such as 'the mentally ill', is that we are effectively taking a step closer to a more realistic situation, by enabling subjects to react to more specific concrete behavioural patterns under circumstances that allow for a great deal of experimental control (Malla and Shaw, 1987). The problem with the vignettes originally used by Star (1955), however, is that the symptomatology displayed in order to represent particular psychopathological states, has now moved on and is no longer in line with contemporary psychiatric thought. Furthermore, most previous authors also failed to present any additional salient non-deviant information about the person in the case descriptions such as their gender, marital status, etc, which would have made the descriptions appear more abstract than real, as Bord (1971) stated, the mentally ill do not exist within a social vacuum. Equally, additional salient deviant identities may also be important factors in determining popular conceptions (Howells, 1984), this point is in fact central to the aims of the present study which is directed towards the measurement of beliefs about mentally ill offenders. Thus each of these factors will need to be addressed during the course of constructing the case vignettes to be used in the current research. Finally, and for the sake of completeness, it should also be pointed out that the treatment variables incorporated into the descriptions were purposely defined in the sense that they were not intended to be representative of other mental disorders or criminal offence types.

The case vignettes were developed by the current author. Essentially, each description was placed within both a social and situational context, which highlighted key features of the referent's symptomatology in relation to a particular type of psychopathology, in addition to information relating to the their status under the type of offence condition.

Type of psychopathology It was decided to use variations on the two types of mental illness that are commonly diagnosed, namely, depressive psychosis and schizophrenia (Clare, 1980). Each description was roughly of equal length and contained standardised information as to the most salient characteristics of that particular disorder. For example, in accordance with the Diagnostic and Statistical Manual (DSM IV), the key signs and symptoms of paranoid schizophrenia are those highlighted in the following case vignette:

" About six months ago (*Time*), however, Tom had started to become increasingly withdrawn and preoccupied. It seemed to both his family and friends as though he was in a world of his own. (*Withdrawal from the External World*) He became less interested in his work and his children (*Volition*). Most of the time Tom would sit upstairs on his own, though on occasion he would stand for hours, in a stiff upright position in the middle of the room (*Psychomotor Catatonic Posture*). Tom's speech was often not clear as he would mutter very quickly and about things that just didn't make sense (*Formal Thought Disorder*). Sometimes he would show sudden outbursts of anger (*Affect*), claiming that his wife was plotting against him (*Content of Thought Disorder*).

During the week before his offence (*Start of Active Phase*) Tom began to complain of hearing voices which he said were getting stronger (*Auditory Hallucinations*), fear of an attack from his wife increased, and generally his whole behaviour become more bizarre (*Active Phase*)".

Type of offence In terms of the offence condition, it was decided to use the most severe form of crime, namely, murder. The reasoning behind this decision was based upon the view that if beliefs were in fact influenced by the presence of an offence, then it is under the most extreme condition that a real difference would be most noticeable.

While the behaviour stimulus remained constant, the offence condition was varied throughout each description. In the two cases which had no-offence attached, comments were added to the beginning and end of the case vignettes, describing the nature of Tom's behaviour just before the 'psychiatrist was called'.

In the cases that described an offence, the opening and closing remarks in the text detailed the fact that before the 'psychiatrist was called', Tom had been arrested for killing his wife with a knife.

The essential difference between the two offence conditions is that, while the severity of the mental disorder in each description is the same, the no-offence condition involves early intervention.

Social and situation context Acknowledging the importance of considering the mentally ill within a more socially familiar context (Bord, 1971), it was decided to include a sentence constant throughout all four descriptions which stated that the referent was married with two children and until recently in generally good health. Such remarks will hopefully go some way towards dispelling the often heard stereotyped reaction that the mentally ill are somehow different to begin with (Miles, 1987). Furthermore, reference to some of the various groups interacting with the mentally ill, such as the police, psychiatrists, family and close friends, helps place the referent within a more realistic situational context.

Discussion of the measuring instrument

Content Entitled 'Beliefs about the Mentally Disordered', the measuring instrument was presented in the form of a schedule, with specific statements and structured response categories. The content of the schedule, which was designed by the present author, is presented in Table 2.3:

Table 2.3
Content of the schedule for each multi-agency group

Schedule Items	Group Surveyed					
	Stud-ents	Polit'l Party	Police	Social Work's	Prob'n Offic's	Mental H.Staff
1 of 4 case vignettes	Y	Y	Y	Y	Y	Y
31 Belief statements	Y	Y	Y	Y	Y	Y
Sociodemog'c items:						
Personal experience	Y	Y	Y	Y	Y	Y
Age	Y	Y	Y	Y	Y	Y
Degree course	Y					
Education		Y				
Gender	*	*	*	*	Y	*
Years of profess'l-experience			Y	Y	Y	-
Rank			Y			
General item on-subject's views	Y	Y	Y	Y	Y	Y

Y Information asked of each respondent
* Information already available on sampling frames
- Information omitted due to clerical error

Belief statements Each of the 31 'belief' statements contained in the schedule relate to the various dimensions of the three scientific models included in the present study. All nine dimensions are represented by at least one item though some of the more complex areas are represented by two specific items. Finally, a separate statement representing the respondents' general view on the patient's likelihood of recovery has also been included.

In order to construct the actual statements, we collected as many items as possible from a search of both textbook and journal literature (Furnham and Bower, 1992; Siegler and Osmond, 1974, 1966). We then set about relating these items to the various dimension of the three models. This involved drafting new questions, where necessary, and revising existing ones. Once satisfied that the substantive nature of the statements adequately represented the appropriate variables of each dimension and were clearly worded, we concentrated on the order in which they would be presented in the questionnaire. This is important, as one item may inadvertently influence a response to another. However, as we are not sure where these influences may lie, it was decided to randomise the order in which each item was presented.

Response categories After framing the items and establishing an appropriate order, we turned to a consideration of the most appropriate likert-type response categories for the schedule. The scale chosen is as follows:

Strongly Agree 6 5 4 3 2 1 0 Strongly Disagree

As with most likert-type scales, the dichotomous bi-polar responses which in this case are 'strongly agree' and 'strongly disagree' have been expanded. Normally conceptual modifiers, such as *partly*, are used to represent the various levels of intensity. However, an ordinate scale with more than five points is difficult to conceptualise in these terms and so for purpose of clarity, a numerical scale was used instead, giving word values to the lowest and highest categories only.

Midpoint An issue that is often ignored by researchers who use likert-type intensity scales is how to deal with the midpoint. Overall, the literature is very piecemeal, thus:

> "in determining the specific categories to employ, common sense and the previous experience of researchers are invaluable aids to decision making" (Sedlack and Stanley, 1992).

In terms of common sense, a fundamental issue to be determined is whether or not to include the midpoint alternative, and if so, how is it being conceptually interpreted by both the researcher and the respondent?

In general, the practice has been to omit the middle category, thus pushing respondents towards one end or the other of the bipolar continuum. The reasoning being that very few people are indifferent and most lean either for or against something. Overall, the literature suggests that it should be included (Sudman and Bradburn, 1983) unless, of course, there is a good reason not to, for example, if it has been clearly demonstrated at the pretest stage that the midpoint forces a response set, or is viewed differently from how the researcher intended.

For statistical purposes we need to understand the scale in terms of a linear intensity continuum, thus the middle alternative would represent a position somewhere near an indifference point between agreeing and disagreeing with a particular statement. It is, therefore, essential that the respondents interpret this scale in the same way if the results are to be considered as meaningful. The matter was extensively pretested and it was decided to include a midpoint represented by the phrase 'do not know'. Information regarding the terms meaning and that this category should be used sparingly was incorporated into the instructions to respondents.

Socio-demographic items Each of the socio-demographic questions were asked using a single item with structured response categories. It will be observed from Table 2.3 that while some of the items are asked of all respondents, others are specific to a particular sample population. This was due to the fact that either the data was already available, or because it was felt that the item would be fairly constant across each group.

Content analysis

Content analysis may be defined as a research technique specifically developed for the purpose of objectively and systematically identifying specific characteristics manifestly present within the content of communication (Holsti, 1969).

In terms of the current research, it is the manifest content of the respondents' communication with regard to the interviews and the open-ended question on general views towards the mentally ill that is of interest.

The length of these written comments, including the general remarks made by the interviewees, ranged from a few lines to several pages of text, though the majority of respondents offered no more than a few short paragraphs within the space provided on the questionnaire.

Content analysis coding procedures The process of coding our qualitative data is essentially guided by three important consideration, namely, selecting the appropriate: response categories, units of analysis and units of enumeration (Sudman and Stanley, 1992; Hagan, 1989). Each of these procedures are highly inter-related in the sense that the quality of the first process, establishing the response categories, will largely dictate the quality of the others. It is essential, therefore, that each stage is established on the basis of sound theoretical considerations.

Response categories The response categories chosen as the basis for our analysis are the three factors that were extracted from the principal component analysis. The structuring of the data set along these lines may be justified on the grounds that they satisfy most of the key elements associated with category construction. The three factors or categories are fairly exhaustive in that they cover a very wide array of issues that may be discussed in relation to the mentally ill, though a general category will also be established in order to cater for any miscellaneous information. The categories have also been empirically shown to be mutually exclusive in the sense that there is a very poor inter-correlational relationship between each, and finally, they collectively reflect the purpose of the current research (Berelson, 1952).

Units of analysis Once the categories have been established, the next step is to develop precise operational definitions for each. This will be achieved through the use of the thematic unit of analysis. Described as 'the most useful unit of content analysis' (Holsti, 1969), the theme essentially refers to the overall point, aim or purpose being expressed within a particular document. In terms of the current study, this unit of analysis seems to be well suited, as the content data from each respondent consists of short comments covering only a few general issues regarding the mentally ill. Furthermore, relating each theme to the various categories will be a fairly straight-forward process, as each of the three categories have been defined along a specific set of dimensions or subcategories, and so have quite specific parameters. For example, the subcategories of factor one are broadly tailored to account for all the thematic dimensions found in the content data that are associated with either a sympathetic or punitive approach towards the mentally ill.

Units of enumeration Finally, as we are primarily interested in establishing the number of times a theme appears in favour of a particular dimension within each category, it will be sufficient for our purposes to employ the most often used frequency system of enumeration.

Pretesting the research design

During the course of designing the various elements of the survey experiment, extensive pretests were carried out in an effort to ensure that any problems or difficulties were identified and resolved. In summary, the pretests showed that: there were no problems with the letter of introduction, the instructions were clear and understandable, and the descriptions caused no problems, in fact, several respondents enjoyed reading the case vignette and commented on how interesting they were. Furthermore, a preliminary analysis of the pretest results showed that responses to each of the items were varied, indicating that the results were probably meaningful in the sense that the respondents avoided a response set regressing around the midpoint and that, technically at least, the factorial design would work in practice.

Reliability and validity

Acknowledging the importance of obtaining both reliable and valid measurements, strenuous efforts were made, during the course of developing and pretesting the present study's schedule instrument, to demonstrate that we could be reasonably confident that both attributes were supported. Measurement reliability was examined at two stages: firstly, we used a test-retest procedure during the course of conducting the actual pretests, and secondly, we tested the alpha reliability coefficients of the composite measures obtained from a principal component analysis. In order to determine the theoretical validity of our measuring instrument, both it's content and face validity were systematically and objectively assessed.[9]

Data collection

The mail questionnaire

Dillman's theory of cost and reward Contrary to traditional claims, there now exists a great deal of evidence which suggests that high response rates can frequently be achieved through the use of the mail questionnaire data gathering technique (Miller, 1991). Probably the most convincing evidence in support of this fact has been produced by Dillman (1983, 1978), who reported on the response rates obtained from 48 different surveys, covering 37 projects, conducted in nine different states and at both a local and national level. His results showed that the most common length for a schedule was 10 pages and that an average overall response rate of 74% was achieved with no survey obtaining a rate of response below 60% (Dillman, 1978).

These high response rates were not achieved by merely capitalising on some unique aspect of the target population, nor through the inclusion of a group specific gimmick such as arranging a prize draw. Rather, they were achieved through the use of a standard set of mail procedures known as the Total Design Method (TDM) (Dillman, 1978).

The Total Design Method (TDM) may usefully be described as a methodological recipe which includes both the ingredients for encouraging response and the directions for combining them. Thus the TDM essentially consists of two parts: Firstly, identifying and designing those aspects of the survey process that may effect the quality and quantity of responses, and secondly, an administrative plan which helps to organise the survey effort so as to maximise on the efficiency of the design intentions.

Searching in the dark for useful factors that might influence the respondents behaviour is clearly unsatisfactory. Thus in order to be able to identify and manipulate the various aspects of a survey project, we need a more constant and stable basis from which to work. Fortunately, such a context is available through the development of social exchange theory (Homans, 1969; Blau, 1964; Thibout and Kelly, 1959). Basically, this socio-economic conceptual model states that people are motivated largely by the returns their actions are expected to bring. This form of social exchange is considerably broader than the notion of economic exchange, from which the concept was originally derived, as the future obligations of one person to another are diffuse, unspecified and not negotiable (Dillman, 1978:12).

Dillman argues that surveys are a special form of social interaction to which this social exchange model is clearly applicable. The basic assumption being that a simple cost-benefit analysis is being applied to the respondent's position in a survey. Most people will only respond to a questionnaire if the perceived costs of doing so are minimal relative to the perceived rewards, and when the respondent is confident enough to trust that the expected rewards will be delivered.

There are a number of ways in which the respondent's costs can be minimised. We can ensure that the schedule is not too long, avoid the use of condescending and difficult to complete statements and ensure that the instructions are clear and concise. In terms of providing social rewards, we can explain how the study could benefit the respondent, accord individual attention to respondents through personalised letters and offer a tangible reward in the form of a copy of the results. Establishing trust, the model's third important concept is a little more difficult, though still achievable through demonstrating that the research is supported by or has approval from a reputable authority.

The second part of the TDM ensures that the good design intentions developed through the social exchange model are fully and effectively implemented in practice. Setting up an administrative plan requires a high degree of forward planing. For example, in order to carry out a precisely timed follow-up sequence, it will be necessary to estimate the likely response rate at each stage, to print enough schedules in advance and prepare all the follow-up letters before the main study begins.

The TDM thus provided the present study with a conceptually stable basis from which to design and implement many of the procedures and strategies associated with the mail-questionnaire data gathering method. The underlying premise at each stage being directed towards reducing costs and maximising rewards in an effort to motivate the respondent to participate in the survey.

Mailing the schedule It can be seen from Table 2.4 that four types of information were unevenly administered to the various sample populations. Three of the survey groups sent out an irnternal letter or memo to their members, giving advance notification of the research and broadly informing them of the study's nature and utility. The initial mailing, which was sent to each sample population, contained a covering letter, the schedule and a pre-addressed stamped return envelope, while the first follow-up simply consisted of a single letter which acted as a reminder. It will be observed from Table 2.4 that this letter was only sent to two of the sample groups, the reason being that contacting the various organisations involved a great deal of time, effort and expense, which had to be taken into account. In some cases, it was necessary for us to weigh up and decide upon a balance between what would have been ideal in procedural terms against the organisations willingness or ability to help in practice. Ultimately, in the case of the political members, probation, social workers and mental health practitioners it was decided to only use one follow-up mailing.

Table 2.4
Type of letter administered to each sample population

Group Surveyed	Type of materials administered			
	Internal Letter/ memo	Main letter	First follow-up (reminder)	First follow-up (remail)
Students		YES	YES	YES
Political Members	YES	YES		YES
Police	YES	YES	YES	YES
Social Workers		YES		YES
Probation Officers	YES	YES		YES
Mental Health Staff		YES		YES

The first follow-up (complete remail) was sent to all those respondents who had not completed and returned the first schedule. Its content included exactly the same materials as the initial mailing except for a modified covering letter, the substance of which portrayed a number of potentually conflictual messages. Overall, the letter's substance was more intensely persuasive, being highly personal in nature and including a tone of insistance at a more pronounced level than was included within the initual introductory letter. Despite this, the content was well balanced within the limits of normal ethical practice in the sense that it did not appear threatening or impatient in its manner.

In terms of timing, those survey groups who had agreed to send out an internal memo announcing the study, did so a week before the initial mailings were sent. The reminder letter was sent a week later, and the complete remailing follow-up approximately three weeks after the date of the first mailing. In general, the whole survey was carried out over a 23 month period from February 1993 to January 1995, while avoiding the holiday periods during the summer and at Christmas.

Rates of response Once a schedule was returned, the respondents' name and contact address were deleted from the sample population's data base so as to ensure that they were not sent any further material. Those names that remained on the computer two weeks after the complete remailing follow-up had been sent out constituted the survey's non-response rate. These remaining respondents included those who were contacted but chose not to complete and return their schedule, as well as those who could not be reached due to an out-of-date forwarding address. All the schedules that were returned could be used, even the small percentage (2.4%) that were incomplete.

The response rate for each sample population is presented in Figure 2.2. [10] It will be observed that the overall mean rate of return was 77.5%, while the response rates for each of the six survey groups ranged between 65% for the mental health practitioners and 89% for the probation officers. In comparison with previous mail questionnaire studies, such rates of return are very satisfactory (Miller, 1991; Dilman, 1983, 1978).

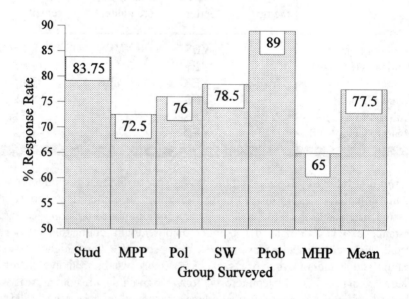

Figure 2.2 Bar chart of response rates for each multi-agency group

While these response rates are encouraging, some consideration should also be given to the nature of those respondents who failed to take part in the survey. In general, it would be reasonable to suggest that most of the groups constitute populations that are fairly homogeneous, thus those who chose not to respond were probably not substantially different, demographically at least, from the rest of their population.

Such an approach is unlikely to constitute an accurate reflection of our political sample, however, as their members are draw directly from the general population. The non-responses from this survey group were, therefore, considered separately through examining the geographical dispersion of those respondents who remained on the political group sampling frame.[11] Through plotting the respondent's location in terms of each of the city's electorial wards, it was observed that a significant minority were geographically located in the northern areas of the city. Coincidentally, these areas are also dominated by estates which typically comprise of District Council and Housing Association owned affordable social housing, thus on the basis of this evidence, it would not be unreasonable to postulate that our group of non-respondents is at least partly made up of those respondents who represent the lower socio-economic boundaries. Such a conclusion would, of course, be very much in line with the research relating to the fact that mail surveys still remain vulnerable to a lower response rate from this section of society (Hagan, 1989).

Processing the data As soon as all the schedules were returned, we began the process of preparing the data for analysis. The main task involved entering the coded information into a fixed format data file in SPSS PC+. As the data were entered manually, rather than via the use of an optical character reader (OCR), several tests were performed on the data in order to determine its level of accuracy. Firstly, we conducted a number of frequency analyses in order to identify any unusual data entries, for example, numbers outside the parameters of the coding set and to ensure that the fixed variable format was in line with the appropriate data set. Secondly, we re-check a 10% sample of the schedules in order to make sure that the data had been entered correctly. Throughout the course of conducting these tests, no significant problems were identified.

The interviews

The interview guide The qualitative data on beliefs about the mentally ill was obtained in two ways. Firstly, through subjects making written comments in response to an open ended question asking for their general views or concerns about the mentally disordered, and secondly, through the use of both unstructured and semi-structured interviews.

The interviews that were carried out with respondents from the two lay samples were generally unstructured in nature and so the interview guide was quite straight forward. The interviewees were simply encouraged to discuss their general views and concerns regarding the mentally ill in general, and any issues associated with the mentally ill that they considered to be important, such as care in the community and the plight of the homeless. The interview guide relating to the respondents from the four professional samples was, however, a little more detailed.

Essentially the guide was divided into two sections. As with the lay samples, part one simply dealt with their general views about mental illness and health, while part two contained a number of specific questions relating to the interviewees' views on the management approach of inter-agency co-operation.

Conducting the interviews All contacts, initiated by the respondent, were made by phone. During the course of our conversation the subject was asked whether they would be interested in discussing the subject matter of the research more fully. The decision to approach a particular respondent in this way was largely a 'judgement call', dependent upon how generally receptive and interested they appeared.

Once a respondent had agreed to participate, arrangements were made in terms of a suitable time and location for the interview to take place. It can be seen from Table 2.5 that subjects from the two lay samples and the police were interviewed in a face-to-face situation. In the case of the lay groups, the interviews took place at the respondent's home, while the police interviews were carried out at the police station during their duty breaks. With regard to the other three professional groups, the respondents were more geographically dispersed and so it was difficult to arrange a suitable place to meet. A decision was made to conduct these interviews over the telephone at a time suitable to the interviewee. On average, the interviews lasted for around 25 minutes and this time frame was fairly constant amongst all the interviewees within each sample population.

Table 2.5
Information relating to the nature of the
interviews for each sample population

Group Surveyed	Nature of Interviews		
	Number	Mean length in minutes	Type: telephone/ face-to-face
Students	4	25	Face-to-Face
Political Members	4	21	Face-to-Face
Police	4	30	Face-to-Face
Social Workers	3	33	Telephone
Probation Officers	2	20	Telephone
Mental Health Staff	2	28	Telephone

With the subject's consent, all the interviews were recorded using a standard audio-tape recorder with a specially adapted built-in voice activated microphone. The telephone interviews were recorded through the use of a slightly modified answering machine. After the interview, the content of each audio-tape was transcribed in detailed note form on to a data base.

Ethical considerations

Table 2.6
Nature of the research ethicality test performed by each survey group

Group Surveyed	Ethicality Screening Process
Students	University Psychological Ethics Committee
Political Members	Internal Executive Committee
Police	Internal Senior Officers
Social Workers	District Health Authorities Ethics Committee
Probation Officers	Internal Senior Staff
Mental Health Staff	District Health Authorities Ethics Committee

It will be observed from Table 2.6 that before permission to conduct any research was granted, each of our study's six organisations subjected the survey's purpose and methods to some form of ethical screening process. In general, each ethical evaluation was conducted within either a highly formal manner, such as through making an application to a well established Ethics Committee, or in a less official way via internal meetings amongst the study populations' senior staff. As a consequence of these ethicality tests, a number of interesting issues arose which require some consideration.

The first point of interest to emerge related to the fact that the responses from both formal Ethics Committees, namely, the University and District Health Authority, generally highlighted similar concerns with regard to several particular issues including: assurances about confidentiality, utility of the final results and duration of the study. The fact that each committee independently arrived at similar conclusions with regard to the ethical nature of the current research is very encouraging, especially in the light of attempts to try and establish a universally standardised Code of Ethics in order to guide and better inform researchers within the social sciences.[12]

One particular point, highlighted by both Committees, related to the nature of the first follow-up letter (complete remail). With regard to its substantive content it was generally felt that the letter's tone was too strong and that several of the phrases used would have to be re-expressed or taken out. For example, the point was made that we should remove a sentence from the first paragraph which stated: 'Unfortunately, to date, I have not yet received your completed questionnaire'. This remark was actually borrowed from the work of Dillman (1978) who suggests as part of his Total Design Method for mail questionnaires, that the use of such a direct approach acts as a subtle form of insistence, designed to try and persuade the respondent to complete the schedule. However, both Committees interpreted such remarks in terms of placing too much pressure on the respondent to reply. Thus as a consequence of this difference in the degree of emphasis, a gap was forged between what is theoretically desirable in research and what is ultimately acceptable in practice. In the final analysis, however, the exclusion and toning down of such 'persuasive' or 'pressurising' remarks appears to have had no discernable effects on our overall response rates.

Within the context of considering the ethical nature of the current research, a further difference in approach may be highlighted. This time, however, the problem was less easily surmountable and related to a degree of divergence existing within an organisation, between what was ethically/morally acceptable and what was considered to be legally enforceable. The organisation involved were the mental health practitioners. Once the Health Authority's Committee were satisfied as to the ethicality of the study, they gave permission for us to approach the Hospital Trust's Personnel Department in order to obtain the required lists of mental health employees. The personnel managers, however, were not willing to make the staff lists available on the grounds that to supply such information would result in a direct breach of the legal criteria governing staff employee confidentiality. The matter was finally resolved through establishing a compromise, which meant that in turn, we would have to approach each line manager directly and ask for their permission to view the lists of mental health staff members under their management. Ultimately, this process took a great deal of time and demonstrates that, in addition to ethical considerations, both legal and bureaucratic obstacles may also impede a researcher's access to a particular sample population.

Finally, a further issue arose with respect to the organisations who adopted a less formal approach towards a consideration of the ethical nature of the research. Their deliberations of the study's purpose and methods led to no specific objections being made, not even with respect to the substantive nature of the follow-up letters. Thus it would have been reasonable for us to retain the letters' original wording despite the fact that they had recently been formally identified as in breach of ethical guidelines. Ultimately, the decision was made to standardise the letters in accordance with the formal Ethics Committees' decisions. The fundamental point to be highlighted here is that without the existence of some form of general guide to ethical standards which is readily available, determinations of ethicality will remain uncomfortably lodged upon moving sands, which invariably may result in unforseen ethical problems and dilemmas for both the researcher and those who are to be the subjects of the study.

Concluding overview

In order to accurately test the research propositions presented in chapter one, it is essential that we develop a methodological approach which takes account of the fact that we wish to study a number of controlled variables, namely, type of psychopathology and type of offence over a highly diverse set of sample populations.

This chapter has responded to this demand through the detailed consideration of how the study's survey experimental design was formulated and justified. It is worth reiterating the fact that applying experimental procedures, specifically within the context of a social setting, is an approach which is rarely adopted within the social sciences. This is actually quite surprising, for as we demonstrated earlier, the design's ability to control both internal and external validity factors clearly enhances its potential for obtaining high quality data, which in turn must surely make such designs one of the most powerful research tools available.

Throughout this chapter, we have also discussed in some detail, the nature and content of the various methodological procedures used within the study. In particular, the actual structure of the survey took on board many of the criticism made about the previous studies, and we also partially tested the theoretical soundness of Dillman's (1983, 1978) Total Design Method and found it to a highly effective process for enhancing mail survey response rates. Finally, in an attempt to overcome the constraints inherent in collecting purely empirical data, we discussed how the research was extended to include the collection of qualitative material via the use of both unstructured and semi-structured interviews.

Notes

1 The use of college students and staff as respondents seems to be a particularly common practice in the research on attitudes towards the mentally ill (Furnham and Bower, 1992; Eker, 1985; Olmstead and Durham, 1976).

2 For a useful summary of the key issues raised by these data gathering techniques see (Miller, 1991).

3 Recently, the cost per interview has been estimated at around £20 (Brockington et al, 1993).

4 The issues arising from these questions will be discussed when we consider the study's data collection methods.

5 This estimate was obtained from private correspondence with the city of Cambridge's Electoral Registrar.

6 Fifty percent of this sample having no further education after leaving school.

7 Dealings with the various Research Ethics Committees will be discussed in more detail at a later point in this chapter (See: 'Ethical considerations').

8 It should be noted, that the partial ordering effect created by the way in which the sampling frame is presented, does not constitute a key feature of this research and so, for the purpose of obtaining a systematic probability sample, will not generate a cyclical effect which would bias the selection process.

9 The coefficients for each composite measure derived from the alpha reliability test will be presented and discussed further in the next chapter.

10 X-axis abbreviations are as follows:

Stud	= Students	MPP	= Members of a political party
Pol	= Police	SW	= Social workers
Prob	= Probation Officers	MHP	= Mental health practitioners

11 As we mentioned earlier, this particular survey group's sampling frame was organised in accordance the 14 Electoral Wards within the city of Cambridge.

12 This point should be qualified in light of the fact that not all academics are supportive of the establishment of such a Code of Practice, citing the view that the Orwellian 'Big Brother' influence will dictate and control future research (Reynolds, 1982). The evidence would suggest, however, that support for the idea in principle is growing and that attempts to develop such a code in practice will continue (Sedlack and Stanley, 1992; Hagan, 1989; Diener and Crandall, 1978).

3 Data analysis and presentation of the results

Introduction

In this chapter, the data obtained from the various sample populations will be analysed using a variety of statistical techniques. The results will be presented in four main sections, each of which will be further divided into a number of subsections in order to account for the various statistical components used within the analysis process.

Section one, which will be divided into two main parts, examines the raw data relating to each of our six sample populations. Firstly, descriptive data in cross-tabular and frequency distribution formats will be presented and discussed on the key socio-demographic variables of interest to the study. In subsection two, we will consider this raw data from a different perspective through examining its distribution across the study's four experimental conditions. At this stage, a correlational measure of association will be used in order to ensure that the data has a random, non-bias spread, suitable for the purpose of conducting statistical tests.

Section two, relates directly to the first main question of interest to the current research and may broadly be divided into three stages. In the first subsection, we will attempt to gain a prima facie understanding of our research sample's responses through a consideration of the descriptive data relating to the questionnaire items associated with beliefs about the mentally ill. Essentially, this will involve looking at both percentage and mean central tendency distributions for each of the various dimensions that constitute the study's three scientific models. The second subsection will focus in more detail on the way our subjects responded to all the items within a particular model. For example, did the respondents agree with the whole range of dimensions that go to make up the medical paradigm? In order to determine whether or not there exists such an internally coherent belief system, separate zero-order correlation matrices were set up within the dimensions of each model, and a significance test performed on their inter-item coefficients. Satisfied that no single scientific theory received an overwhelming level of support, we decided to search for the existence of a distinct multi-agency approach which may actually underlie the three formally expressed paradigms. Subsection three was, therefore, concerned with the various processes associated with conducting a principal component factor analysis.

An important point to note in relation to section two is that, in order to expedite our analysis, a conscious decision was made at the outset to assume that all null-hypotheses were true. The logic of this decision is sound (Levey and Howells, 1995; Roskin et al, 1988) and it has enabled us to: firstly, reduce our data set to a more manageable form through the development of composite measures, and secondly, establish an overall multi-agency approach which can then be used as the basis for comparatively analysing the possible existence of differences between the various independent variables included in this research.

In section three, a series of multivariate analyses were performed on the studies various treatment and socio-demographic variables, the central aim being to try and establish which factors were most likely to influence multi-agency thinking. At this stage, the plethora of ANOVA results obtained were organised, presented and discussed in terms of the studies remaining propositions.[1]

The Fourth and final section will be concerned with structurally analysing the thematic content of our qualitative data. In essence, this data will be organised around the various comments association with the three factors that were found to constitute our multi-agency approach towards the mentally ill.

In concluding this overview, a number of juxtapositions germane to this chapter should be presented. It was decided, throughout the analysis, not to accept as significant any finding above $p < 0.01$. The establishment of such a strict significance level was based on the view that, as there are almost 1000 cases within this research, a probability level set at a higher rate would substantially increase the chances of generating a Type I error. Thus, if the normal probability level $p < 0.05$ were used, there is a chance that at least 50 significant results would occur by random chance alone. This is simply not acceptable. By examining only those results at $p < 0.01$, we can be sure that a real difference has occurred even though we may be running the risk of creating a Type II error ie, rejecting other differences that exist at a lower probability level.

Throughout the analysis we were also conscious of how we dealt with any missing values. In each case they were either excluded or deleted on a pairwise basis, depending upon which process was most appropriate for that particular statistical test.

Finally, in an attempt to clarify the findings, the overall presentational structure of the chapter is such that all tables, graphs and matrices, along with any additional information relating to a particular analysis, are displayed in a technical appendix at the end of the book.

The nature of the sample populations

The sample populations' distribution

It can be seen from Table A1, that in total 961 subjects responded to our questionnaire on beliefs about the mentally ill. As expected, these respondents were unevenly distributed amongst the six survey populations that go to make up our overall multi-agency sample. The smallest number of responses came from the social work subsample (N=81) which accounted for only 8.4% of our total sample, while the largest proportion of responses came from the student population accounting for just over one third (34.9%) of the total sample size. Around forty-five per cent (45.6%) of the questionnaires returned were evenly distributed amongst the second lay sample - political members - and two of the professional groups - police and mental health practitioners - while the remaining 11.1% were accounted for by respondents from the probation service.

Table A2, shows how the demographic variable gender is represented across the whole sample. By looking at the *Row Totals*, it can be seen that overall, a little under two-thirds of the respondents (61.8%) are male. A cursory look at the *Column Percentage* cell differences within Table A2, clearly shows that there are considerably more males in both lay groups, the police and probation samples, while the remaining two professions display a higher proportion of females, with social workers showing a female/male ratio at around 2.5:1 (71.6% and 28.4% respectively).

The descriptive statistics provided by Table A3a, inform us that the age range for the whole sample is between 18 and 80 with an overall mean of 34.5 and a standard deviation of 11.4. It can also be seen that respondents from the student population were the youngest overall with a mean age of 26.4 years, and that the political members sample were the eldest with a mean of 44.2 years.

Table A3b, which is a cross-tabulation of age with group surveyed, offers a more detailed picture on how the age variable is distributed throughout each of our sample populations. In this table, the quality of the age variable has been reduced from ratio to nominal level data by dividing the individual ages into two manageable categories. The dividing point between the two categories is, in fact, roughly in line with the total sample's mean age of 34.5. This data reduction exercise is justifiable for a number of reasons. Firstly, using the age cut-off point of 35 years will enable us to measure whether or not their exists a difference in beliefs between those in the lower age category, who we might expect to have been brought up during an era of community mental health care since the 1960s, and those older respondents who were socialised at a time when a more restrictive and demeaning ideology dominated (Nunnally, 1961). Secondly, for statistical reasons, it is essential that we reduce the data levels so as to ensure a reasonable sample size within the categories of each variable.

Judging from Table A3b, some noticeable differences in the distribution of ages between each of the subsamples may be observed. It can be seen from the *Column Percentage* figures that both the student and police samples have the greatest proportion of respondents within the younger age category 18-35 at 94.3% and 63.7% respectively, while in the remaining four samples the greater proportion of respondents appear to be older.

In reply to the questionnaire item regarding whether or not the respondent had ever personally known someone who had received treatment for mental disorder, just over half (53.2%) said that they had (*Row Totals*, Table A4a). Of those respondents with some personal experience, the *Row Totals* in Table A4b inform us that 36.7% said that the person had been their friend, and 34.5% stated that it was someone in their community. Over a quarter (26.5%) stated that they had known a close/distant relative who had received treatment in a mental hospital, while 2.2% (N=11) admitted that they themselves had suffered from some form of mental disorder in the past.

Overall, just under a third of all respondents (30.6%) offered further comments regarding their views/concerns about the mentally disordered (Table A5). It can also be seen from the *Column Percentage* figures in Table A5, that, with the exception of mental health staff, roughly between a quarter and a third of the respondents within each sample population offered additional information.

Table A6, provides descriptive data on how the three professional samples - police, social workers and probation officers - responded with regard to the questionnaire item relating to the number of years respondents had worked within their profession. From this table, it can be seen that the mean number of years for the entire population was 11.5 and that the social work sample had the most experience with a mean of 12.4 years.[2]

Finally, some of the subsamples were asked about particular issues directly relevant to their group. Table A7, provides information regarding the student sample's course of study, 77.6% of the respondents stated that they were carrying out a doctoral degree, 15.2% a master's and 6.3% another type of post graduate course, for example, a PGCE certificate.

The political sample were asked about the number of years formal education they had received. Table A8, shows that a high proportion of respondents were educated to at least degree level with 48.3% being in full time education over the age of 20.

Table A9, illustrates the various rankings of the police sample. It can be seen that the majority (73.6%) had the status of constable, 19.6% were ranked as sergeant, while 6.1% had the professional title of inspector or above.

Testing the random assignment of subjects to experimental conditions

In the previous subsection, we examined some basic descriptive statistics in an attempt to gain a more detailed understanding of how the study's key socio-demographic variables were distributed throughout the whole sample. The primary concern at this stage is to deal with the important issue of ensuring that our subjects' responses were independent of the survey's research design.

In principle, when treatments are randomly assigned to subjects or subjects are randomly assigned to treatments, we expect and hope that such an arrangement will randomise individual difference between the treatment groups. Under such circumstances, any significant difference found between two treatment means may be interpreted, with some degree of confidence, as being produced by the difference between the two treatments themselves, rather than differences between the subjects within the two treatment groups.

In practice, however, a wide array of incidents may distort the assignment of subjects on a truly random basis. In laboratory experiments, treatment formulas may become contaminated before they are tested, and subjects may not turn up. In social experiments, subjects who have been randomly assigned to a particular condition may refuse to respond, thus distorting the number of subjects within a particular treatment. For example, if we found that the nature of the case vignettes used in the current research design were approached differently by different groups, then we would end up with a distorted, non-random, assignment of subjects. Perhaps women objected to the fact that Tom attacked his wife and so refused to respond to the questionnaire. If such a situation did occur, then we would expect disproportionatly fewer responses from women under certain experimental conditions. Consequently, the effect of such a disproportional response on our results would be considerable as we would be forced to make major statistical adjustment to our data, perhaps through weighting certain categories of responses.

Bearing in mind the possible problems that could arise as a result of a bias response rate, it would seem appropriate at this stage to test our data to ensure, with a reasonable degree of confidence, that the loss of subjects due to non-response is random and in no way related to the experimental conditions themselves.

The most appropriate way of examining such an issue would seem to be through statistically considering how the main variables of interest to the study are distributed amongst the four experimental conditions that make up the survey's factorial design. Thus through testing our data with a statistical measure of association, we will be able to determine whether or not responses within particular categories of a variable and overall are biased. If a non significant result is achieved then we may conclude that our response rate, and hence non-response rate, is random in the sense that it was not dependent upon the nature of the particular experimental conditions. It is to a consideration of this issue that we now turn.

The main variables of interest in this research ie, the independent variables are: type of disorder, type of offence, age, gender, group surveyed and previous experience of mental illness. We must, therefore, look at how these variables are distributed across each treatment condition. Our null hypothesis is that within each variable, there will be roughly an equal number of responses across each condition. This would suggest that our subjects' non-response was not influenced by the experimental conditions per se, and was, therefore, randomly distributed.

It will be observed from Table A10, that each of the main variables has a small Pearson's chi square value which is associated with a sizable significance level, statistically demonstrating that we are in a position to retain our null hypothesis of no difference. Thus our subjects' responses were random and not determined by the presence of a relationship between the studies main variables and the four experimental treatments.

Summary

In summary, the primary concern of this section has centred around two issues: firstly, to gain a clearer understanding of the nature of our overall research sample through a detailed consideration of the key socio-demographic variables associated with each sample population, and secondly, to test via a the Person's measure of association the random assignment of subjects to each of the study's four experimental conditions.

Satisfied that our data requires no further statistical adjustments, we may now turn to consider the first of the study's main propositions, which requires us to examine the relationship between our respondents' beliefs and the three formally stated scientific models of mental illness presented earlier.[3]

Proposition 1 How do multi-agency and scientific theories of the mentally ill in general compare?

Descriptive data on beliefs towards the mentally ill

The descriptive data presented in Table A11, displays a mean and, in parenthesis, a percentage agreement score for each of the questionnaire items used to describe the various dimensions of the three models of mental illness. It should be noted that some of the dimensions of these models were described by using more than one questionnaire item, and so they are described by using more than one mean and percentage value. Furthermore, the same questionnaire item was used to represent the prognosis dimension for all three models.

The mean and percentage scores were collated on the basis of all the respondents (N=961) who answered the questionnaire after reading one of the four case descriptions about a mentally disordered person. Thus, as it was mentioned earlier, the mean values represent an overview of the whole research sample's beliefs about the mentally ill in general.

It can be seen from Table A11, that respondents were willing to accept, to varying degrees, almost all the dimensional aspects of the medical model. Respondents strongly felt that Tom's behaviour clearly showed that he was suffering from a mental illness (mean 4.20, 71.1%) and that those afflicted were entitled to sympathy (mean 4.79, 86.4%) and had a right not to be held responsible for their illness (mean 4.03, 68.1%) or blamed for any consequential actions (mean 4.54, 78.7%). The highest mean value was for the item describing society's right to restrain Tom against his wishes while he is a danger to the public (mean 4.82, 88.9%), while the strongest level of disagreement was shown with regard to the statement which claimed that surgical treatment would have a beneficial effect (mean 1.06, 6.3%).

Of the eleven items used to describe the moral (cognitive behavioural) model, only 4 had mean values which were above midpoint, with the highest value referring to the patient's right to be released when their behaviour is once again acceptable to society (mean 4.63, 79.8%). The more contemporary cognitive aspects of the model do appear to be more acceptable, however. It was felt that society had a duty to provide people and places in order to teach mentally disordered patients how to conform (mean 3.51, 62.8%) and, although still low in intensity, a substantial minority of the total sample supported the view that treatment (mean 2.80, 43.2%) and hospital care (mean 2.28, 35.5%) orientated towards teaching/conditioning the patient's behaviour was more appropriate than punitive sanctions (mean 1.40, 13.8% and mean 1.54, 22.7%).

Ten questionnaire items were used to describe the psychosocial model of which 7 mean values were rated above midpoint. Respondents generally supported the psychosocial model's beliefs that society in general may have been a contributory factor in the onset of mental illness through agreeing with the dimensions: aetiology, treatment, function of the hospital, and the rights and duties of the patient, though they firmly disagreed with the more 'purer' view that Tom's behaviour indicated a society out of control (mean 1.68, 18.2%) and that society is solely to blame for Tom's condition, and should, therefore, have no rights over him (mean 1.17, 9.0%).

While these findings are of general interest in themselves, they tell us nothing about how the respondents actually replied to the questionnaire items. In particular, are the sample's responses to the items within any one theory sufficiently consistent to form an internally coherent model? In order to test this question, correlations were computed between the item scores of each model's dimensions.

Tables A12a-c, present zero-order correlation matrices for each of the three models of mental illness. The entry in each cell is the Pearson's r correlation coefficient, a measure of association which informs us about both the direction and strength of an association between two items. The table is symmetrical and so only half of each matrix has been displayed for ease of reference. The values on the diagonal all equal one since a variable is perfectly correlated to itself. Finally, it will be observed that the significance levels are displayed underneath each correlation matrix.

From the first matrix, it can be seen that 66 inter-correlations were computed for the various dimensions that make up the medical model. Of these 48 (72.7%) were statistically significant, 11 at $p<0.01$ and 37 at $p<0.001$ level. Overall, aetiology was significantly correlated with every dimension, except those relating to the rights of the patient and the duties of society. The inter-relationship between aetiology, behaviour and treatment:2 appears to be reasonably strong with coefficient values around 0.40. Though, interestingly, the association between these three dimension and those relating to the respondents' level of sympathy and understanding appears non-existent. For example, the non-significant coefficient values between aetiology, the rights of the patient and the duties of society are less than 0.06 in every case.

The moral (cognitive-behavioural model correlation matrix shows that out of the 55 inter-correlations calculated 50 (90.9%) were significant, 4 at $p<0.01$ and 46 at $P<0.001$. Within this model the aetiology dimension was significantly correlated with all the other dimensions except the duties of the patient. Furthermore, the item referring to the rights of the patient dimension (ie, that the patient has the right to be released when his behaviour becomes acceptable) was negatively correlated with all the other dimensions, except treatment:2 (ie, teaching Tom the proper way to act and behave) where there exists a small but nevertheless significant correlation. In fact, some of the other coefficients provide additional support for suggesting that there is a degree of consistent support for the new approach of cognitive learning therapy ie, that the patient's treatment (Treat:2), should be via teaching conducted in a learning environment (F-hosp:1, $r=0.34$) that society has a duty to provide (Dts-Soc, $r=0.47$). Other inter-relationships between dimensions associated with this more modern approach are far more spurious, however. The presence of inter-relationship between the old punitive and new psychological aspects of this model could be due to the offence condition associated with some of the case descriptions.

There were 33 significant results out of 45 inter-correlations of the psychosocial model (73.3%), 2 were at $p<0.01$ and 31 at $p<0.001$. Aetiology was highly significant with regard to each dimension except: function of the hospital, prognosis and duties of the patient. Furthermore, the coefficients show that the aetiology dimension correlates reasonably well with both social treatment factors ($r=0.38$ and 0.44 respectively). Overall, within each of the three models, the prognosis dimension was negatively correlated with the dimensions of aetiology, behaviour and treatment, which suggests that our respondents may not be very optimistic about the long term benefits of each separate approach.

An overview of Tables A12a-c, may lead us to conclude that, as there exists a significantly high degree of inter-correlation within each of the three models, our respondents are indeed viewing these academic theories as internally coherent paradigms. However, while this may be a fair comment to make, it is not very informative, as the bivariate coefficient patterns are generally inconsistent. As we mentioned earlier, a quick scan of the coefficient values within each model demonstrates that some dimensional sets inter-relate reasonably well and others show a very poor association. Thus, while the overall relationship between a set of variables is greater than one might expect through mere random association, the coefficients do indicate that complete internal coherence within each model is fairly spurious.

As no single model coherently represented a multi-agency approach towards the mentally ill, the next most logical step would seem to be directed towards the possible presence of inter-model associations. If we look again at Table A11, it can be seen that there exists the possibility for inter-relationships which have not yet been considered. Thus by looking within dimensions and across models, rather than within models and across dimensions, it would be reasonable to conclude that there may exist a pattern of beliefs which actually underlies the three scientific paradigms expressly stated in this research. It is to a consideration of this possibility that we now turn.

Underlying beliefs about mental illness

To recapitulate, we concluded our examination regarding the internal coherence of each model by suspecting that several of the variables may be related to each other in a way which is not directly observable, that is to say, some, or indeed all of the variables, may possibly be measures of an underlying currently hidden set of dimensions, factors or components which may help explain contemporary multi-agency theories of mental illness.

Working with a large number of variables in an attempt to discover patterns of relationships is tedious. Therefore, if such implicit factors were found to exist, measures of these general factors could be constructed and then used as key variables throughout the course of our data analysis. Thus trying to isolated these 'hidden' factors, would greatly facilitate and clarify the current research.

Principal component analysis The statistical technique that will be used in order to analyse the internal structure of our set of variables is principal component factor analysis. There are many kinds of factor analysis, however, the principal component technique has been chosen as the methods and procedures it follows in order to identify, extract and present any underlying factors appear to be the most straightforward.

Examining the correlation matrix In order to ensure that our data set was suitable for the principal component factor model, several statistical procedures were applied to a complete zero-order correlation matrix set up through combining all the variables that relate to each of the study's three scientific paradigms. The computations from these tests showed that our coefficient values satisfied both Bartlett's test of sphericity (Norusis, 1992) and Kaiser-Meyer-Olkin measure of sampling adequacy (Kaiser, 1974).

Factor extraction Once satisfied that we may comfortably proceed with the use of the factor model, we analysed the correlational data with a view to determining whether or not there exists key explanatory factors underlying the data set.

In terms of varimax (an orthogonal rotation algorithm) the factor matrix converged (arrive at a solution) in just 7 iterations (rotations). The number of useful factors contained within this solution was determined by the scree test which extracted three factors collectively accounting for 45.3% of the total variance.

Interpreting the factors In an effort to ensure that our three factors are substantively meaningful, we will only concern ourselves with those variables which have a real relationship, as opposed to a merely spurious association, with each principal component. Thus, as it can be seen from Table A13, only those items with a coefficient value greater than 0.45 were retained. In fact, the lowest coefficient score was 0.48 and most of the variables were above 0.50 in value, thus demonstrating fairly strong levels of association within a single factor.

Factor 1, accounted for over a fifth of the variance (21.4%) and included 10 variables covering both the medical and moral (cognitive-behavioural) models (Column one, Table A13). Four of the items were positively related to the factor and the remaining six had a negative association. Of the four positive coefficients, two referred to the rights of the patient to be freed from responsibility for their illness (item 21) and blame for actions consequential of their state of mind (item 4). It was also felt that the mentally ill should be shown sympathy and understanding and that they had the right to be released when their behaviour was more acceptable to society (items 28 & 25). The six negatively associated variables came from the moral (cognitive-behavioural) model and referred to the fact that Tom's behaviour was bad (item 13), that he should be punishment and imprisoned for his immoral behaviour (item 6 & 10) in a hospital with an oppressive environment (items 3 & 17) and that society had a right to treat Tom in this way as he has a duty to take responsibility for his own deviant actions (item 31). As these items were negatively associated with this factor, it can be assumed that the views held by respondents were the reverse ie, they did not agree overall. Thus our first factor may be described as eliciting a generally sympathetic response towards the mentally ill.

The next factor to emerge from the analysis (factor 2) accounted for 12.5% of the variance and was expressed by eight items (Column two, Table A13). Three referred to the aetiology, behaviour and treatment within the context of the medical model, and the remaining five spanned various dimensions of both the psychosocial and medical model, referring to the rights of society and the duties of the patient. Thus society clearly should have rights (item 27), including the right to restrain Tom against his will while he is a danger (item 15) and to force him to take medication (item 12). The patient is also seen as having clear duties to co-operate with any help offered (item 18) and a duty to take medical treatment (item 23). Overall, this factor seems to support the medical paradigm though within a highly restricted and controlled context.

The final factor (factor 3), accounting for 11.4% of the variance, was positively correlated to six variables mostly from the psychosocial model, though one item represented the more contemporary aspects of the moral model. The dimensions of aetiology, illness was caused by social stress (item 24), treatment, by producing a generally more comfortable and less stressful society (item 16 & 30), rights of the patient to care as a victim of stressful circumstances (item 2) and the duty of society to change for the good of the patient (item 14) were all found within the items of this factor. The item relating to the more modern cognitive aspects of the moral (cognitive-behaviour) model referred to the duties of society to provide people and places in order to help teach the mentally ill how to modify their behaviour (item 8). It would, therefore, appear that factor 3 is orientated towards a more community based approach for dealing with the mentally ill.

Computing composite measures The final stage of the analysis involves reducing the items associated with each of the factors into three separate composite scores which can then be calculated for each respondent in the survey. However, before such a data reduction technique is implemented, it is essential we ensure that each set of items is reasonably well inter-related, thus justifying their treatment as an indice measure suitable for the development of a single composite score.

In order to test the internal coherence of the items within each index, alpha reliability tests were performed on each of the three factors (Table A13). The results showed high reliability coefficient levels for each respective factor, clearly demonstrating that the items associated with a particular principal component are fairly strongly related to each other, thus justifying their use as composite measures.

Summary

In this section, we have demonstrated that on the whole our sample's beliefs do not directly conform to the approach adopted by any single scientific model. Instead, via the use of principal component analysis, we have highlighted three unique factors that appear to underlie implicit multi-agency beliefs towards the mentally ill in general.

In the remainder of this chapter we will use these factors as the basis for exploring the possibility of significant differences existing between the various treatment and socio-demographic variables included in this study. The statistical technique most appropriate to such a comparative analysis is the parametric test analysis of variance (ANOVA).

Proposition 2 How does behaviour defined as psychopathologically (depression/schizophrenia) and/or criminally (presence/absence of an offence) deviant influence multi-agency thinking?

In order to respond to this question we will need to consider the ANOVA data for each of our three factors as it relates to the main and interaction effects obtained from both of the study's key treatment variables, namely, type of disorder and type of offence.

Type of disorder: main effects With regard to the 'sick' role factor, it will be observed from the first main effect statistic in Table A15, that there is a significant difference between the two levels of the treatment variable disorder type ($F=14.88$, $p<0.0005$). The descriptive data in Table A14a, under the *main effects* column, informs us that the mean score for the depressive person is 4.15 and that for the schizophrenic the mean score equals 4.35. Thus it would appear that subjects are significantly more prepared to offer the status of 'sick' role to those suffering from schizophrenia.

A significant main effect was also found for the disorder treatment variable under the medical-control factor (Table A15). Furthermore, judging from the descriptive mean data in the *main effects* column of Table A14b, it would appear that the schizophrenic (mean 4.00), rather than the depressive person (mean 3.73), is considered by respondents as more appropriate for this type of restrictive medical approach.

In terms of the social-treatment factor, the difference between the two types of disorder is again statistically significant (Table A15 - F=8.21, p<0.004). In this case, however, it is the depressive person (mean 3.60) rather than the schizophrenic (mean 3.40) who is considered as more suited to some form of community based care (*Main effects* column, Table A14c).

Thus the overall findings from each of the three factors, as they relate to the type of disorder, suggest that a significant 'real' difference exists in the way our subjects generally perceive both the schizophrenic and depressive person.

Type of offence: main effects A consideration of the main effects for the treatment variable offence type shows a statistically significant result in the case of each of the three dependent variables (Table A15). In terms of the 'sick' role factor, the descriptive data from Table 14a, informs us that the mean score for the no-offence condition equals 4.71, while for the criminal offence condition the mean value is only equal to 3.80. Thus subjects are significantly more willing to offer the status of care and sympathy to the mentally ill in general, as opposed to the mentally ill offender.

Judging from the mean scores (Tables A14b-c) and significant levels relating to the type of offence in terms of both the medical-control and social-treatment factors (Table A15), it would appear that respondents are significantly more likely to view the mentally ill offender as requiring greater medical control (F=150.79, p<0.0005) and less social management (F=11.782, p<0.001) than the mentally ill in general.

On the basis of these findings, we may, therefore, accept the conclusion that a real difference exists in the way both the mentally ill and mentally ill offender are perceived.

Type of disorder and offence: interaction effects Now we must consider the disorder×offence interaction effect for each of the three dependent components. The findings from each of these interactions will enable us to determine whether or not the results obtained for the separate main effects of both disorder and offence exist independently of each other. For example, do the differences found between the levels of the disorder variable remain constant, within the limits of random error, while controlling for the type of offence only?

From the data relating to the 'sick' role factor presented in ANOVA summary Table 15, it can be seen that the F-ratio for the disorder×offence interaction is not significant. This indicates that the difference found between the two levels of the disorder variable - depression and schizophrenia - over (controlling for) the first level of the offence factor - no-offence condition - is not significantly different from the mean score between depression and schizophrenia for the second level of the offence variable - the criminal offence condition. Thus with a non-significant interaction effect between disorder×offence we may conclude that the significant mean difference in levels of support for the sympathy factor found between the depressive and schizophrenic person remains true even when controlling for the type of offence.

The disorder×offence contingency matrix presented in the ANOVA summary Table A14a clearly illustrates this point. From the first mean scores in the second data column in this table it can be seen that the schizophrenic non-offender (mean 4.81) is viewed more sympathetically than the depressive non-offender (mean 4.60), a position which holds in terms of both the schizophrenic and depressive offender.[4]

With regards to the medical-control model, the two way interaction between the treatment factors of disorder×offence appears to be highly significant at $F=7.620$, $p<0.006$ (Table A15). This result and the two-way contingency matrix presented in the second data column of the ANOVA summary Table A14b, suggests that the two main effect results for disorder and offence are to some extent dependent on each other in the sense that the differences found in the levels of one treatment variable are partly determined by the effects of the other.

The nature of the significant interaction between these two treatment variables is more clearly presented graphically in Figure A4. Having plotted the mean scores for each level of the disorder factor across categories of offence, it can be seen that the lines drawn between the depressive and schizophrenic means are not parallel. There is clearly a linear relationship for both types of disorder which suggests that there is an increase in support for the medical-control model as we move from a no-offence to criminal offence condition. It is evident from the graph, however, that the rate of support for this model dramatically increases in the case of the depressive person to the point where there is very little difference between the depressive person and the schizophrenic under the offence condition.

No significant first order interaction effect was found between the two treatment factors in terms of the social-treatment model (Table A15). Therefore, the significant differences that were found for both the disorder and offence main effects appear to hold. Thus as the disorder×offence contingency matrix in ANOVA summary Table A14c clearly illustrates, under both offence conditions the depressive person is viewed as more appropriate for this model than the schizophrenic.

Overall, in addressing this proposition we have been concerned with both the main and interaction effects as they relate to the study's two main treatment variables, namely, type of disorder and type of offence. The issues raised by the next proposition move our attention away from these treatment factors and instead provoke a consideration of the differences existing between the study's main organismic variables.

114

Proposition 3 How do the socio-demographic factors (age, gender, group surveyed and experience of mental illness) influence multi-agency thinking towards the mentally ill in general?

In this question we will be primarily concerned with the ANOVA main effect results for each of our three factors as they relate to each of the key socio-demographic variables included in the study.

From the ANOVA statistics presented in the first data column of Table A15, it can be seen that the 'sick' role main effects for both independent variables age and gender failed to achieve a significant F-ratio. In the case of gender, this result tells us that the mean difference between male (mean 4.17) and female (mean 4.36) subjects are not statistically different from one another (Table A14a). On the basis of a non-significant F-ratio for the variable age, we can also conclude that the there is no difference in the overall level of sympathy offered by either of our two age categories.

The main effects for both remaining independent variables are, however, highly significant at $p < 0.0005$ (Table A15). Thus as the mean scores from Table A14a inform us, subjects who have had some degree of personal experience with the mentally ill (knownMDP) tend to be more sympathetic and understanding towards their plight (mean 4.46) than those subjects with no previous involvement (mean 3.99). In terms of the group surveyed main effect, the significant F-ratio ($F=18.523$ $p < 0.0005$) supports the research hypothesis that there is a real difference in the mean scores of at least two of the six multi-agency groups (Table A15).

In order to determine roughly where the main differences between our multi-agency groups may lie, a Tukey HSD multiple range test with $p < 0.05$ was carried out using one-way ANOVA on the appropriate data set.[5] The data pertaining to this main effect are presented in the form of a Bar Chart in Figure A1. The results of the differential test are presented below the abscissa. Those groups that do not differ significantly from one another are linked by lines on the same level. Thus judging from the three lines presented in Figure A1, it would appear that there exists three separate sets of significant differences in our group surveyed data set. The police have the lowest mean sympathy score at only 3.76 and are shown by the bottom line to be significantly different from the other five multi-agency groups. The middle line indicates that while the two lay samples were similar to each other, they were significantly different from the other four groups. Finally, the top line indicates that the three caring professions were not significantly different from one another but statistically different from the other three multi-agency samples.

In terms of the medical-control factor, of the four subject variables, two main effects have reached a satisfactory level of significance (Table A15). The mean scores for the significant age main effect presented in Table A14b inform us that respondents over the age of 35 (mean 3.96) are more supportive of this approach than younger subjects (mean 3.79). The significant group surveyed result suggests that there is a difference in the level of agreement with this factor amongst at least two of the groups.

The information presented in Figure A2 informs us that both the social workers and probation officers stand apart from the other four multi-agency groups who are similarly minded. From a visual inspection of the Bar Chart, it can be seen that both the dissenting groups are fairly unsupportive of this approach with mean scores only around 3.40.

In terms of the two non-significant main effects, namely, gender and experience of mental illness, we can conclude that these variables do not influence subjects' views towards this factor.

Both group surveyed and gender showed a highly significant difference in approach towards the idea of social-treatment. In terms of the significant gender difference ($F=11.12$, $p<0.001$ - Table A15), it would appear that men (mean 3.62) are more willing to accept this form of management for mentally ill patients than women (Table A14c) who seem fairly apposed to the idea (mean 3.32).

From the group surveyed Bar Chart (Figure A3) it can be seen that mental health practitioners were significantly different from the other five multi-agency groups and are strongly opposed to the ideas contained within factor three, generating a mean score just below the scales midpoint at only 2.99. In contrast, both the social workers and probation officers showed the highest level of support with mean scores of 3.74 and 3.77 respectively, though their level of support for this social-treatment factor was not shown to be significantly different from that held by the remaining three groups, namely, the two lay samples and the police.

Finally, neither of the socio-demographic variables age or knowing a mentally disorder person reached an acceptable level of significance and so we may conclude that these organismic variables are not important influential determinants of respondents' support for this social-treatment factor.

Thus in terms of the socio-demographic variable's main effects, it would appear that there exists a number of differences across each of our three underlying factors. In particular, we have shown that there are key differences between several of our multi-agency groups across each implicit model as well as differences within other socio-demographic variables which are unique to a particular underlying paradigm. In our fourth and final proposition, an attempt will be made to examine whether or not these main effect differences hold across both treatment variables - type of disorder and type of offence.

Proposition 4 How do the socio-demographic variables (age, gender. group surveyed and experience of mental illness) influence multi-agency thinking towards behaviour defined as psychopathologically or criminally deviant?

The issue which is of concern in the context of this question is whether or not the significant differences found between the various levels of the study's two treatment variables - types of disorder (depression/schizophrenia) and type of offence (presence/absence of a criminal offence) - hold over the various subject variables - group surveyed, age, gender and experience of mental illness - also considered by this research.

Type of disorder and subject variables: interaction effects It will be observed from the 'sick' role column in ANOVA summary Table A15, that all the two-way interaction effects between disorder and each of the four subject variables are not significant. The interpretation of these non-significant interactions with respect to each main effect, will be similar to that described for the non-significant result found in the case of the disorder×offence interaction with respect to the separate main effects of disorder and offence. Thus we may conclude that the significant difference found between depression and schizophrenia remains unchanged by the independent influence of the various levels within each of the four key subject variables. As we mentioned earlier, the symmetry of this fact also holds true so that the status of each organismic variable remains constant irrespective of disorder type. For example, according to the disorder×group surveyed first order effect for the 'sick' role model, the significant differences found between the various multi-agency groups in terms of their view of the mentally ill in general appears to hold constant under both types of psychopathology - depression and schizophrenia.

With regard to factor two, the only subject variable to have a significant first order effect with the type of disorder is group surveyed (F=2.76, p<0.008 - Table A15). The disorder×group surveyed interaction tells us that the mean differences found for both the disorder and group surveyed main effects no longer hold.

A graphical illustration of the two variables (Figure A5) shows a number of anomalies from the parallel lines we would have expected if the variables were independent of each other. The first point of interest is in relation to both the police and mental health practitioners' mean scores for each type of disorder, which suggest that generally neither tends to differentiate on the basis of psychopathology alone and that both groups believe a controlled form of medical management would be most appropriate for both disorder types. The point of intersection between the two line does indicate, however, that the police tend to view the depressive person, rather than the schizophrenic, as more suitable for this form of management, an approach which is the reverse of all the other five multi-agency groups.

A further interaction effect illustrated by the graph is the dramatic change in approach adopted by both the social worker and probation officer groups regarding each disorder type. In terms of the depressive person in general, it is very clear from the mean scores that both of these professions strongly disapproved of the medical-control factor (means 3.16 and 3.15 respectively). Yet in the case of the schizophrenic, there are clear signs of support from both agency groups (Figure A5).[6]

The only first order interaction to produce a significant result in terms of the social-treatment factor is again between disorder×group surveyed (Table A15). From the line graph presented in Figure A6, it is quite evident that there are several deviations from parallelism. The significant group surveyed main effect showed that the mental health practitioners were strongly opposed to this method of dealing with the mentally ill in general. In terms of the two-way interaction effect it would appear that the strength of their opposition increases dramatically in the case of the schizophrenic, while in terms of the depressive patient their overall approach shifts slightly to a position mildly supportive of some form of social care.

In terms of the social worker and probation officer groups, the difference in support for this factor, as we move from one type of disorder to the other, is fairly small. Thus it would appear that the type of psychopathology per se does not seem to influence their overall view which is fairly supportive of the social management approach. In contrast, both the lay groups show some degree of decline in support for the idea of social care as we move from the depressive to the schizophrenic patient. In fact, the decline is sufficient for the Tukey multiple range test to suggest that, in terms of the schizophrenic, both the social worker and probation officer groups are significantly more in support of the social-treatment factor than the other four multi-agency groups. Finally, it should be noted that the police again failed to differentiate between the two types of psychopathology with both means scores indicating a fairly small degree of support for any form of community based care.

Type of offence and subject variables: interaction effects In terms of the 'sick' role factor, the two-way interactions between type of offence and each organismic variable reveals one significant result, namely, offence×group surveyed (Table A15 - $F=3.912$, $p<0.002$). Thus as we mentioned earlier, this interactive effect suggests that the significant differences found between the respective levels of each main effect are not independent of one another.

From a graphical illustration of these two variables (Figure A7), it can be seen that in the case of the two lay samples and the police there is a substantial decline in the level of sympathy and support offered under the criminal offence condition.

118

In contrast, this difference between the two levels of the offence condition is considerably reduced in the case of the three caring professions. Thus we may conclude that, to some extent, social workers, probation officers and mental health practitioners are not greatly influenced by the additional salient deviant identity of a criminal offence. In each case the level of sympathy and understanding offered is still high. This is particularly the case with mental health practitioners where the mean difference between the two offence conditions is marginal.

We will now turn to consider the effect the treatment factor type of offence has upon each of the subject variables in terms of the medical-control factor. Judging from the data presented in Table A15, it would appear that there are no two-way interactions which have reach a satisfactory level of significance. Thus the main differences found between the levels within each variable appear to hold in the case of both the mentally ill and mentally ill offender.

Despite this fact, there does seem to exist a point of substantive interest regarding the first order interaction between offence×group surveyed. The non-significant result suggest that the group surveyed main effect holds across both levels of the offence condition with both the social worker and probation officer groups generally opposing this way of dealing with the mentally ill. This does indeed still seem to be the case under the no-offence condition, with both professions showing strong resistance to the medical-control factor. With regard to the criminal offence condition, however, it can be seen from the mean scores presented in Table A14b that there is a dramatic increase in support for the medical-control model by both professions. This shift is particularly prominent in the case of probation officers who moved from a position of outright rejection of this approach in terms of the mentally ill non-offender (mean 3.03) to a high degree of acceptance in the case of the mentally ill offender (mean 3.91).

No first order interactions with the offence condition produced a significant effect under the social-treatment factor (Table A15). The only substantive point that should perhaps be highlighted here relates again to the offence×group surveyed interaction. In accordance with the offence main effect, there is indeed a substantial decline in support for this community based approach as we move from the mentally ill to the mentally ill offender (Table A14c). However, this reduction in approval seems disproportionably high in the case of probation officers whose shift from being this factor's most enthusiastic exponent (mean 4.11) to only a minimal degree of acceptance (mean 3.39) clearly demonstrates the influential effect the presence of a criminal offence has on this profession's overall beliefs. In contrast, this additional deviant identity appears to have played no part in structuring the views of mental health practitioners whose approach towards some form of social management was generally unenthusiastic to begin with.

The influence of within-group variables

A key finding prominent throughout our analysis of the data relates to the clear impact the variable group surveyed has had on perceptions of the mentally ill.

It may be the case, however, that the differences found between groups are simply the product of deviations already existing within groups. For example, the perceptual approach adopted by the members of a political party could be spuriously related to the socio-demographic variable of education.

Earlier we mentioned that data was collected on a few socio-demographic variables that were associated with each specific organisation. Thus in order to determine whether or not each of these within group factors had an influential effect on the views adopted by a specific multi-agency group, we carried out a series of one-way ANOVAs across the levels of each specific socio-demographic variable.

The one-way results showed that no within group variable reached a satisfactory level of significance. Thus it would appear that being a member of an organisation per se is the strongest determinant of perceptions, at least when compared to the socio-demographic factors considered by this research.

Thematic content analysis

Structure of the analysis

The first data column in Table A16 is a cross-tabulations of the thematic data obtained from our content analysis of the qualitative material relating to the study's interviews and the open question included at the end of our measuring instrument. The data presented in the following columns display the same information after controlling for the type of psychopathology. Thus data column two contains the qualitative data obtained in response to the case vignettes of depression, while the final column refers to the cases describing the disorder of schizophrenia.

It was clear from the empirical data that several of the multi-agency groups had very similar beliefs about the mentally ill. As a result, the decision was made to try and simplify our analysis by collating the information relating to both the lay samples - students and political members - and to do the same for the two social service professions - social workers and probation officers.

The rows of the cross-tabulations are represented by the three implicit models extracted from our principal component analysis. Each of these response categories were then broken down into a set of relevant themes. For example, it can be seen from Table A16 that the 'sick' role model was subdivided into four thematic areas: sympathy, responsibility, individual disorder and previous experience. Finally, in order to gain a more detailed understanding of the substantive content of our data, Table A16a sets out a brief description of the key issues and dimensions which broadly represent the nature of each theme.

Key findings of the analysis

While a more comprehensive picture of our results will be presented during the course of the discussion, it will be helpful at this stage to highlight a few of the most salient points.

It can be seen from data column one in Table A16, that a total of 511 usable responses were identified as classifiable under the key themes representing our content analysis.[7]

The first point of interest arises within the context of the 'sick' role model and relates to the fact that while a number of comments were made expressing a degree of sympathy for the mentally ill, considerably more referred to the fact that patients should be held responsible for their behaviour. Furthermore, when the responsibility theme is broken down by type of psychopathology, we find that there is a disproportionately high number of such responses for the depressive patient. A fact which holds across each of our multi-agency populations.

In terms of this thematic model, it is also interesting to note that a number of respondents were prepared to openly discuss their encounters with the mentally ill. Furthermore, several of these accounts were quite sensitive in nature, describing the respondent's own personal experiences resulting from problems such as a 'break-down' or depression.

A willingness to discuss such matters in a frank and open manner with a researcher who is a complete stranger, strongly implies that the stigma traditionally associated with the mentally ill may be less of an issue. Our evidence relating to the stigma theme of the medical-control model does not, however, add support to such an implication. Within this context, we find that each of our multi-agency groups tends to stigmatise the mentally ill to some degree and this seems to be particularly so in the case of the schizophrenic.

With regard to the aetiological nature of mental illness, a clear distinction can also be seen between respondents' perceptions as they relate to both the depressive and schizophrenic patient. In terms of each multi-agency group, perhaps with the exception of the mental health practitioners, it would appear that depression is viewed as arising primarily as a consequence of social factors, while schizophrenia is more frequently considered to be a product of internal physio-chemical problems.

Concluding overview

The data obtained from our measuring instrument was systematically analysed in accordance with the various propositions of the current research. In order to maximise on our ability to be able to manipulate each of the experimental design's independent variables, our analysis employed a wide range of powerful statistical measures at both a bi-variate and multi-variate level.

In general, the results have shown that implicit beliefs do not reflect any single scientific paradigm and are influenced by a whole range of factors including: the type of psychopathology, the nature of the offence condition, as well as a number of socio-demographic variables.

In chapter four, we will build upon these findings through discussing in some detail how they may contribute to our understanding of a whole range of issues and concerns associated with the management and care of the mentally ill and mentally ill offenders.

Notes

1 These propositions were set out in chapter one and constitute this chapter's main headings.
2 Due to an administrative oversight, information was not collected on 'Years of service' for the mental health practitioners.
3 See chapter one 'Models of mental illness'.
4 The disorder×offence interaction is symmetrical to the offence×disorder interaction. We may also conclude, therefore, that the significant offence main effect also holds across separate levels of disorder. Thus, it is also true to say that subjects are more sympathetic towards both the schizophrenic non-offender than the schizophrenic offender, and the depressive non-offender than the depressive offender.
5 It should be emphasised that the results obtained from the Tukey HSD multiple range test will only be used as a very rough guide to assist in the location of possible differences between the various multi-agency groups. Sole reliance on this approach would be erroneous, as the ratio of between and within group variances has been substantially manipulated in order to conduct the test on the appropriate data sets.
6 In fact, a Tukey HSD multiple range test, carried out on the medical-control data set relating specifically to the schizophrenic, showed that the significant group surveyed main effect no longer holds.
7 These qualitative responses were made up of 294 statements from the open-ended question at the end of the measuring instrument and the statements obtained from the 19 interviews. The reason why the number of themes exceeds the number of statements is because several respondents commented on more than one issue.

4 Discussion

Introduction

The propositions of this research as presented in chapter one set out to explore three central issues, of which the first was to examine the underlying pattern of beliefs held by our multi-agency population towards the mentally ill in general. Secondly, the study set out to determine the extent to which this overall approach towards the mentally ill was influenced by various forms of psychopathologically and criminally deviant behaviour. Finally, an attempt was also made to examine the degree to which certain socio-demographic variables re-shaped this general structure of implicit beliefs. The primary purpose of this chapter will be to draw our findings together and make sense of them within the context of these key concerns.

The measuring instrument appears to have a clear and interpretable factor structure, which suggests that our overall sample population holds a relatively complex and multi-faceted belief system. Thus in an attempt to gain a coherent understanding of this underlying approach, section one will consider in some detail the three implicit theories extracted from the principal component analysis. In particular, we will examine the substantive nature of each factor relative to the study's three scientific models and the degree to which our unconsciously held approaches towards the mentally ill inter-relate with each other on a structural level.

As the three-way interaction effects associated with each implicit model were non-significant, the general pattern of findings discussed specifically in relation to the study's two treatment variables - type of psychopathology and criminal offence condition - seem to be representative of our overall multi-agency approach.[1] As a result, it would appear that there exists a degree of common ground between each of the lay and professional groups. In section two, with supporting evidence obtained from our content analysis, an attempt will be made to explore these similarities through identifying a number of key concepts and issues that are omnipresent throughout the entire sample.

In section three, we will start to examine the effect certain socio-demographic variables may have upon implicit theories towards the mentally ill and mentally ill offenders. In this section, we will look exclusively at the way in which our overall multi-agency approach differs across each of the six lay and professional groups included in the study. Through the use of our qualitative data, an attempt will also be made to gain a general understanding of some of the underlying reasons why a particular organisation adopted a specific way of thinking about those suffering from some form of psychopathology and we will conclude by looking at each of the professional groups' perceptions as they relate to the practice of inter-agency co-operation.

At this point it should be made clear that through the use of multivariate statistics we are not only able to examine the effects of our multi-agency population vertically - through dividing our sample by each group surveyed - but also horizontally - by isolating factors such as age, gender and experience across group boundaries. Thus our discussion, with regard to the influence of various socio-demographic variables, will continue in section four where we will focus on the specific impact of age, gender and previous experience on respondents' implicit theories of the mentally ill.

In section five, we will concern ourselves with some of the most important implication that may be derived from these results. As with the earlier discussion, the structure of this section will be representative of the study's three principal components. Furthermore, the significant points to be raised will be broad in nature, discussing at both a theoretical and practical level the impact our findings may have on various criminological and clinical issues encompassing both the mentally ill and mentally ill offenders.

Finally, in section six an attempt will be made to place the discussion of our results within a more realistic context. This will be achieved through pointing out some cautions and limitations to the nature and parameters of the present research which need to be borne in mind when considering the depth and scope of the findings. Once these factors have been raised, an attempt will be made to direct future research in the area of multi-agency beliefs towards behaviour defined as psychopathologically and criminally deviant.

En passant, some comment should also be made regarding the discursive approach adopted in this chapter. During the first four sections the results will be considered at a level which may be defined as closely related to the primary concerns of the current research. Thus while the findings are discussed within the context of previous studies on perceptions of the mentally ill, no serious attempt has been made at this stage to broaden the debate further. The adoption of such a narrow approach may be justified on the grounds that it will enable us to focus more specifically upon clarifying and presenting the key issues to be derived from our complex mesh of multivariate data. Once this has been achieved, it will be appropriate for us to widen the debate in order to include a more detailed consideration of the central findings within a much broader context.

Comparing multi-agency and scientific theories towards the mentally ill

It is evident from the findings relating to both the correlational and principal component analyses that no single scientific model neatly reflects the view of our sample population towards those who suffer from some form of mental illness. Instead, the results suggest that our overall multi-agency approach centres around three quite distinct implicit theories of how this minority group should be understood and managed.

The 'sick' role model

The most dominant principal component to emerge from our data set was a bi-polar factor consisting of ten dimensions.[2] The actual nature of these dimensions suggests that the pattern of beliefs adopted by respondents is loosely structured through the formulation of a continuum which seems to pivot around the notion of responsibility.

At one end of this continuum there exists four positively related items which clearly demonstrate support for the ascribed status of the 'sick' role (Parsons, 1958, 1951), while at the continuum's opposite extreme, the six remaining dimensions represent a highly moralistic approach towards the mentally ill.

The pivotal nature of the responsibility element is clearly demonstrated by the fact that the degree to which respondents progress along this continuum depends largely on how willing they are to accept the view that the patient is not to blame for their circumstances.[3] According to Parson (1958, 1951), the status of the 'sick' role, which bestows upon the patient the qualities of sympathy, care and compassion, is only ascribed on the implicit understanding that physical illness affects people indiscriminately so that anyone may become ill. It is something a person gets, or 'catches', through some kind of external agent and so is considered as not the responsibility or fault of the sick person themselves (Miles, 1987). If however, respondents prefer to accept the claim that the mentally ill are responsible for their own behaviour, then support for this caring role will rapidly diminish and be replaced by the belief that the mentally ill are merely social deviants who should be treated in the same way as all morally bad individuals through some form of punishment.[4]

It is quite evident from the overall grand mean score for the composite measure relating to the bi-polar nature of this principal component that respondents are more willing to judge the mentally ill in sympathetic rather than moralistic terms.[5] A similar type of implicit approach has actually been identified by several earlier studies, using both comparable and divergent measuring instruments (Wolff et al, 1996b; Brockington et al, 1993; Murphy et al, 1993; Furnham and Bower, 1992). In particular, Furnham and Bower (1992) noted that one of their factors was associated with items which entitled the patient to sympathy and to be spared moral judgement.

The medical-control model

The second factor to emerge from our principal component analysis consisted of eight internally coherent dimensions which, for explanatory purposes only, may be subdivided into two implicit components or submodels.[6] The first of these components deals with the aetiology, behaviour and treatment dimensions associated with the medical model, while the second submodel strongly exerts both the rights of society and the duties of the patient.

Thus within the context of this implicit theory, respondents are prepared to label the bizarre behaviour exhibited by patients as mental illness and accept that the origin of this behaviour is organically based within the individual which in turn is susceptible to treatment through the use of medication. In the same breath, however, respondents also favour the use of extreme measures directed towards ensuring that such patients are forcibly restrained and controlled. On several occasions, this latter point has been identified as representing a distinct factor in itself and is often referred to as 'authoritarianism' (Brockington et al, 1993; Taylor and Dear, 1981) or 'social control' (Wolff et al, 1996b)

In these terms, it would appear that this multi-agency view is strongly supportive of the highly traditional medical paradigm which dominated mental health care prior to the 1960s (Thompson, 1994; Jones, 1972). Such an approach was based solely upon authoritarian and restrictive principles practised within the context of secure 'total institutions' (Goffman, 1961).

The origins of such an approach are, however, difficult to isolated at this early stage in our discussion. At a first glance, such an underlying pattern of beliefs may seem rather draconian in nature. This would be especially so if we were to discover that such a restrictive position was adopted simply because: certain types of psychopathological behaviour (Levey and Howells, 1995; Kirk, 1974; Phillips, 1963), the label mentally ill (Nieradzik and Cochrane, 1985; Link, 1982; Nunnally, 1961), or indeed both referents provoked high levels of fear, stigma and consequently intolerance amongst our respondents (Arkar and Eker, 1994; Nieradzik and Cochrane, 1985; Bord, 1971). On the other hand, when we take into account the fact that several of our case vignettes actually contained detailed information relating to a fatal stabbing, respondents may feel justified in asserting that such an implicit approach is a fairly realistic way of managing those patients who are both psychopathologically and criminally deviant.[7]

The social-treatment model

The third and final underlying principal component accounted for only slightly less variance than the medical-control model and so should be considered as an equally important multi-agency approach towards dealing with the mentally ill.

Six dimensions were associated with this underlying factor and in contrast to the medical-control model, this approach was dominated by the role society itself has to play in the cause and treatment of mental illness. Essentially, patients are perceived as victims who were simply unable to cope with the stressful circumstances in which they found themselves. The underlying pathology is believed to exist within a social rather than medical context, hence treatment is approached in terms of reducing or alleviating those factors which are perceived by the patient as highly stressful and generally difficult to manage. Consequently, within this implicit theory there also appears to exist some support for the use of psychotherapeutic treatment techniques directed towards teaching the patient how to cope and adapt to situations within their own environment.

Overall, by emphasising the importance of socio-environmental factors in the process of managing the mentally ill, this approach demonstrates some support for a number of the main ideological and strategic aspects underlying the practice of community based care (Taylor and Dear, 1981), an initiative which, as we mentioned earlier, has been highly prominent in the field of mental health during the last few decades (Thompson, 1994; Taylor and Taylor, 1989).

The inter-relationship of implicit theories

The fact that these three multi-agency factors are poorly inter-correlated suggests that they each function as quite distinct and independent approaches towards dealing with the mentally ill.[8] As a result, there exists the possibility that the overall structural pattern of beliefs associated with either a treatment or socio-demographic variable may comprise of any one or more of these implicit theories. For example, in the case of the variable group surveyed, we may find that the police are only supportive of the traditional medical paradigm, while the probation service advocate the use of all three implicit models during the course of managing this minority group.

It is also worth pointing out that on a substantive level an important distinction may be made between the nature of factor one and the remaining two implicit paradigms. The first principal component may be considered as identifying a belief system which deals specifically with the shape of our cognisance towards the mentally ill themselves. Thus in effect, this dominant multi-agency view measures our respondents' perception, knowledge and understanding of this minority through testing their commitment towards issues such as responsibility, culpability, sympathy and morality. In contrast, the two remaining principal factors offer a more tangible approach in the sense that they each present solutions directed towards constructively managing, rather than idealistically perceiving, those who have suffered from some form of mental illness.

The influence of psychopathological and criminal deviance on multi-agency thinking

So far, we have discussed both the substantive and structural nature of the three theories that implicitly underlie our multi-agency approach towards the mentally ill in general. In this section we will take things a step further by considering how this overall approach is influenced specifically by the type of psychopathology - depression or schizophrenia - and the presence of a criminal offence condition.

The 'sick' role model

From a consideration of the multivariate results pertaining to the disorder and offence main and interaction effects, it would appear that the schizophrenic is perceived as more entitled to the 'sick' role than the depressive person under both the no-offence and criminal offence conditions. Conversely, the findings relating to the first order symmetrical relationship between these two treatment variables inform us that in terms of both types of psychopathology, the no-offence condition is viewed with a significantly higher degree of sympathy and understanding than the mentally ill offender.

Judging from both the empirical and qualitative evidence, there would appear to exist a great deal of general support for the 'sick' role in the case of each type of mental disorder. In particular, there were a large number of accounts describing individual experiences of depression resulting from bereavement, work and family related stresses, and other distressing problems. Furthermore, numerous accounts were also offered which remarked upon the need to treat both the depressive and schizophrenic patient in a caring and humane way.

However, while the adoption of such a generally sympathetic approach is encouraging, the fact that the depressive patient is perceived as significantly less entitled to the 'sick' role than the schizophrenic is actually quite surprising. Previous evidence from studies which have examined implicit beliefs towards individual psychopathological states suggests that there exists a great deal of consensus as to the pathogenesis of depression, and that in general this disorder is widely experienced and well understood (McKeon and Carrick, 1991; Rippere, 1981, 1977), a claim which also appears to be supported by our qualitative data.

Conversely, for decades evidence has been produced demonstrating respondents' ignorance and contempt for the schizophrenic (Levey and Howells, 1995; Bhugra, 1989; Rabkin, 1974). Thus, on the basis of these results we would reasonably expect our respondents' sympathy to lie firmly with a disorder which we all, to one degree or another, may empathise. The fact that our expectations with regard to the depressive person have been transposed requires some clarification.

One possible explanation which may be justly formulated from the evidence suggests that many people's experiences of depression are actually associated with symptoms which are very mild and fairly short lived (McKeon and Carrick, 1991). As a result, the nature of the empathetic approach adopted towards other sufferers may become distorted to the point where common-sense notions of depression are suddenly understood in terms of each individual's own personal way of dealing with or overcoming their generally minor condition ie, perhaps through thinking of happier thoughts (Rappere, 1981) or "talking his problems through with friends" (LAY-d2-25).[9]

It would, therefore, appear that greater emphasis is being placed on the ability of the depressed patient to actually take control of there own problems. A view also substantiated by our qualitative data which shows that a considerable number of the substantive comments pertaining to this implicit theory relate to the degree to which the mentally ill, particularly the depressive person, should be held responsible for their behaviour. Thus within the context of our earlier remarks on the pivotal importance of the responsibility element, it could be argued that it is the degree to which the depressive patient is perceived as more responsible for their own condition that largely accounts for the lower level of 'sick' role status ascribed.

Further evidence in support of the possible existence of such a perceptual process may be obtained from our empirical data pertaining to the fact that the case vignettes describing the presence of a criminal offence condition were believed to be significantly less entitled to sympathy, and thought of more in terms of how responsible they were for their behaviour and culpable for any consequential actions. This fact is particularly evident in the case of the depressive person where the level of support as we move from the no-offence to the criminal offence condition drops dramatically. Furthermore, the substantive evidence also shows that more respondents were prepared to see the depressive patient, rather than the schizophrenic, as punishable for any criminal offence.

The medical-control model

In terms of this implicit theory, the significant two-way interaction results between disorder and offence would lead us to conclude that the traditional medical paradigm is viewed by respondents as a more appropriate way of managing the schizophrenic than the depressive patient. In fact, the mean scores clearly demonstrate that there exists very little support indeed for the application of such an approach in the case of the depressive non-offender.

The inverse findings from this first order effect inform us that in general, the mentally ill offender is perceived as more suitable to this underlying multi-agency theory than the mentally ill. This is particularly so within the context of the depressive patient, where a highly significant increase in favour of the medical-control model is revealed as we move from the depressive non-offender to the depressive offender.

Thus on the basis of this empirical data and the numerous general and specific substantive comments pertaining to the belief that schizophrenia has an internal physio-chemical, and in particular genetic origin, it would appear reasonable to postulate the view that our respondents may be prepared to think of schizophrenia as an illness just like any other to the extent that the behavioural symptoms are generally being interpreted as signs of an underlying disease.

However, as a consequence of this approach towards the schizophrenic, an important issue emerges as to why such a seemingly informed medical view was generally rejected with regard to the symptomatology associated with the disorder of depression. It is to a consideration of this point in question that we now turn.

Judging from the overall evidence, this markedly different perception of each psychopathological disorder may be partially explained in terms of the actual nature of certain behavioural patterns elicited by the schizophrenic. For example, the reference to a psychomotor catatonic posture - 'stands for hours, in a stiff upright position in the middle of the room' - may have proved too difficult for many of the respondents to comprehend. As a result, such behaviour may have provoked a degree of fear and unpredictability which in turn led to the patient being labelled as mentally ill (Levey and Howells, 1995; Miles, 1987).

In contrast, the reason why the depressive person is not seen as mentally ill may partly be explained in terms of our earlier remarks relating to the fact that most people can identify, to one degree or another, with the symptoms associated with depression and so are able to make sense of the patient's behaviour using alternative terms to mental illness (McKeon and Carrick, 1991). Furthermore, it could also be argued that respondents may not wish to associate their individual experiences of depression with a mental condition.

Additional support for suggesting that to some extent respondents may have been provoked into defining certain behaviour as mentally ill may be obtained from our qualitative evidence which reveals that the two key themes common to each sample population centre around the stigmatic nature of mental illness and the need to ensure a high degree of secure provision.

Furthermore, the fact that the depressive offender is suddenly viewed within a medical-control context at a similar level of intensity to that of the schizophrenic offender, strongly implies that respondents are no longer able to rationalise and understand in everyday terms the depressive patients behaviour. Concurrent

130

findings have noted that perceptions of such unusual behaviour have been described as 'strange and mysterious' (Fracchia et al, 1976) and akin to 'a foreign country' (Porter, 1987). In general, the decision does not appear to have been made on rational medical grounds but because the depressive offender's actions which are viewed as disruptive, bizarre and troublesome can no longer be tolerated (Rabkin, 1974), consequently there exists the need to provide a degree of restraint and control.

The social-treatment model

It is evident from the first order interaction effect between the study's two treatment variables that the depressive person is viewed as significantly more suited to some form of community based care than the schizophrenic. Furthermore, within the context of each type of mental disorder the findings clearly show that this implicit approach is considered as more appropriate to the mentally ill as opposed to the mentally ill offender.

The fact that the depressive patient is generally perceived within a social-treatment framework neatly compliments our earlier empirical evidence and conclusions. Collectively, these findings clearly show that the depressive non-offender is not viewed in medical terms but is instead understood and identified within a socio-environmental context (McKeon and Carrick, 1991). This approach is also quite evident from the substantive data relating to the depressive case vignettes, which in general, centres around comments relating to the causal effect environmental factors have on depression and the role of society as a mechanism for the effective prevention and treatment of such conditions. The fact that the depressive non-offender is perceived within a purely social context also suggests that there exists a high degree of tolerance for their behaviour. This is quite surprising given the clinically serious nature of the condition described in the case vignette.

In terms of the schizophrenic non-offender, however, our previous findings do not appear to conform so systematically due to the fact that there also exists some support for this condition under the social-treatment model. The reason why the schizophrenic commands a degree of approval within this implicit model is difficult to ascertain at this stage, though it would not be unreasonable to suggest that this support may have arisen as a product of possible differences in approach between the various multi-agency groups.

In terms of the criminal offence condition, it is quite evident that in general respondents disagree with the adoption of this management approach in the case of the schizophrenic offender. Such a view is very much in line with both the perceived incomprehensible nature of the behaviour and the respondent's general desire to be protected from any further harm. In the case of the depressive offender, however, a small degree of support for this implicit social-treatment model may be found. A finding which offers further weight to our earlier comments relating to the fact that, although the offender-patient should initially be managed within a controlled environment, there exists a degree of tolerance for the behavioural symptoms associated with depression which may help in the course of re-integrating the patient back into the community at a later stage.

The inter-relationship of implicit theories

Thus far an overview of both the empirical and substantive evidence has shown that there exists a number of concepts and issues which appear to be common across our entire multi-agency population. In general, these issues seem to unconsciously influence and shape the differential perceptual approach adopted by our respondents towards each type of psychopathological and criminal condition. Within the context of these key concepts and issues, however, it is highly likely that there exist marked differences in interpretation across each of the study's key socio-demographic variables. It is to a consideration of this possibility that we now turn.

The influence of group surveyed on multi-agency thinking

In this section we will examine both the quantitative and qualitative evidence relating to each of the study's six survey samples. The central aim will be to firstly, identify and locate the main difference between the various multi-agency groups in terms of their general beliefs towards each type of mental disorder and criminal offence condition, and secondly, gain a clearer understanding of the most important reasons influencing the particular approach adopted by each multi-agency population.

The 'sick' role model

The findings, generated by the two-way interaction between the variables of disorder and group surveyed, suggests that within the context of both types of psychopathology, the various sample populations may be differentiated from one another in terms of the level of overall support each has for the 'sick' role model. Essentially, this difference is characterised by two clusters or subset of multi-agency groups: firstly, the two lay samples and the police who in general demonstrated a moderate to low level of support and, secondly, the three caring professions - social workers, probation officers and mental health practitioners - who were significantly more in favour of this approach.

In terms of the first order interaction between offence and group surveyed, a similar conclusion may be reached regarding the difference between the two group clusters. However, in this case a significant interaction effect was also found which was generally highlighted by the fact that with regard to the mentally ill offender, the three caring professions remained firmly supportive of the 'sick' role.

On the basis of this evidence, and given the pivotal nature of the responsibility concept in determining levels of support for the 'sick' role, we would expect to find that respondents within the two lay groups, while showing some degree of sympathy, are generally ready to perceive the depressive patient as predominantly in control of their own behaviour and, therefore, more blameworthy for any consequences. Support for such a view is evident from the qualitative data which highlights the fact that depression is typically understood in terms of a transitory condition in which recovery depends "partly on the will power of the patient to ... start thinking of more optimistic things and not dwell too much on the past" (LAY-d2-105) and the ability of individual sufferers to "hang in there and get through the most unhappy times, perhaps through talking his problems through with friends" (LAY-d2-25). More generally, it was felt that in order for their condition to improve, "the greatest effort should be made by the patient himself, only when the patient wants to, can he recover" (LAY-d2-236). He should "get himself some help" (LAY-d2-44) for only when he "asks for it, does society have a duty to look after him" (LAY-d2-125). Furthermore, the view that the depressive patient should be held culpable was also substantiated by several remarks made with reference to the offence, the strongest claim being:

"... it's ridiculous ... the idea that society should bare the crime and he [Tom] should be excused punishment simply because he couldn't cope" (LAY-d1-98).

In terms of the schizophrenic, the general emphasis of opinion was less on the patient's likely level of responsibility and more directed towards the need to stress that:

"people suffering from mental illness should be cared for with respect, dignity and as a person who has individual needs just like everybody else" (LAY-s2-142).

However, in the case of the schizophrenic offender, respondents tended to talk less about the patient's right to care and more on the importance of blame and punishment for the offence, in particular it was generally felt that "Tom should take some responsibility between his periods of illness" (LAY-s1-04) and that he should "perhaps receive some type of punishment once recovered" (LAY-s1-21).

The police actually afforded a significantly lower level of support to the 'sick' role model than any multi-agency group. Overall, it would appear that the respondents within this profession were generally prepared to view everyone as initially responsible and to blame for their actions, the presence of a mental disorder only serving to partially mitigate such a finding. This point was frequently highlighted in the case of both the depressive and schizophrenic offender where it was felt that:

"While I accept that Tom is mentally ill I find it difficult to ignore the moral/legal issues involved ie, that Tom planned to kill his wife thus he deserves some sort of punishment" (POL-d1-75).

"While the welfare and rehabilitation of the offender should be borne in mind, society's overriding duty is to protect itself ... In respect of those responsible for committing serious offences society has a right to gain retribution ... Society should ensure that there is an element of punishment" (POL-d1-6).

This is not to say, however, that the police were totally unsympathetic towards the plight of the mentally ill. Rather it would appear, judging from the evidence, that the issue was hidden by numerous other competing concerns which were given a higher degree of priority such as the need to protect the public and consider the views of the injured party, "... it is no comfort to the victim to find out that the culprit was mentally disordered." (POL-s1-58)

In contrast, an analysis of the remarks made by the three caring professions within the context of the responsibility theme showed there was very little discussion directed towards developing an association between responsibility, culpability and punishment. Instead, the notion of patient responsibility was seen more in terms of how it might be used during the course of treatment. Generally, it was felt that some effort should be made to try and make the patient aware of their illness so that they could start to learn and understand its nature:

"When well enough they should try and look at why they became unwell (SW-d2-190) and 'They can control symptoms some of the time and so should be encouraged to manage their behaviour where possible" (PROB-d2-45).

The analogy was often drawn with physical illness where the patient is responsible for doing what is in their best interest, for example, staying in bed, keeping worm, taking medication, etc.

In these terms, it could be argued that the increase in support for the 'sick' role may only be partially associated with the decline in beliefs about the degree of patient responsibility. There also appears to exist a case for saying that the level of perceived responsibly still exists but primarily on the understanding that any attempt at removal would in effect disempower the patient.

"They may not be responsible for all their actions but we have no right to deprive them of the responsibility they do have, this ... [however] is not to say that we avoid showing them compassion" (SW-s2-21).

Thus it would appear that the three caring professions are to some extent, actually re-defining the concept of responsibility by detaching it from issues such as fault and punishment, and instead re-interpreting the notion within a more positive context orientated towards the future treatment and well-being of the mentally ill.

Empirical support for these two differing approaches can be found when one considers the significant two-way interaction between offence and group surveyed. Here the results show that in the case of both the depressive and schizophrenic offender, there is a dramatic decline in support for the 'sick' role model by both the lay groups and the police. Thus substantiating our earlier claim that the presence of a criminal offence is associated with an increase in the perceived level of patient responsibility and blame. In the case of the three caring professions, however, this significant decrease in support no longer holds, hence, further demonstrating that the notion of responsibility is possibly being re-defined to the benefit of the patient.

The medical-control model

The most prominent feature of the disorder by group surveyed interaction effect relates to the significantly lower level of support for this implicit model found in the cases of both the social workers and probation officers under the condition of depression. In fact, both lay groups also appear to generally disagree with the application of this approach in the case of the depressive non-offender.

In contrast, the empirical findings relating to the schizophrenic show that, while the police and mental health practitioners generally agree with the medical-control model in the case of each type of mental disorder, there is a considerable increase in support for this implicit approach by the remaining four multi-agency groups. In fact, in the case of both the social workers and probation officers the increase was sufficient to remove the significant difference that had existed between the various groups under the psychopathology of depression.

In terms of the non-significant two-way interaction between offence and group surveyed it will be observed that all six survey groups are supportive of this implicit theory with regards to both the depressive and schizophrenic offender.

On the basis of this evidence it would appear that four of our six multi-agency groups are not prepared to see the depressive non-offender within a medical context. In terms of the two lay groups the view that it is "ridiculous to explain it [depression] in terms of chemicals" (LAY-d2-53) was offered further support by the substantive evidence which showed a general reluctance by respondents to directly label this condition as 'mentally ill'. Instead, alternative terms such as 'sad', 'very unhappy', 'distressed', 'non-conformist' and 'misguided' were used. Some respondents made a particular effort to avoid the 'mental illness' term by suggesting quite poetic alternative such as that "we need to help those who have lost their way" (LAY-d2-358) or that they are "specialised in a particular aspect of their psychology"(LAY-d2-39). Conversely, the fact that the depressive offender was suddenly perceived within a medical context was also apparent from the labels used by respondents. Thus rather than being seen as 'sad' or 'unhappy', the patient was suddenly perceived as 'mentally', 'seriously', 'clinically' or even 'chemically' depressed. With regard to the depressive offender there was also a clear need to enforce a degree of control either through some form of detention or medication:

> "for potentially violent individuals a form of sedation will of course be required - I approve the use of drugs under such circumstances." (LAY-d2-148).

In the particular case of the schizophrenic, the majority of comments tended towards the view that the condition's aetiology was biological in nature, based upon "chemically related problems in the brain" (LAY-s2-44), which a large number of respondents were convinced was related to 'hereditary' and 'genetic' factors.'

It is also quite apparent from the lay respondents comments that a modest degree of stigma still exists regarding the schizophrenic patient and the mentally ill offender in general. The substantive evidence suggests that such individuals are generally seen as potentially dangerous, violent and unpredictable, a view typically found in previous studies of the mentally ill (Levey and Howells, 1995; Steadman and Cocozza, 1978; Rabkin, 1974). An interesting feature about these remarks, however, is that many were made within the context of a third person:

> "There is a tendency for *many people* to think of all mentally ill people as being eccentric and unpredictable and to fear that they could be violent. ... They raise fear of disorder and danger and make *us* anxious about how *we* live" (LAY-s2-121).

> "The *public* holds a strong stigma against the mentally ill ... they should not be allowed to roam freely in society where they can be a danger ... they are likely to either commit suicide or assault someone" (LAY-d2-48).

Such an approach strongly suggests that our respondents are conscious of the fact that to hold a negative perception towards the mentally ill is inhuman and wrong. Consequently, in an attempt to try and emphasis this point but hide their own prejudices and appear more moderate, the issue is expressed in terms of a 'neutral' referent, the avoidance of such a psychologically conflicting position is common particularly on sensitive issues.[10] The qualitative data offers two points which help substantiate such a claim. Firstly, the fact that so many people wrote that this view is common in 'many people', logically implies that there must exist some degree of overlap, and secondly, as is evident from the above quotes, several respondents although starting in terms of a third person either unwittingly, reverted to the referent of self or expressed their negative views at a later point.

Possibly as a consequence of this stigma and out of a concern for public safety, both the empirical and substantive data clearly indicated a perceived need to manage such patients within a controlled environment. Overall, it was felt that "with an unknown quantity such as schizophrenia, society does have the right to be protected from potential harm" (LAY-s2-14) and that "society should protect itself at all costs" (LAY-s2-206) by locking the schizophrenic patient up, even "If prison is the only place to restrain them" (LAY-s2-173). Furthermore, while such an approach was viewed as in the best interests of the patient as well as society, for such actions to be deemed necessary, it was sufficient that the patient is only "likely to cause harm" (LAY-s1-263) and "If wife/family felt threatened" (LAY-d2-98). With regard to the patient's long term prospects it was envisaged that they should remain institutionalised "until they were better" (LAY-s2-32), "permanently" (LAY-s2-128), "as long as they are ill" (LAY-s2-284) or "until sure that such a mental relapse will not re-occur" (LAY-s2-121).

The reason why the two caring professions - social workers and probation officers - objected so strongly to this approach in the case of the depressive non-offender, appears to be largely motivated by concerns about the over-indulgent use of medication and confinement. The evidence from their comments suggested that an approach orientated towards the specific use of drugs and restrictive regimes would not, in the long term, be of great benefit to the patient. The social workers in particular, emphasised that imposing too high a level of control over the patient tends to:

"produce a treatment system that is primarily symptom focused with a view to repressing the patients behaviour" (SW-s1-4).

According to this profession, such a narrow approach ignores the numerous benefits and achievements that can be gleamed from psychotherapeutically based schemes which actively involve the patient:

"I am concerned that drugs are frequently given for depression when techniques such as counselling and befriending would really be more helpful" (SW-d2-92).

General concern with the fact that current practice has not yet managed to strike a balance between the emphasis on the need to control and on the patient's needs within the community was frequently mentioned by those professionals within the probation service where the belief was strongly held that:

"... many mentally ill patients languish in prison tormented and abused or discarded on the streets without any official offer of help" (PROB-d1-92).

Such situations were understood to arise particularly in the case of minor offenders:

"I have notice that a number of mentally ill offenders are not bad enough to be sectioned and have refused psychiatric treatment while in custody, which has meant that they end up in ordinary prisons" (PROB-d1-72).

As with the social workers, it was generally felt that drugs, while of some help initially, should not be viewed as a matter of course, the general view being that they tended to encourage dependency and:

"... often cause unpleasant side-effects which are difficult to cope with and make the task of resolving any underlying social problems that much tougher" (PROB-d2-27).

In terms of these two professions, the fact that the empirical data points to a highly significant shift in support for the medical-control model under each of the three remaining psychopathologically and criminally based conditions, suggests a clear shift in policy towards such individuals. From the substantive data it would appear that the schizophrenic is viewed as generally less likely to benefit, at least initially, from community based treatments such as counselling and that in the case of both the depressive and schizophrenic offender there appears to exist a clear need to protect the public and to believe generally that medication would be more appropriate as there is "really little else that can be done during such episodes of serious illness" (PROB-s1-100). In the particular case of the schizophrenic, it was also clear that a stigma was on occasion associated with this condition which may have amplified the respondents' desire to ensure that these patients were securely managed:

"schizophrenics are clearly a risk, you only need to hear the news to find out about all the cases of psychiatric patients committing murder when they are set free" (SW-s1-83).

However, this fact should not be overstated for, while the schizophrenic was negatively perceived, there exists some evidence to suggest that the nature of this stigmatic perception, or at least the way these professions dealt with it, is somewhat different to the approach of 'self denial' generally adopted by both the lay and police respondents. Instead, several accounts showed that these two caring groups (as well as the mental health practitioner) were more prepared to openly acknowledge that such views were occasionally held:

"... I would be lying if I said that I never feel uncomfortable around certain mentally ill people, in my mind I tend to stereotype them ... I am also conscious of the need to ensure that I am not prejudice" (MHP-s1-25).

"even though I have suffered from depression, I still tend to negatively look upon certain mentally ill people" (PROB-d1-88).

As a result of this conscious reaction towards the presence of a stigma, respondents are more aware of the potential for prejudices and so are more likely to positively re-define their approach towards such patients, rather than unwittingly avoid the issue altogether or displace such negative evaluations to a third person.

The most interesting feature about the results obtained from the police and the mental health practitioners is that, while both multi-agency groups generally agreed on the appropriateness of this approach for each of the four psychiatric conditions, they did so by starting from quite differing perspectives. The substantive data relating to the police shows that their primary concern was for the protection of the public from harm. Towards this goal it was felt that there needs to be "an increase in the amount of places and hospitals that offer a high level of security" (POL-s1-41) and that they spent a disproportionate amount of their time dealing with 'escapees' and 'offenders':

"who are allowed to wander out of wards and hospital grounds, causing concern to local residents" (POL-s1-38)

With regard to the mental health practitioners, however, the general view was that a degree of secure provision was essential to the well being and effective treatment of the patient. Some respondents even suggested that the traditional 'total institution' approach should be brought back:

"I strongly feel that asylum, in the original use of the word, continues to be vital as a refuge for disturbed people, for understanding, support and medication ..." (MHP-d1-220).

139

"... for the seriously mentally ill asylums must be developed in which the best aspects of the mental hospital tradition must be preserved - compassion, help, support, proper medical care and security" (MHP-s1-35).

"Victorian hospitals with all their faults, and indeed there were many, at least provided a roof, food and warmth, today many don't have this" (MHP-s2-135).

The social-treatment model

The significant results from the disorder by group surveyed interaction effect highlight two key issues. firstly, that both the social workers and probation officers have the highest overall degree of support for this model, this fact is statistically evident in the case of the schizophrenic. Secondly, the means suggest that, while the mental health practitioners disagree with this implicit approach in terms of the schizophrenic, they do never-the-less offer a small degree of support in the case of the depressive non-offender.

In terms of the non significant first order effect between offence and group surveyed, it is quite evident that there is very little support for the mentally ill offender amongst any of the multi-agency groups, with the mental health practitioners showing a particularly strong level of disagreement with this form of managment.

With regard to the two lay samples, there was some degree of emphasis in their comments demonstrating support for the view that the causes of depression were very much related to social issues such as "family stresses and responsibilities" (LAY-d2-121), "pressures of work" (LAY-d2-355), "small petty frustrations that can build up" (LAY-d1-28) and "the highly individualistic nature of our society" (LAY-d2-145). In terms of the schizophrenic, support for the social-treatment approach appears to be based largely on the grounds that a good environment would not do any harm. More specifically, socio-environmental changes were seen as helping to prevent the condition from getting any worse and/or having a 'soothing', rather than a direct causal effect on the schizophrenic:

"I always thought that schizophrenia was due to a chemical disorder in the brain ... I guess that a stable living environment cannot hurt" (LAY-s2-57).

"social change by making life less stressful would help relax and sooth the schizophrenic as it would do us all [sic]" (LAY-s2-233).

With regard to the content analysis theme, care in the community, a substantively prominent feature throughout each or our multi-agency groups referred to the fact that, while the idea of providing community based care was accepted as good in principal, it was generally perceived as hopelessly inadequate in practice. In terms of our lay samples, particular concern was shown for the increasing number of homeless people on our streets with either mental health, alcohol or drug related problems. Typically, it was felt that:

"the number of mentally ill people on the streets is appalling. They are homeless and deprived of welfare benefits and help" (LAY-s1-17). "Care in the community is thought of as leave-them-alone-and-they'll-go-away policy" (LAY-d2-63). As a result "many mental people [sic] taken out of institutions, have been disregarded and are now homeless" (LAY-s2-218)

Other comments related to the patients' generally disruptive nature, and included: "shouting and arguing in the streets late at night" (LAY-s2-311), "aggressive begging" (LAY-s2-187) and a general fear of threats and intimidation.

Overall, the police tended to offer some degree of support to this implicit theory in both cases of depression. Judging from the qualitative data, there appears no obvious reason for this. Though a possible explanation may rest with the fact that retrospective information about a depressive patient may reduce the level of stigma and perceived unpredictability relative to the schizophrenic and those labelled mentally ill, which in turn makes the depressive condition seem more tolerable. The negative view associated with the schizophrenic appears to be consistent with that held by lay respondents, thus such patients are generally perceived as more aggressive, dangerous and unpredictable:

"dealing with call-outs to scenes where all you know is that someone is behaving strangely, can be frightening ... at least normal offenders are predictable" (POL-s2-49).

"There are always jokes over the radio about calls to attend a scene in which someone is behaving in a weird way, it's a shame because it really gives the mentally ill an image problem" (POL-s1-117).

For the police the policy of community base care also causes a great deal of problems, partly due to the fact that there appears to be a large minority of patient which:

"no-one is prepared to take responsibility for looking after and so they roam the streets, get arrested for minor offences, and are dealt with by the courts, once they are back in society the cycle starts again" (POL-d1-47).

In addition, it was generally believed that the inadequate number of secure facilities available means that:

> "care in the community all to often equates with care in the custody office" (POL-d1-6), and it was felt that, "the frequency with which mentally disordered persons are held in police custody is disturbing as the law and codes of practice are woefully inadequate ... [furthermore] ... supervising them is dangerous for both the patient and the police" (POL-d2-173).

Typically, the general opinion was that these problems resulted in a great deal of police time being 'wasted' dealing with minor issues such as "baby-sitting people while waiting for the duty doctor to arrive" (POL-s1-34). In particular, there existed the belief amongst senior staff that given the new business environment, under which the police now have to work, dealing with these issues took valuable police resources away from more serious issues and pre-established target areas:

> "... an increasing burden has fallen on to the police by being called to incidents involving the mentally disordered. This takes us away from our primary roll and with difficult/persistent cases budgets can become stretched" (POL-d1-49).

Furthermore, it was quite clear from the qualitative evidence that the day-to-day management of the mentally ill, within the context of a front line service perceived as wholly inadequate, often led to difficulties and frustrations, not only for the police, but also for the victim and the patient:

> "Care in the community is crap. It's a cop out - a waste of my time. I've had the responsibility of sectioning someone - knowing that she would not get the help she needed. I felt pathetic and useless knowing that I couldn't help her. All I could do was get her off the streets for a week or two to give her ex-boyfriend a break from her threats and assaults" (POL-d2-21).

As depression is generally viewed within a social context, it is, therefore, not surprising to find that both the social service professions - social workers and probation officers - are supportive of this form of management. The fact that the schizophrenic is also perceived as being able to benefit from this approach, does to some extent contradict our earlier findings with regard to the medical-control model ie, that "really little else can be done during such episodes of serious illness" (PROB-s1-100). Judging from the substantive comments, there appears to exist two key issues which may help explain this anomaly. Firstly, there was a great deal of support for the idea of a continuous programme of care, which essentially acknowledged the need for the initial use of medication in order to stabilise the condition, but which then moved on toward more socially orientated programmes such as teaching the patient coping and adaptation skills within their environment:

> "Medication often plays a vital role in the process of getting better, even if it just calms the patient down so that he can think more clearly about what he wants to do ..." (SW-s2-33).

> "Treatment needs to have a social input but I would never discount the value of appropriately prescribed medication" (PROB-d2-41).

Secondly, it was generally felt that there needs to exist a high degree of surveillance over such individuals during the course of social integration, this appeared to be based on ensuring that the patient did not relapse and become a danger:

> "there should exist a continuum of treatment/care appropriate to the patient's illness which takes into account their risk via supervision in the community" (PROB-d2-63).

Once again, present programmes of community based care were viewed as hopelessly inadequate in the sense that:

> "patients get moved on from place to place, live in poor accommodation and turn to drink" (PROB-d2-43), furthermore, there was "concern for the strain that is put on families and voluntary services who have to cope with a mentally disorder person" (SW-s2-81) and a social worker of twenty years in the job felt that, "there has been a deterioration in the standards of care since the 1970s" (SW-d2-11).

Numerous suggestions were made as to how the system could be improved. For example, it was felt that there existed a need for:

> "a far greater external mix of specialised hospitals, clinics, half-way houses, group homes and hostels" (SW-d2-63), "more facilities particularly at night and during the weekends, so that help should only be a phone call away" (PROB-d1-28), a greater emphasis on working with families, "families should not be made to feel guilty if they can't cope and should be given money to take on the responsibility" (PROB-d1-33) and help was needed to "gain re-integration into jobs" (SW-s1-171).

Although mental health practitioners offered a minor concession to the depressive non-offender, it seems generally to be the case that this profession was opposed to the use of any form of social-treatment model for both types of psychopathology. It was observed earlier that in general they were supportive of the asylum, however, judging from their comments, this does not seem to be because they object to the initiative of community care. In fact, as with the social service professions, there was some support for the notion of a continuous programme of care amongst practitioners. However, the overwhelming emphasis was on the hopelessly inadequate state of the present community based system. Generally it was felt that:

"The approach is enlightening but has been irresponsibly managed and inadequately resourced particularly the transition from institute to the community" (MHP-s2-143).

It was also felt that a great deal of pressure was being placed on "voluntary services who often have to pick up the slack" (MHP-s2-92) and that "not only do patients suffer, but also their families who find it difficult to cope with them" (MHP-d2-11). In particular, it was highlighted that many of the after-care provisions that are essential to patients on leaving hospital have, in many areas, yet to be "identified, never mind implemented" (MHP-d2-41). Furthermore, several practitioners felt that the whole exercise was nothing more than a way of saving money:

"It [care in the community] is a cost cutting exercise ... CCT is determining care in the community and not a real incentive to improve their [the patient's] condition" (MHP-s2-59).

"Care in the community will only be used as a dumping ground for difficult patients who do not fit neatly into the new business environment of the NHS or private mental health facilities" (MHP-s2-33).

Thus on the basis of this overwhelming evidence, it would appear that for the mental health profession the pendulum has swung back in favour of hospital care, not because it is necessarily perceived as the best way, but largely because many mental health practitioners are hopelessly disillusioned by what they see as the real failures of the community based care alternative.

"Society will pay a heavy price for the care in the community failures at a later date" (MHP-s1-87). "Care in the community will ultimately end in disaster due to poor planning and the traditional stigma that still exists" (MHP-s1-43).

It is clear from the evidence presented in this section that there are a number of important similarities and differences between the various multi-agency groups, in terms of the level of agreement each has, both within and across the three implicit theories of mental illness. Furthermore, the qualitative data suggests that there also exist major differences in the underlying reasons why a particular group supports or otherwise a particular pattern of beliefs towards the mentally ill. Within the context of these belief systems, it is interesting to note the way in which each profession views the notion of inter-agency co-operation.

On a general level, it was felt that multi-agency working was in principle the best way forward both for the purpose of exchanging ideas and for maximising the use of available resources. It was clear from the evidence, however, that implementing such an approach in practice, although to a limited extent successful, often broke-down and led to tensions and difficulties between various professions.

In particular, the police felt that their relationship with duty psychiatrists could be greatly improved, the general view being that psychiatrists treated what the police had to say "with a pinch of salt" (POL-s1-99) and would often not section a mentally ill patient in custody on the grounds that they did not feel the condition to be bad enough. In such cases the police felt powerless and:

"As a result we are left to deal with the problem ... which means giving him a caution or sending him to court; either way they won't get noticed until they do something really serious, by which time there is little point in saying 'I told you so' ... custody officers should have more power to section when they think there is a risk to public safety" (POL-s2-14).

The most common problem, identified by probation officers, related to the fact that there exists a group of mentally ill offenders "which is not interesting to psychiatrists" (PROB-d2-105). As a result, no-one takes responsibility for them, and the court, reluctant to give a prison sentence, places them on probation so that:

"the probation service is increasingly becoming 'piggy in the middle' as a last alternative. This will remain the case if roles and responsibilities remain so fuzzy" (PROB-s1-17).

Our social worker sample were also critical of psychiatrists, arguing that there are frequently disagreements between both professions over the nature of a case, in particular, "the seriousness of the disorder and the degree of patient responsibility" (SW-d2-79). The general feeling being that psychiatrists tended not to listen and assumed that they were better placed to decide issues such as patient dangerousness, while the general view of approved social workers was:

> "predicting dangerousness is not a precise art and so requires
> consideration from several stand-points ... it is clear that they
> [psychiatrists] are no better at doing this than the general public, research
> would support this claim" (Sws214.

It was also felt that psychiatrists often ignore the views of the patients and that:

> "clients/patients are being listened to only as a tokenistic gesture rather
> than as a real and genuine shift in mental health practice" (Sws241).

Mental health practitioners appear to be feeling the pressure of discontent from other agencies and in turn are concerned that:

> "There is a clear lack of appreciation/understanding of mental illness
> among court staff, probation officers, magistrates, solicitors and the
> police" (MHP-d2-127).

In particular, it was felt that most other professions view the hospital as:

> "the ultimate place of disposal for all psychiatric cases ... particularly the
> courts who view hospitals as the only alternative to prison ... the courts
> divert patients to hospital as it is seen as an easy option" (MHP-s2-155).

The agency with which the mental health profession had the greatest level of discontent was actually the government. Claiming that their 'chaotic' policies with regard to closing the old mental hospitals and the introduction of radical NHS reforms has had the effect of creating a shortage of available beds for psychiatric patients, which has meant that decisions relating to sectioning are often made on "a selective basis" (MHP-d2-127). Furthermore, it was generally held that certain psychiatric patients and offenders:

> "simply cannot be accommodated outside RSU environments as they
> create difficult and destructive cultures on the wards" (MHP-s1-188).

The influence of age, gender and previous experience on
multi-agency thinking

Thus far we have considered differences within our multi-agency population by vertically cross-sectioning our overall sample into the study's six survey groups.

Judging from our findings, however, there also appears to exist divisions within each model which actually cut horizontally across the various multi-agency samples, in particular, the influence of socio-demographic variables such as age, gender and personal experience of mental illness.

The 'sick' role model: the influence of previous experience

The significant main effect for the variable, known a mentally disordered person, informs us that those respondents, who have had previous experience or contact with the mentally ill, tend to be much more prepared to afford the patient the status of the 'sick' role than those, who have had no direct involvement. The fact that this main effect remains stable across each two-way interaction informs us that this difference holds regardless of the type of mental disorder or offence condition. Furthermore, a one-way analysis of variance showed that the actual nature of the respondent's experience, for example, friend, relative, etc, had no significant impact on the degree of sympathy shown.

The conclusion, that contact with the mentally ill can help to promote a more positive perception, is generally consistent with the findings of several previous studies (Brockington et al, 1993; Malla and Shaw, 1987; Link and Cullen, 1986). In terms of the patient's relationship with the respondent, however, our finding of no significant effect seems to conflict with the earlier research which managed to find both a positive association between contact and a more favourable view (Phillips, 1963) and a negative association (Swingle, 1965). Thus evidence has now been established for each possible permutation in the association between experience and perceptions of the mentally ill. The fact that no clear conclusion has been reached could, nevertheless, be helpful in the sense that the overall findings may by implication be suggesting that any differences that do exist are highly spurious and that by itself previous contact with the mentally ill is generally not important (Murphy et al, 1993).

After a consideration of the non-significant first order effects between previous experience and the two treatment variables, it could also be argued that the actual behaviour elicited by the patient has no influence on beliefs and that ultimately contact per se is sufficient to generate a more favourable view. Such a conclusion, however, feels uncomfortably simplistic and does not seem to be substantiated by our earlier comments nor by some of the qualitative data.

Earlier in the discussion, we suggested and produced evidence in support of the view that, while previous experience of depression may result in a more sympathetic approach, this degree of empathy dramatically changes the longer the condition lasts or the more serious is becomes, as people begin to associate their own common-sense notion of depression with the patient. Furthermore, in the case of the mentally ill in general, it has been demonstrated that, while respondents feel sorry for and pity the patient more after contact, they still fail to show them any increased degree of respect (Johannsen, 1969). Thus, while contact with the mentally ill may have an impact on improving both attitudes and beliefs, it would appear that in some cases the changes are only temporary and in many instances changes are made to the least functionally appropriate cognitive states ie, feeling sorry for the patient is not terribly helpful. On the basis of this evidence, it may be argued that experience alone is not sufficient to bring about a real change in thinking. In fact, some of our substantive comments suggest that direct contact alone may be highly detrimental to both the care-giver and the patient.

> "I found the whole experience extremely upsetting and the views, which I did have with regard to issues like responsibility, were shattered and became even more confused" (LAY-d2-44).

The medical-control model: the influence of age

Of the three sources of variation, the only socio-demographic variable to reach a satisfactory level of significance within the context of the medical-control model was that of age. In this case the age main effect informs us that those respondents over the age of 35 were statistically more likely to support this implicit approach than members of the younger age category. Furthermore, the results obtained from the higher order interactions inform us that this effect holds regardless of the nature of each treatment variable.

The negative association between age and tolerance of the mentally ill has been frequently demonstrated (Wolff et al, 1996b, Phillips, 1966; Freeman, 1961; Whatley, 1959). The main argument put forward to explain this finding centres around the existence of some form of culturally generated liberalism amongst younger people which is generally promoted by the fact that society is more open and democratically accountable. The division of our sample into two age categories offers further support to this view by demonstrating, that those born after 1960 have generally been exposed to a mental health policy orientated towards a higher level of community integration for persons suffering from some form of mental disorder, while the older category of respondents possibly experienced a more 'traditional' approach towards the mentally ill.

It would be unwise, however, to consider such an explanation as conclusive. Clearly, numerous other variables such as education, socio-economic status, etc, may act as important determinants which, if controlled for, may account for this difference (Wolff et al, 1996c). Furthermore, while the medical-control model appears generally supportive of the more traditional perspective, it also provides evidence that our respondents are medically informed about certain mentally disabilitating conditions. As a result, the notion that younger respondents are more informed and are, therefore, more humane in their approach no longer holds as older members' support for this model demonstrates that they are equally, if not more, knowledgable themselves.

In an attempt to account for this anomaly, it may be helpful to suggest a view which has seldom been considered. Thus, rather than or in addition to, the notion of a generally more liberal culture which could quite easily influence older respondents, there exists the possibility of psychological conservatism being produced by the process of aging (Murphy et al, 1993). Tenuous evidence in support of such a claim may be obtained from our empirical data which shows that the variables normally associated with a generally more humanitarian attitude, namely, groups surveyed - particularly the caring professions - and knowing a mentally disordered person, failed to significantly interact with the age variable, hence demonstrating that there is possibly something about this factor which is independent of the others, namely, the development of a more conservative approach associated with the psychology of growing old. [11]

The social-treatment model: the influence of gender

In terms of the social-treatment paradigm, only the gender main effect reached a satisfactory level of significance. This shows that regardless of the type of mental disorder or offence condition, men tend to be more supportive of this implicit management approach than women.

Judging from the previous evidence, it would appear that very little attention has been directed towards the influence of gender on beliefs towards the mentally ill. There does exists a modest degree of evidence, however, which suggests that women are generally fearful of crime and more intolerant of the mentally ill which, once placed within the context of this implicit theory, may partially account for the gender difference revealed by the current research.

As we mentioned earlier, the impetus behind the social-treatment theory loosely stems from the belief that such patients would benefit substantially from improving the general nature of their own social environment. However, directly or otherwise, the success of such an approach also partly depends on society's willingness to accept the presence of the patient within the community and it would appear that it is on this issue that the two gender groups seem to disagree.

Within the specific locality of Cambridge (Naylor and Wincup, 1994) as well as nation wide (Last and Jackson, 1989), there exists a great deal of evidence to show that women are generally more fearful of crime. Some of the previous research has also suggested a perceived degree of association between mental illness and the commission of serious crimes, particularly sexual offences such as rape (Levey and Howells, 1995; Steadman and Cocozza, 1978; Swarte, 1969). Thus on the basis of these findings, it could be argued that women may be less willing to accept the idea of mentally ill patients living unrestrained within the community as it generates strong feelings relating to the fear of attack. Support for such a view may be obtained from a series of studies conducted during the

1960s on a sample of 300 housewives, the findings from which showed the respondents to be highly rejecting of those they believed to be mentally ill (Phillips 1966, 1964, 1963). More recent research suggests that this level of fear may also be generated out of concern for someone close to the respondent themselves. In particular, Wolff et al (1996b) has produced evidence to show that having children in the family is a strong determinant of fear and exclusion, hence, by implication, it may also be the case that women are less supportive of treating the mentally ill within a social context out of concern for the potential threat to their children.

Finally, we should not dismiss the possibility that the difference may simply be an artifact of the study itself. For example, each of the case vignettes related to the fact that it was the wife who was either under threat or stabbed, a "not uncommon situation in my experience of dealing with mentally ill offenders" (MHP-d2-36) but, nevertheless, it is, as one respondent points out, "still violence against women" (LAY-d2-54) which may have provoked a generally more defensive reaction from the study's female respondents.

Summary

The primary concern of this chapter thus far, has been to present and discuss the key research findings within the context of the study's main propositions. Throughout this debate a number of important differences in beliefs about the mentally ill have been highlighted between the study's various treatment and socio-demographic variables. The aim in the next section will be to build upon this new knowledge through a broader consideration of their impact at both a criminological and clinical level.

Criminological and clinical implications of the current research

Ever since the importance of considering community attitudes and beliefs in relation to mental illness was officially remarked upon (Royal Commission, 1957, para 63-73), a number of studies from various perspectives have been carried out in Britain (Wolff et al, 1996a; Bhugra, 1989; MacLean, 1969). However, this study represents the first systematic attempt to comprehensively examine multi-agency beliefs towards various types of psychopathologically and criminally deviant behaviour.

The findings discussed earlier are profuse, and suggest a number of important consequences for the way in which this minority group is managed. Essentially, these issues broadly span both the criminal justice system and the field of mental health and are significant at both a theoretical and practical level. In order to demonstrate the applicability of our research within these parameters, an attempt will be made to generally consider a wide range of these issues.

The fact that the structural nature of our multi-agency approach towards the mentally ill appears to defy reduction or classification into any single scientific model, should probably be looked upon favourably, for to find that a single scientific paradigm is supported without question, would most certainly be disadvantageous to both the nature of clinical care and the general development of knowledge within the field of mental health (Roskin et al, 1988). However, as we mentioned earlier, our overall approach is comprised of three mutually exclusive implicit theories of which any one or more may be supported within the context of each treatment or socio-demographic variable. Thus at any stage, it is possible for the structure of our multi-agency approach to show itself to be generally: narrowly defined, poorly organised, tentatively held and contradictory in nature, as is believed to be the case with many implicit theories (Valentine, 1982). Consequently, there still exists a great deal of scope for concern, regarding the management of the mentally ill.

In terms of the substantive nature of these multi-agency theories, it is interesting to note that the first implicit model - the 'sick' role - challenges the key ideological premise behind the medical paradigm. As we mentioned earlier, the general impetus behind promoting the virtues of this paradigm has been to re-educate (Crocetti et al, 1974) or implicitly orientate (Pilgrim and Rogers, 1993; Miles, 1987) people into understanding mental illness in terms of an illness just like any other, in the hope that they would be more prepared to grant the mental patient all the rights and privileges currently enjoyed by the physically sick. Yet, the 'sick' role factor exists as a coherent model in itself and clearly promotes the belief that one should offer the mentally ill care and sympathy as a matter of course. Furthermore, its dominant status relative to the other two implicit theories suggests that respondents are prepared to grant the status of the 'sick' role without automatically accepting the existence of an organic cause or indeed, that any form of illness in the medical sense of the word exists at all. On the basis of this evidence it would, therefore, appear that the protagonists of the medical approach have for some time been pushing though an open door, a view supported by the findings of another recent study on implicit theories in which the authors conclude:

"... it seems the lay respondents wish to confer the benefits of the 'sick' role on the schizophrenic patient without necessarily agreeing that the disorder has an organic origin" (Furnham and Bower, 1992:206).

The fact that the 'sick' role is available to the mentally ill regardless of the nature of their condition is encouraging, as it implies that policies directed towards the management of this minority are being developed within a highly discerning perceptual context, conscious of the need to safeguard and promote the civil rights and interests of the patient. Such an approach has been clearly demonstrated over the last decade or so with the introduction of numerous legislative instruments such as the Mental Health Act 1983, the Police and Criminal Evidence Act 1984 and the NHS and Community Care Act 1990, each of which contain extensive provisions for the better care and more humane treatment of the mentally ill.

The difference in support for the 'sick' role generally held by our multi-agency population across each type of mental disorder and offence condition implies that, while this approach may be available to the mentally ill regardless of the nature of their condition, the extent to which this level of sympathy is sustained over time or after a worsening of the condition, may possibly depend to some extent on how each particular psychopathological state is perceived. Thus there exists some evidence to suggest that while the 'sick' role is granted per se, its continuance needs to be justified ie, the onus of proof is to some extent on society to justify why the patient should no longer be given sympathy.

As discussed earlier, support for the 'sick' role is primarily shaped by the degree to which the mental patient is believed to be responsible for and so in control of their own behaviour. In the case of the schizophrenic, we found that the condition is generally thought of as resulting from physio-chemical processes over which the patient has very little control. Thus by implication, this fact may help respondents justify and make sense of the need to maintain the view that the schizophrenic should continue to be judged in sympathetic rather than moralistic terms, an approach supported by the fact that the schizophrenic offender retains a moderate degree of 'sick' role support. In contrast, our evidence has shown that the problems associated with the state of depression are more readily understood within a psychosocial context and as such, patients tend to be viewed as having a higher degree of control over managing their behaviour. Consequently, the more serious the condition, as in the case of the depressive offender, or the longer it lasts, the less applicable the 'sick' role becomes, which in turn generally implies that the depressive patient may become more vulnerable to moral exhortation.

With regard to the aetiological nature of schizophrenia, a particularly prominent feature supported across the entire sample population and highlighted by other recent studies (Furnham and Rees, 1988) is the general belief that the condition is genetically determined. Scientific evidence in support of such a belief has been found (Gottesman and Shields, 1972), and indeed over the last few years enormous strides have been made in the field of eugenics, however, the conviction with which this view is held in some cases seems to be far in excess of our current scientific understanding of the schizophrenias. This point is significant in the sense that if the strength of such a belief continues unchecked, then it could quite possibly have a considerable impact on certain modalities of treatment. In particular, psychotherapeutic techniques such as cognitive learning therapy may start to be considered as ineffectual on the grounds that there is little point in trying to manipulate cognitive-behavioural states perceived to be the product of genetic deformities, consequently the employment of psychotherapeutic procedures in general would appear to the holders of such a belief about as useful as trying to talk brown-haired people into having blonde. Instead, in the long term, preventative treatments directed towards genetic manipulation or sterilisation of the patient may become the preferred alternative. Such approaches have been supported in the past (Kallmann, 1959) and more recently several American states, in particular, North Carolina and Virginia have passed laws supporting the practice of sterilising some schizophrenic patients (Farina and Fisher, 1982).

In a further attempt at promoting a generally more favourable disposition towards the mentally afflicted, the medical paradigm promotes the belief that understanding mental disorders as illnesses just like any other, will have the implicit effect of reducing the generally negative stereotyped image that surrounds the mentally ill (Levey and Howells, 1995). Our evidence, however, shows that in general the schizophrenic is still strongly stigmatised and believed to require a high degree of controlled management.

Judging from previous research, there is evidence to suggest that generally negative attitudes towards the mentally disorder are consistently held regardless of socio-demographic differences (Nunnally, 1961) and that they have always existed (Bhugra, 1989; Prins, 1984). Furthermore, it has also been shown that a degree of stigma exists even when the cause of the problem is not questioned as in the case of physical illnesses such as multiple sclerosis (Miles, 1987). Thus by implication, it would appear that viewing the aetiology of schizophrenia within a biological context does not appear to clarify anything in the eyes of the respondent. In fact, as we mentioned earlier, the inability of some respondents to comprehend the behaviour of the schizophrenic may have provoked the 'mental illness' explanation simply as a response to an already existing stigma, in which case such a conceptualisation to some extent may only serve to make the condition appear even more mysterious, unfathomable and 'spoilt' (Porter, 1987; Goffman, 1963).

The fact that the schizophrenic is viewed within a medical context may also be viewed as unhelpful in promoting a generally more tolerant approach towards such patients. While the notion of an internal cause may benefit the schizophrenic in the sense that they are able to hold on to the 'sick' role and so not be viewed as morally responsible, perceptions of an inability to control one's actions inevitably provokes the detrimental feeling that the patient is unpredictable, the most salient hallmark of the mentally disordered (Nunnally, 1961). A belief which has the consequence of engendering the need to restrain and control those so identified. An approach which by implication could have a profound effect upon the liberty of the schizophrenic (Thompson, 1994).

In terms of the depressive patient, the above issues appear to be inversely supported by our evidence which shows that as the condition is generally perceived within a socio-environmental context, the mental patient is afforded very little negative press. Depression appears not to be so highly stigmatised largely due to the fact the most people can either relate to or make sense of the condition in everyday terms. As we have shown, one consequence of this fact is that the patient runs a higher risk of loosing the 'sick' role status as they are perceived as more responsible for their condition. However, despite this fact, this element of perceived control does make them more predictable, which in turn affords the depressive patient a higher degree of tolerance in the community, even after a serious offence has been committed.

With specific regard to the type of offence condition, it is quite clear from the findings that the mentally ill offender is perceived differently under each of the three implicit models. Overall, the mental patient-offender is afforded significantly less sympathy than the mentally ill in general and is also viewed as requiring a high degree of medically dominated care and control which is to be administered within a secure environment.

The fact that the inclusion of an offence condition provokes such a response should probably not be considered as all that remarkable, especially in the light of recent criminological research which has shown that the public are fearful of crime (Last and Jackson, 1989) and would generally prefer to see an increase in the use of prisons for normal offenders (Walker and Hough, 1988). What is interesting, however, is that such a markedly different response was evoked, despite the existence of only a very small qualitative difference in the case vignettes between the no-offence and criminal offence conditions. Essentially, the main symptomological distinction between the two descriptions centres around the progressive nature of the mental disorder's active phase over time.

Thus our findings clearly demonstrate the fundamental importance of mental health programmes orientated towards primary prevention and early intervention. The ability to identify mental conditions in their early stages would undoubtedly benefit both the patient and society, not only through reducing any possible risk to the public, but also by manifesting the opportunity of dealing with the patient's problems at a time when both lay and professional organisations are less restrictive and morally judgmental in their ideological approach.

A further issue provoked by this finding centres around the question as to why such a markedly different approach was found despite the existence of such a qualitatively small difference between the experimental conditions? It could of course be argued that our sample populations' beliefs are so unstable that even the smallest difference in the nature of the referents is sufficient to provoke a change in beliefs (Farina and Fisher, 1982; Nunnally, 1961). While such a conclusion does not appear to be warranted from the evidence, which clearly shows that our multi-agency population possesses a coherent pattern of beliefs about the mentally ill which may be clearly and logically defined in terms of three meaningful implicit theories, the very existence of a difference between the no-offence and offence condition does highlight some rather worrying anomalies in the way respondents think about particular psychopathological states.

In the case of the depressive patient it will be observed that there is a remarkably high degree of tolerance for his behaviour, despite the fact that in clinical terms the patient's active phase is so serious that it is only a matter of time before his delusional state provokes him into killing his wife. Once the criminal offence has been committed, the perceptual approach adopted by the respondents alters dramatically in support of a more restrictive practice ensuring that the patient is medically controlled. On the basis of such a marked transition in beliefs, it would be reasonable to postulate the view that it is not only tolerance that allows such depressive patients to go unnoticed, but also ignorance of the potential harm that they could inflict. Evidence outside this research which adds further support to such a claim stems from the work of Lerner (1980) who has observed that people generally want to believe in a 'just world' philosophy in which other's motives and goals are perceived as positive. Thus, unless someone's identity is overtly labelled deviant in some way, they are generally not perceived as a threat (Goffman, 1963). With regard to each specific multi-agency group, this approach conforms admirably with the evidence. Here we find that each group demonstrates this change in beliefs as we move from the depressive patient to the depressive offender, with the exception of the police and the mental health practitioners. In the case of the latter two groups, the depressive patient was perceived as requiring a degree of medical care and control at the outset. Thus it may be argued that these groups were not so ignorant of the fact that the patient was a potential threat to public safety as the other four survey groups. Furthermore, it is interesting to note that while both the police and mental health practitioners were able to identify the patient as a threat, each used their own unique blend of professional expertise. As we mentioned earlier, both professions reached a similar conclusion with regard to the medical-control model but from differing ideological positions. Thus it would appear that the police overcame their ignorance of the patients condition through a consideration of his potentially unlawful behaviour, while the mental health practitioners identified the depressive patient through considering the severity of his symptomatology. The remaining four groups appear not to have a yardstick against which to measure the seriousness of such behaviour, a position which some might argued could be easily remedied through learning to understand such forms of social deviance in medical terms (Crocetti et al, 1974).

Within the context of this last statement, the notion of medically taxonomising behaviour does seem to have some merit. Unfortunately, the use of diagnostic terms such as mentally ill or schizophrenia have their own limitations which, when applied to patients, have been shown to be highly detrimental (Arkar and Eker, 1994; Appleby and Wessely, 1988). The beliefs held by our respondents in relation to both the schizophrenic patient and the schizophrenic offender offer further support to this claim. For example, in terms of the medical-control model, a nonsignificant increase in support for this approach was observed as we moved from the no-offence to the criminal offence condition, in each case the level of support being fairly high.

Such evidence tends to confirm the generally held view that paranoid schizophrenia appears to be the behaviour pattern most widely recognised as mental illness (Arkar and Eker, 1994; Malla and Shaw, 1988) and that patients identified as such, tend to be contemporaneously associated with violence and serious crime (Levey and Howells, 1995; Tringo 1970). On the basis of this evidence, it can be clearly seen why the identification of an offence with the case description had very little effect on beliefs. Essentially, the schizophrenic patient was evaluated in fairly negative terms to begin with and the addition of a further deviant identity only served to confirm and reinforce what the majority of our respondents had already perceived to be the norm.

Summary

In this section we have considered some of the possible implications that may arise from the way in which both the depressive and schizophrenic patient are perceived. In general, we have shown that the way in which a particular type of psychopathology is viewed could have a fundamental impact in terms of a whole variety of issues including: the degree to which the patient is morally judged for his behaviour, the nature and type of treatment deemed appropriate, the level of stigma and tolerance associated with a particular condition, the societal awareness of danger, and the negative consequences arising from the use of particular psychiatric terms.

The significance of multi-agency theories across groups surveyed

In this subsection we will highlight some of the most important ways in which our research findings may impact upon or shape the lives of both the schizophrenic and depressive patient-offender. This will be achieved firstly, by considering in turn the implications arising from the particular pattern of beliefs held by each of the studied six survey populations, and secondly, through developing our understanding as to how this collective multi-agency approach may be guiding the nature of inter-agency co-operation towards the management of the mentally ill in general.

Lay beliefs As we mentioned earlier, ideological changes within the field of mental health during the last few decades have encouraged an important shift in social policy towards those who are mentally ill. The care of such persons has moved away from the old techniques associated with custodialism and instead, the development of community based psychiatric services has been encouraged (Taylor and Taylor, 1989; Jones, 1972). However, the practical success of this ideologic and strategic principle clearly depends, at least to some degree, on the reception society is willing to accord this minority (Wolff et al, 1996a; Dayson, 1993; Furnham and Bower, 1992).

Both the quantitative and substantive evidence presented in the current study persuasively demonstrates that those generally labelled mentally ill and the schizophrenic in particular are likely to encounter a hostile reception by a society which is still fearful, intolerant and generally of the view that, even if the considerable inadequacies of the present system of community care were markedly improved, it would not have that great an impact on either alleviating the symptoms of schizophrenia or on the public's concern for safety. Other recent studies have confirmed this view by showing that to some extent both the mental patient and facilities for their care are unwelcome by society (Hall et al, 1993)[12] and that former patients have also been refused jobs, housing and general civil rights simply because they have a medical history (Miles, 1987). Furthermore, it has been argued that the only reason why their presence has not been so strongly opposed is because of the poor cohesive nature of many neighbourhoods (Segal et al, 1980), residents often do not know they are there (Rabkin, 1981). The fact that Wolff et al (1996b) found that residents required information about new mental health facilities in their area does suggest, however, that it is possibly the mental illness per se that is being rejected and not so much the patient.

Judging from our earlier remarks in relation to respondents' general perception that schizophrenia has an internal/genetic aetiology, it is hardly surprising that there exists some degree of public rejection. A commitment to such a belief appears to be unhelpful in reducing stigma, provokes a greater sense of patient unpredictability and seems to generally re-enforce the belief in a poor prognosis. From the perspective of our lay samples, the whole situation appears even more ambiguous and confusing due to the fact that their commitment to a bio-genetic aetiology for schizophrenia appears to have been arrived at without the slightest comprehension of the condition's key symptomatology. This fact is evident from our findings which show that several respondents were surprised at the label 'schizophrenia' used in the case vignettes, believing instead that the condition usually defined individuals possessing a "split personality" (LAY-s2-88) or "competing people in one body" (LAY-s2-74). Such an implicit misconception has been highlighted by others (Furnham and Rees, 1988) and in some cases it continues to be held with conviction:

"I am somewhat surprised by the fact that you refer to Tom as a schizophrenic ... I think you will find on asking a psychiatrist that he will tell you that [sic] schizophrenia has more to do with a person having two, or in some case more, different personalities competing with each other. A rather obvious, though extreme example, of course, would be Stevenson's Jekyll and Hyde" (LAY-s2-286).

Conversely, the implicit belief that depression is generally associated with psychosocial factors appears to help considerably in generating a favourable opinion towards the suitability of community based care for such patients. Emphasising the psychological and social aspects of everyday life is clearly understood and it is quite possibly this fact that encourages our respondents to view the patient as more in control and so more socially acceptable. Whatever the origin, mental disorders perceived as having a psychosocial cause have been shown in other countries to be evaluated more positively (Arkar and Eker, 1994; Eker, 1985) and rejected less (Norman and Malla, 1983; Townsend, 1975). In terms of the present findings, it would appear that the main obstacle to the increased use of community based care in the case of most depressive patients, relates primarily to the perceived inadequacies of the current system.

The lay public, in its capacity as indicators of deviant behaviour in society, as juror, as lay representative on Mental Health Review Tribunals and as supporter of the presence of former psychiatric offenders within the community, has occasional involvement in how the criminal justice system deals with both the schizophrenic and depressive offender. In particular, implicit lay theories appear to have a great deal of practical significance with regard to the policy of diverting such people away from the criminal justice system and into care by health and social services (Watson and Grounds, 1993).

During trials involving mentally ill offenders, one of the jury's main tasks will usually centre around determining from the facts the degree to which the accused may be held responsible for their crime. In particular, expert testimony will be presented in relation to either the defence of insanity or a plea of diminished responsibility (Bluglass and Bowden, 1990). With regard to the schizophrenic offender, the implication from our findings is that such defences are likely to succeed to the extent that the offender-patient is not viewed as morally responsible for their condition. This view is also likely to hold for both serious and less serious offences (Howells, 1984). It is quite clear from the substantive data, however, that in recognition of the fact that the situation involved a very serious offence, namely, murder, some form of punishment should be administered once the schizophrenic had recovered. Thus it would appear that although a jury is comfortable with the idea of schizophrenia mitigating the offender-patients degree of responsibility, in really serious cases the effects of this mental illness are dominated by a need to administer censure. This fact was quite apparent in the case of Peter Sutcliffe where a guilty verdict of malice aforethought was passed, despite declarations of schizophrenia from both the defence and prosecution (Pilgrim and Rogers, 1993). If this is the case, then perhaps there exists some grounds for suggesting a change in the law to a defence of 'guilty by reason of insanity', an approach which has received support from other countries such as Canada (Mackay, 1991).

With regard to cases involving a depressive offender, it appears that the defence would have a much tougher task convincing a jury to support such pleas by virtue of the fact that such offender-patients are viewed as having a significantly higher degree of control over their behaviour. However, while the depressive patient was viewed as more morally responsible for their offence, it is interesting to note that they were perceived as equally appropriate for the medical-control model as the schizophrenic offender. Thus it would appear that both punitive and therapeutic measures were deemed appropriate, the general view being that some form of help should be given on the basis that "the depressive patient should perhaps not be blamed entirely" (LAY-d2-53). Interestingly, on several occasions the justification for treatment was also likened to the perennial smoker or drug addict, the approach being that where treatment is required, then it should be given regardless:

"society has always treated those who act irresponsibly such as smokers who get lung cancer" (LAY-d1-378).

One of the most important measures introduced to safeguard the liberty of the psychiatric patient or offender who has been involuntarily admitted to hospital is the regular review of their case by a Mental Health Review Tribunal (Peay, 1989). With regard to the way lay members on this panel may respond to certain psychiatric conditions, some very general remarks may be implicity drawn as a consequence to our findings.

In terms of the lay group's perception of the schizophrenic, although the patient will continue to be stigmatised, the key issues appear to be the predictability of their behaviour and the availability of a 'helpful' and 'soothing' environment outside the hospital. In the case of the schizophrenic who has been admitted for treatment prior to the commission of any offence, the patient will have a better chance of being granted a discharge, if it can be shown that their condition has been stabilised and that their behaviour while in hospital was calm and predictable, furthermore, that there exists a good network of support within the community to ensure that their condition remains stable. Our findings with regard to the schizophrenic offender are less optimistic, however, the commission of a serious offence seems to confirm the 'all things bad' view, thus making it very difficult for the patient to 'undo-the-loss' associated with 'normal' behaviour (Cumming and Cumming, 1965; Nunnally, 1961).

It could be argued that, as the depressive offender's behaviour is deemed appropriate for management within the context of the medical-control model, their chances of release will be similar to that of the schizophrenic. This may to some extent be true, however, the fact that our results show some level of support for the social-treatment approach suggests that such patients may be more readily re-integrated and accepted back into society. A possible reason for their acceptance seems to be based on the fact that as the condition of depression was originally thought of in terms of a social, as opposed to some form of mysterious internal process, it is generally more comprehensible, which importantly ensures that the patient's behaviour appears more predictable.

The general success of formal policies orientated towards the re-integration of former psychiatric offenders will depend to some degree on the status of a whole plethora of conflicting issues associated with how this minority is generally perceived. This research, in line with previous findings, has shown that the mentally ill are negatively evaluated, numerous studies have also demonstrated that crime is feared by various strata within our society (Last and Jackson, 1989; Box et al 1988) and to complete the circle, the mentally ill are often associated with violence and the commission of serious crimes (Levey and Howells, 1995; Appleby and Wessely, 1988). Given this pattern of attitudes and beliefs, it is hardly surprising that the former mentally ill offender-patient is feared and rejected (Steadman and Cocozza, 1978).

There also exists further evidence to suggest that these popular conceptions are frequently re-enforced either through the commission of horrific crimes by the mentally ill, for example, Michael Ryan, Christopher Clunis, Beverly Allitt and more recently, Thomas Hamilton or via the extensive sensationalist reporting and speculation of such events that takes place in the media (Williams and Dickinson, 1993). Thus on the basis of such a persuasive account, it is actually quite surprising that any policy motivated by the goal of producing some form of community based care for the former mental patient ever manages to get further than the drawing board.

The fact is, however, that although progress is slower than was generally envisaged, policies such as diverting the mentally ill offender away from the criminal justice system and the eventual deinstitutionalisation of such patients back into the community are progressing (Taylor and Taylor, 1989) and the actual public reaction to such events seems to be far less reactionary or consensually negative and more demographically diverse than previous evidence would suggest (Wolff et al, 1996a; Hall et al, 1993; Howells, 1984; Nuehring and Raybin, 1986).

Taking this matter a step further, we might speculate as to why such negative popular perceptions about the mentally ill in general and the former offender-patient in particular have not manifestly shaped behaviour in favour of actively rejecting any attempt to re-integrate such individuals. In response to this, we might refer to a whole range of issues that may contribute towards this current position: attitudes and beliefs may be only partially related to actual behaviour (Wicker, 1969), the highly individualistic nature of modern societies may be generating a degree of passivity and learned helplessness in the face of those deemed to be in a position of authority, and it could also be argued that often residents don't even know that a home for the mentally ill has already been established near by (Wolff et al, 1996a). It is this author's contention, however, that dominating all these issues are two highly significant classes of beliefs about mental illness and crime which collectively shape and develop our long-term approach towards those who are both psychopathologically and criminally deviant. Firstly, there exists the belief that the public should be protected from those who are dangerous regardless of its manifestation, and secondly, there is a deep moral concern for the well-being of those who are emotionally disturbed, whether offenders or not (Hill, 1982).

The presence of these two emotional issues have been clearly demonstrated by our findings which show that while our sample strongly believe that the offender-patient, particularly the schizophrenic, should be controlled, there still exists a reasonable degree of sympathy and concern at both an empirical and qualitative level directed towards ensuring that the patient's human and civil rights are maintained.

Recently, the public's concern for how the mentally ill are cared for was highlighted by the case of Ben Silcock, a mentally ill patient who was severely mauled after climbing into the lions den at London zoo (Daily Telegraph, August 5th 1993). Thus on the basis of this evidence it would appear that the public's primary objection to the mentally ill living within the community rests not with a blanket unwillingness to tolerate such individuals, but largely on the belief that they are likely to be a danger to society. Hence, by re-assuring the public on this issue and through the development of monitoring programmes for those patients in the community considered to be most at risk from relapse, such public concerns may to some extent be alleviated. Recently, as part of the Secretary of State for Health's Ten Point Plan, guidelines have been issued on the proposed establishment of a supervision register and on the introduction of new powers associated with providing effective care and supervision in the community after being discharged from hospital. In the longer term, the enforcement of such policies should help improve not only the quality and safety of community based care programmes, but also alleviate levels of public anxiety, which in turn will help reshape the currently negative image of the mentally ill.

Police beliefs The low level of 'sick' role support ascribed to both the depressive and schizophrenic patient-offender suggests that the police are generally uncaring and unsympathetic to the needs of the mentally ill. However, judging from the qualitative data and some previous evidence, a far more complex picture emerges. In the first instance, we must keep in mind the fact that the rules and regulations that govern the activities of the police with regard to issues such as arrests, detention and the preparation of cases for the Crown Prosecution Service are largely determined within a highly legal context. As a result, their initial perception of the mentally disorder offender is more likely to be shaped by the need to ensure that the public is protected from further harm (Dohrenwend et al, 1967) through lawfully charging and collating evidence against the accused.

It should also be kept in mind that the primary task of the police is to protect the public and as a front line service they are often the first authority to come into contact with instances of serious psychiatric disturbance. Previous studies have shown that the police do not object to this (Bean, 1986), however, it is clear from the present findings that such situations are viewed as frightening and difficult to handle:

"We are often forced to deal with someone who we are told over the radio is behaving strangely, that's all the information we get ... before we get to the scene I am wondering what to expect ... we don't know what they will do or how they will react ..." (POL-s1-187).

Furthermore, it could be argued that constantly dealing with the mentally ill under such conditions ie, only while they are at their worst, may serve to reinforce the police's generally stigmatic view which in turn makes them more intolerant and less willing to excuse the patient's behaviour on the basis of their mental state.

It is also quite possible that the quality of the interaction between the police and the mentally ill may significantly deteriorate as a result of the coming together of several conflicting factors. As we mentioned earlier, due to the new business orientated approach towards policing, there exists the growing perception that dealing with persistent offenders with minor psychiatric problems drains resources. Such concerns have come at a time when there are an increasing number of vulnerable psychiatric patients roaming the streets and a strong level of police discontent for the current system of community based care. As a result, the police may feel under an increasing degree of pressure to view prosecution as the only way to cost-effectively protect the public in such cases.

In connection with this, there exists some justification for asserting that the present conflicting approaches existing within the police may have serious consequences for the specific policy of diverting such offender-patients away from the criminal justice system, a point highlighted by our empirical and substantive evidence which shows that this profession would prefer to manage both the depressive and schizophrenic patient within a controlled environment and support punitive sanctions where a serious offence has been committed.

Despite this rather gloomy outlook, there does appear to exist evidence which implicitly suggests that the police are aware of these conflicts and are conscious of the need to avoid prosecution where possible. In particular, several comments were made with regard to how the present system of diversion could be 'streamlined' through giving:

"custody officers the power to be able to refer for assessment" (POL-s2-157), "increasing the role and responsibilities of GPs" (POL-d2-33) and "providing more secure places other than the police cell for us to make referrals" (POL-d1-101).

Our findings also appear to offer some degree of optimism in relation to the police's power of arrest under S.136 of the Mental Health Act 1983. Essentially, this section states that a constable may detain a patient 'who appears to him to be suffering from mental disorder and to be in immediate need of care and control'. This means that, initially at least, the police have to become diagnosticians in the sense that they must determine whether or not the patient is in need of some form of care and control.

In general, it would seem that such legislation makes little sense as it places the police in a position whereby they are forced to pronounce on medical matters for which they have no more formal training than an unqualified lay person. However, it has been argued that such low level diagnoses made on first contact between the police and the patient depend as much on a consideration of social and moral criteria as they do on psychiatric factors (Bean, 1986). This fact is further substantiated from our evidence which shows that even though the police use indicators other than clinical symptoms, such as their likely risk to public safety, in order to reach decisions about particular patients, their conclusions are markedly similar in the case of both the depressive and schizophrenic patient-offender to those of mental health practitioners. A finding which has received support on numerous other occasions (Bean, 1980; Sims and Symonds 1975; Kelleher and Copelan 1972).

It should be noted, however, that while there exists some support for suggesting that the police may be a competent and efficient source of referral, this does not necessarily mean that other agencies are entirely happy with the police adopting such a role. Ideological differences between the various groups has tended to lead to professional rivalries. For example, we have already shown when discussing multi-agency working that the police often feel that they are too quickly dismissed by psychiatrists and furthermore, evidence from elsewhere has shown that within this context both the police and social workers are critical of each other:

"social workers, for example, are critical of the police because they say the police lack the professional training of social workers and are,therefore, unable to deal sensitively with the mentally ill. The police in retaliation, merely assert that social workers do not have a monopoly of sensitivity in this matter" (Bean, 1986:60).

Mental health and social welfare staff Of the study's three caring professions, only the mental health practitioners were prepared to view the depressive patient specifically in terms of a mental illness. The social workers and probation officers preferred instead to associate this condition with psychosocial explanations. Thus, by implication, it could be argued that the use of medical terms such as 'mentally ill' to describe the nature of depression generally stems from their use by medical personnel and are only adopted by the majority of society as a matter of convenience rather than as a result of any implicit commitment to this approach (Furnham and Bower, 1992).

Our evidence also suggests that the existence of such implicitly conflicting paradigms amongst the various professions may unconsciously have a significant impact upon the nature of community based facilities and the type of patient care available, which ultimately may result in a considerable degree of inconsistency, confusion and patient distress. For example, if we examine the structure of the two most prominent organisations designed to replace the asylum, namely, Community Mental Health Centres (CMHC) and District General Hospital Psychiatric Units (DGHPU) (Samson, 1992), it will be observed that there exists a marked contrast in their basic underlying ideology and the services they provide. According to Sayce (1989), the motivating force behind CMHCs is a wish to reject a medicalised model of psychiatry in favour of a new eclectic approach. In contrast, DGHPUs were established in an attempt to fully integrate psychiatry into medicine which consequently encourages the specific use of physical treatment (Pilgrim and Rogers, 1993). It is perhaps no coincidence that the former approach would seem ideally suited to the broader ideological beliefs of our social welfare respondents, while the latter would be more suited to the medically based views of our sample of mental health practitioners.

With regard to the specific needs of depressive patients, self referral to a CMHC for advice, if one is available and well publicised, may result in an approved social worker or psychologist suggesting a course of treatment consisting of counselling and other forms of psychotherapy. The same patient could, however, have equally first sought advice elsewhere perhaps from a GP, psychiatrist or other mental health practitioner who might have instead recommended anti-depressant medication, paid less attention to the possible psychological causes of the condition and not seen the patient for several weeks (Roskin et al, 1988). Thus, the way in which a patient is dealt with could become a little like a lottery, dependent partly upon the accessibility of certain professionals within a given area and their commitment to a particular paradigm.

To re-iterate, the point is not to establish which of these particular methods of care is right, but more importantly to recognise that without an over-arching ideological strategy to the notion of community care, the power of the paradigm within each particular profession may start to dictate, at least to some extent, the quality and type of provisions available to certain psychopathologically disturbed individuals. The fact that the majority of carers perceive the depressive patient within a social context, may be partly responsible for the recent claims that CMHCs only concentrate on the 'worried' well, rather than those with severe or long term mental health problems (Thompson, 1994). Furthermore, such centres are frequently opposed by some medically orientated psychiatrists who have seemingly managed to persuade the government not to include their expansion in formal plans to replace asylum beds (Goldie et al, 1989).

With regard to the most appropriate method of treatment, there does exist some evidence implicit within our data and elsewhere which suggests that the way in which both the depressive and schizophrenic patient perceives their own care is an important aspect to the success of certain treatment programmes and that the views of professionals may actually create additional complications. Generally, it has been shown that mental patients prefer the experts they consult to view their condition as a result of inter-personal problems (Colson, 1970). Thus, as there exists a reluctance to associate depression with mental illness, it might be inferred that such patients would actually have a higher degree of therapeutic affinity with the views of social welfare staff rather than medically orientated practitioners. A clash in the nature of underlying beliefs held by both the patient and consultant can be unsettling as one respondent states:

"I felt really depressed ... I visited my GP who didn't listen to anything I said and just proscribed me these [anti-depressant Diazepam 2mg]. I haven't taken any because I don't really feel ill as such and they might make me worse and become dependent on them ... the trouble is I'm not really sure what to do next" (LAY-d2-371).

With regard to the schizophrenic offender-patient, each of the three caring professions are prepared, at least initially, to view the behaviour as resulting from a biomedical anomaly which requires a high degree of controlled management. Given the nature of the condition and the current options available for dealing with such individuals this approach may seem reasonable. In fact, viewing the patient as suffering from an illness can have numerous advantages by both engendering a degree of respectability to the schizophrenic through helping sustain the view, that they were not at fault for any criminal behaviour, and by reducing any feelings of guilt that the patient's family may have felt. However, encouraging the notion that the patient is sick, may also give rise to other unintended consequences.

Some experimental studies, carried out in another context, have shown that it is possible to manipulate the views that a patient holds about their condition by altering the nature of the treatment given (Wehler, 1979; Whitman and Duffey, 1961). Thus it would not be unreasonable to suggest that the schizophrenic, after being exposed to the view that they are sick, as held by professionals within both the mental health and social services, may begin to think of their difficulties as due to a medical problem. As a result, their whole approach may change in the sense that they may start to perceive themselves as having less control over their condition (Morrison et al, 1977) and so will be more prepared to leave the healing process to others. We have mentioned earlier, however, that all three professions believe that the schizophrenic, regardless of the presence of an offence, should take some responsibility for and exercise a degree of control over helping to improve their condition. Thus implicitly, a highly contradictory message is being relayed to the patient which suggest on the one hand, that they have a degree of control, while on the other, that because they are ill, they do not. Of course, the ideal goal would be to get the patient to accept both messages and although this may be happening, it is difficult to determine and so remains a possible area for conflict. Certainly one of the many reason for the failure of the asylums in general and the high levels of staff "negligence and indifference" (Martin's Hospitals in Trouble, 1985) in particular, could be partly due to a build up over time of staff frustrations provoked by the contractions between the nursing staff's wish for the patient to exert some control and so help maintain an orderly asylum, while the hospital environment itself and the underlying beliefs held by mental health staff implicitly led the patient to believe that they were sick and so not able to help themselves.

The consequences resulting from the schizophrenic patient's perception that they are sick may also have an impact with regard to the way in which they cope within a community based care setting. It will be observed, that in the case of both the social workers and probation officers the schizophrenic patient is viewed as able to benefit from being cared for within a social setting. However, evidence has also been presented which shows that these two professions are concerned about the potential for the excessive use of medication and, in particular, that too much can actually inhibit their relationship with the patient and the effectiveness of programmes designed to help the patient cope better with day to day tasks. This break down in relations is normally associated with the fact that many minor tranquillisers, used along-side learning based programmes, hinder progress because of their unwanted side-effects, in particular, these drugs have addictive qualities and sedative effects each of which is made worse by the fact they only succeed in reducing symptoms for short periods of time (Tyrer, 1987). However, a case may also be made for suggesting that the reason why some general psychotherapeutic techniques are often unsuccessful (Bergin and Lambert, 1978) could be due to the difference in ideology existing between the mental health practitioners and social service personnel, which ultimately leaves the patient in a position whereby they not only have to cope with their symptoms, but also make sense of the contradictory messages relating to how they should approach their condition. As one respondent commented about a relative who had been in hospital for some time with schizophrenia:

"When she was allowed to leave the hospital she was very pleased ... that's when the problems started, she wouldn't take her medication claiming that she was better and she wasn't interested in attending a day centre which taught skills such as cooking and shopping because she felt insulted, claiming that she already knew how to do them ..." (LAY-s2-163).

Judging from the evidence, however, it is not only the beliefs of the patient that may be influenced by forces around them. In the specific case of the mental health practitioners, it is interesting to note that while their qualitative evidence suggested that they have some degree of support for the establishment of continuous programmes of care for the mentally ill, their empirical data clearly demonstrates support for the medical-control model under each of the four experimental conditions. From these results a rather significant implication may be drawn. It has been established that beliefs can be easily changed (Nunnally, 1961; Whitman and Duffey, 1961) and there also exists strong substantive evidence to suggest that overall, our sample of mental health staff are strongly disillusioned with the current system of community care. Thus it would be reasonable to suggest that their general level of disappointment with the way things in this area have progressed has had the effect of altering their underlying beliefs towards the whole idea of community based care. If such an process holds true, then the continuation of a poorly resourced and structured system of community treatment could be starting to fundamentally undermine certain professionals' ideological commitment to this approach, which suggests that failure now could seriously damage future progress in social care initiatives. As we mentioned earlier, the pendulum may start to swing the other way in favour of perceiving controlled environments as generally more suitable in certain cases. Recent evidence to support such a claim may be obtained from Samson (1992) who notes evidence suggesting that we have moved from deinstitutionalisation to reinstitutionalisation, and Thompson (1994) who argues that a new 'dark age' for the support of secure psychiatric services may be dawning.

Multi-agency working It is quite evident from the results that there exists a degree of overlap between the underlying beliefs held towards the mentally ill by a particular profession and their concerns with regard to certain aspects of inter-agency co-operation.

With regard to the working relationship between the police and mental health practitioners, it is interesting to note that, while they both held roughly the same view with regard to each of the study's experimental conditions, they frequently reached differing opinions as to whether or not a particular offender-patient should be sectioned. As we mentioned earlier, this could possible be due to the fact that, while each profession reached the same conclusion, they did so for markedly differing reasons. In terms of their working relationship, it is fairly clear from the findings that, on a practical level, practitioners' judgements about the need for hospitalisation are made largely by considering the seriousness of the psychiatric condition and the patient's suitability for hospital care, while the decision of the police is based on the belief that such an action is necessary primarily as a means of protecting the public.

Furthermore, the fact that the social worker sample tended to be more supportive of both the depressive and schizophrenic within a social context, implies that they view each condition as less likely to cause harm to the public. A difference in opinion to that held by mental health staff, which could go some way to accounting for why the existence of a clash between social workers and psychiatrists, was highlighted over the issue of dangerousness and perceived level of patient involvement in the treatment process.

There also exists some support for claiming that, not only do beliefs impact on multi-agency co-operation, but that inter-agency demands, amongst other issues, could to some extent be shaping beliefs. It could of course be contested that the restrictive approach adopted by mental health practitioners is correct and that the other professions are naïve in their position. Right or wrong, however, we cannot ignore the findings drawn from the evidence which suggest that the mental health profession is currently under a considerable strain. Their ability to accurately predict a patient's level of dangerousness has frequently been questioned (Monahan, 1981; Ennis and Emery, 1978) and it would seem that they are under an increasing degree of pressure, particularly from professions within the criminal justice system, to find an alternative to prison for the mentally ill offender. This emphasis on diversion comes at a time when the number of hospital beds are being reduced and mental health staff are becoming extremely disillusioned with the current system of community based care. Consequently, it is not surprising that they appear cautious in their approach towards both the mentally ill and mentally ill offenders.

Thus, within the context of practical problems such as the shortage of hospital beds and the absence of a clear policy objective for community care, it generally appears to be the case that certain normally hidden professional beliefs may become important factors in generating conflict and misunderstanding at a multi-agency level.

The nature of the inter-relationship between the various professional groups may be complicated further by the fact that several other socio-demographic variables, namely, previous experience, age and gender have also been shown to influence the way in which our overall sample population perceives each psychopathological condition.

Thus, with regard to the issue of inter-agency co-operation, differences may exist as a product of any one or more of these factors, rather than specific professional beliefs per se. For example, differential perceptions regarding a patient's risk to the public may be more pronounced between a senior psychiatrist and a younger approved social worker due to the more conservative approach associated with age. Furthermore, our evidence suggests that most multi-agency meetings are conducted at a senior level, hence, there exists scope for arguing that to some extent their overall approach may start from a fairly restrictive position. This point becomes highly significant in situations such as Mental Health Review Tribunals, where the liberty of a patient is being determined, for if the committee generally consists of members over a certain age and perhaps mostly female, the patient may have an immediate disadvantage due to the tendency for such individuals to be generally more supportive of adopting a secure environment for the mentally ill.

A particular finding which has not yet been mentioned, relates to the high number of respondents who felt that they required educating as to the nature of mental illness and related issues. This was reflected across each group surveyed and generally related to the need for an "increase in the number of TV documentaries about mental problems" (LAY-s1-274), "more police training" (POL-d1-146), "additional skills perhaps the same as ASWs" (PROB-s2-37) and generally "more information and advice and details on where to obtain it from" (LAY-s1-338).

In fact, conclusions such as 'the need for more education' are frequently sighted as an important implication arising from research on beliefs towards the mentally ill (Wolff et al, 1996a; Bhugra, 1989). The present study also confirms this need. However, our evidence additionally highlights the fact that we must be very conscious about a number of issues relating to the nature of the information that is disseminated. In particular, we need to be more aware of both the format and content such education/information programmes may take.

The original belief was that the processes associated with community care such as outpatient treatment and deinstitutionalisation would increase the presence of mentally ill patients in the community, which in turn would generate a greater degree of public acceptance (Crocetti et al, 1974). However, evidence now exists which suggests, that knowledge of such mentally disturbed people living near by, may actually have the reverse effect (Rabkin, 1981, 1980b). Furthermore, research on the influence of previous experience with the mentally ill is equivocal and at best the present findings suggest that knowledge of such patients may increase public sympathy but do very little to enhance their level of tolerance. Thus, educating the public, via simply decanting the mentally ill into the community, is not sufficient to induce general acceptance and understanding.

In the past, attempts at educating communities about mental health issues have met with strong resistance (Willcocks, 1968; Gatherer and Reid 1963; Cumming and Cumming 1957). Their failure may partly be explained by the fact that these attempts tried to impose certain beliefs, generally about the medical model, which directly conflicted with the views already held by the community. It is probably true that people will "accept any seemingly factual and authoritative-sounding information on mental health" (Nunnally, 1961:233), however, if this information does not "relieve an immediate personal threat" (Nunnally, 1961:234) or help make sense of the world around them (Furnham, 1988), then the messages may only serve to raise public anxiety and intolerance (Cumming and Cumming, 1957).

Recently, Wolff et al (1996a) announced that they:

"... are currently evaluating the effects of an educational campaign ... to determine whether attitudes can be changed in a positive direction ..." (Wolff et al, 1996a:70).

However, given the highly complex nature of beliefs held by our current sample population, the most pertinent questions seems to be, what exactly should we include in such a programme and consequently what constitutes the baseline from which a positive direction may be determined? For example, would such a programme have succeeded if it managed to change beliefs about depression so that this condition was increasingly viewed as a type of mental illness? Some authors would agree (Howells, 1984), while others (Furnham and Bower, 1992), including the present study, have shown that commitment to the notion of mental illness may be advantageous in certain respects but problematic in others, as it is still associated with highly negative connotations, in particular, stigma and intolerance. Educational programmes are further hampered by the fact that there does not appear to exist a definitive body of knowledge about mental health issues and our findings have shown that there is frequent disagreement amongst the 'experts'.

Despite many uncertainties, there does, however, appear to exist a way forward which is helpful. The public remains 'misinformed' and 'uninformed' (Nunnally, 1961) and the way around this would appear to be through the collation of a set of facts, or close facts, about the aetiology, behaviour, treatment and social effects of mental health problems. This approach needs to be didactic in the sense that information about different possible aetiologies needs to be disseminated and that their importance depends upon the nature of the mental disorder itself (the use of medical language is obviously a problem but a point that can be highlighted). At a more general level, professionals need to work more closely amongst themselves and with the media in order to ensure that an unbiased and factual approach is adopted; the association between schizophrenia and films such as 'Jekyll and Hyde' clearly demonstrates that the present approach is misleading. Finally, any educational campaign should not seek to impose ideas, but instead be honest and informative, leaving the recipient of the information to shape their own beliefs as is the situation with most other issues, such as the AIDS campaign of the 1980s.

Research limitations and future directions

The methodological structure of the current research centres around the use of a survey experiment, designed to obtain both empirical and qualitative data about multi-agency beliefs towards various psychopathological states. The principles behind the use of such a design have been justified and its implementation in practice has demonstrated that this approach represents a comprehensive and worthwhile way of conducting research. As a result, the data presented and discussed in this chapter encompasses a wide array of issues at both a criminological and clinical level and promotes numerous indicators which may help direct subsequent research. However, before embarking on a consideration of possible future hypotheses, it is important that we pay some attention to the present study's key methodological constraints, for it is these limitations which may, to some extent, offer caution against placing our findings within too broad a context.

Some circumspections and limitations

The first area in which a degree of circumspection should be exercised centres around the extent to which these results may be generalised. Overall, it would be accurate to suggest that the study's sample population represents the major lay and professional groups likely to be involved in any Cambridge-based multi-agency approach towards both the mentally ill and mentally ill offenders. Consequently, the results may only be considered as reflecting the views held by this particular community and any attempt to extend the findings beyond this point should be treated as largely speculative. Of course, the primary intention of the study was to focus specifically on perceptions held within a single particular locality. The justification for such an approach originates from the work of Sydiaha (1971) who showed that each community had its own way of thinking and dealing with minorities such as the mentally ill.

Occasionally, throughout the discussion, reference has been made to agencies in general, such as the Criminal Justice, Mental Health and Social Services. Such terms must be treated with some degree of caution for within the context of the current research only a small selection of the personnel representing each agency have been considered. For example, the approach of the Criminal Justice System as a whole is based primarily on our findings regarding the police, and although previous research offers some degree of support to our conclusions, we do not actually know whether other professional groups such as lawyers and magistrates adopted a similar implicit pattern of beliefs.

Finally on the generalisable nature of our findings, a word of caution should be expressed concerning the actual referents used. Although the case vignettes went a step further than most studies in that they accounted for the psychopathological states of depression and schizophrenia as well as the influence of a criminal offence, it would be unrealistic to generalise the findings beyond this point. Given the differences identified between these two mental states, it would be unreasonable to expect implicit theories to be the same in situations where the referent is described as having the symptoms of 'brain damage', 'mental handicap', 'alcoholism' or 'psychopathy'. Furthermore, it is questionable whether we would find similar interactions between a particular mental state and the nature of the offence. For example, if we replace the account of a fatal stabbing with other incidents such as 'aggressive begging', 'minor theft', 'rape' or 'arson'. It is also highly likely that adjustments to the nature of certain non-deviant identities held by the referent would also have an effect (Board, 1971). In particular, describing the patients type of employment (Malla and Shaw, 1987), altering the person making the diagnosis (Kirk, 1974) and re-defining the gender of the case vignettes (Phillips, 1963) are all likely to effect the way in which respondents think.

On the basis of these comments research using case vignettes could perhaps be criticised on the grounds that such descriptions are not realistic enough to fully account for all the possible variations that could influence an individual's perceptions. Even in clearly defined situations such as describing information obtained from a psychiatric interview, important nuances are lost such as how the patient looks, their body language and general interaction skills. In an attempt to overcome these limitations, some authors have shown respondents videoed interviews (Jackson, 1988), however, what such methods gain on internal validity, they lose on generalisability as the process is extremely costly and time consuming, which dramatically reduces the likely sample size. Furthermore, with regard to the case vignettes, there is no indication from our respondent's comments to suggest that they did not believe the descriptions to be genuine and there was some evidence to suggest that respondents were interested in the subject and took the task seriously. A large number of respondents made an effort to add further comments and several suggested that more detailed information would have been useful.

With regard to the actual questionnaire, it should be mentioned that while the items were shown to have satisfactory psychometric properties, the measuring instrument itself was designed within a fairly narrow framework. Thus the principal components representative of our sample population's underlying beliefs towards the mentally ill were only measured in terms of three scientific approaches, namely, the medical, moral (cognitive-behavioural) and psychosocial. Using such a narrow set of paradigms is acceptable, especially when we consider the fact that in Britain most programmes designed to manage the mentally ill originate from any one or more of these paradigms (Taylor and Taylor, 1989), however, it is quite possible that the inclusion of other key models such as the psychoanalytic approach may, to some extent, distort our results.

Future directions

It should perhaps be emphasised that despite the exploratory and preliminary nature of this research, the actual findings and their implications are highly pertinent to the task of directing future research in the area. In particular, it should now be clear that research on beliefs towards basic labels such as 'the mental patient' are likely to produce unhelpful results as such terms simply provoke negative sentiments and ignore the wide range of characteristics, including the variable of differential psychopathological states, which clearly influences general perceptions. Furthermore, rather than focusing specifically on the views of the public, future research should take more account of the beliefs implicitly held by other groups who are involved in dealing with the mentally ill, as the implications arising from our findings suggest that the approach adopted by particular professions could have a serious impact on several fronts including: the nature of inter-agency co-operation, the type of treatment methods and facilities available and the way in which patients perceive their own condition.

In terms of the loci of future studies, it is important to ensure that it is focused, with both clear and specific objectives. Within this context the greatest benefit from studying implicit beliefs would probably be gained through carrying out applied research. Understanding multi-agency thinking towards a specific project or programme directed at managing the mentally ill, particularly in the community, will help considerably in elucidating conflicting assumptions at the outset which in turn could be helpful in terms of both the maximum utilisation of scarce resources and measuring the likely success of the scheme. Furthermore, if differences in perception are to be found, then this will act as a useful guide towards either re-shaping the project or re-educating/re-assuring those participants who appear to hold reservations.

Within the parameters of such projects, the measuring instrument could be altered accordingly. For example, if a halfway house for psychiatric patients is to be established, then it may be worth while local lay and professional groups actively interacting with the new residents, and then their beliefs with regard to this particular experience could be measured instead of through the use of a case vignette. There is certainly evidence in support of more information being made available on the establishment of such projects (Wolff et al, 1996a) and although the arguments in support of the mentally ill's anonymity in the community are commendable, the fact that some patients are quickly and quietly located within communities, probably merely adds to the general air of mysticism that surrounds them. In fact, interaction with others in the community is quite normal and natural as almost everyone wishes to know at least something about their neighbours in order to form an opinion. Also within this context, future research should be cautious about the excessive use of scientific models in order to gage implicit beliefs. Clearly, there is very little to be gained from including a psychoanalytic approach in the measuring instrument unless the scheme that is to be established actively involves such a treatment option.

On a slightly broader level, the study's findings also appear to offer guidance on a number of other important research avenues germane to the management and care of the mentally ill. For example, our evidence has shown that regardless of a respondent's degree of professionalism in relation to the mentally ill, feelings of stigma still seem to remain an unconscious feature of their perceptual disposition. Thus we should not be surprised by the fact that so much of the previous research, which set out to simply discover the extent to which their sample stigmatises the mentally ill, identified the presence of a generally negative view (Steadman and Cocozza, 1978; Osmond and Durham, 1976; Nunnally, 1961). The stigmata concept is clearly far more complex in its nature than these early studies would have us believe. Future researchers should perhaps start from the point of accepting its existence (Miles, 1987) and instead turn their attention towards a consideration of how respondents intellectually and behaviourally identify and manage the negative stereotyped images that they may hold. For example, in this study we have shown that both the lay and several of the professional groups deal with the presence of stigmatic notions in a very different way, and learning more about the origin and nature of these differences seems to be far more worthwhile than the rather limited goal of searching/hoping for a generally more optimist perceptional evaluation of the mentally ill.

A further area of concern highlighted by this research relates to the way in which the patient perceives their own condition. We have shown that the ideological position the patient learns to adopt regarding their illness, could have a fundamental impact on the way in which they approach particular treatment programmes. Within this context it would, therefore, seem helpful to direct future research towards gaining a clearer understanding of how the mentally ill perceive themselves. Such research could be carried out through experimentally manipulating the mode of treatment they receive and examining the impact this has upon their optimism about treatment modalities and willingness to actively participate in particular programmes of care.

Any discussion about research on beliefs towards a particular issue should always bare in mind the problem of their relationship to actual behaviour. Earlier, we justified the use of beliefs as opposed to attitudes as the most prominent attribute of this research on the grounds that beliefs were more useful to our understanding of behaviour (Farina and Fisher, 1982). This is acceptable, however, future research should be conscious of the potential chasm between words and deed. Furthermore, attempts should also be made to try and test this relationship, perhaps through examining both perceptual and 'real' responses of a neighbourhood to the residents of a newly established home for the mentally ill.

Finally, it should be openly stated that although the results on underlying beliefs towards the mentally ill produce interesting and potentially useful information, future research into the actual causes of or treatments for such psychopathological conditions should still continue. Improvements in our understanding of implicit theories are important and should, of course, be encouraged, however, such an approach will never replace research directed towards empirically testing scientific theories as such studies represent our most accurate method of collecting knowledge.

Concluding overview

In this chapter we have shown that the implicit pattern of beliefs held by our respondents is highly complex and not directly related to any one particular scientific model, though at the same time still clear and meaningful at both a structural and substantive level. We have also demonstrated that these views are not constant and are influenced by a whole range of factors which ultimately result in fundamental differences in approach towards both the depressive and schizophrenic patient as well as between the mentally ill in general and mentally ill offenders. Furthermore, it is also evident from the findings that there are major ideological differences in the way various multi-agency groups approach the management of those who suffer from some form of mental disturbance.

The implication of these results were discussed and some directions for future research suggested. Overall, it would appear that the way in which an individual or an organisation perceives a particular psychopathological state could have a fundamental impact on the way in which that particular mentally ill patient-offender is treated.

Notes

1 The non-significant three-way interaction effect between disorder×offence×group surveyed, which is not reported in our data set, essentially informs us that the differences found between disorder×offence for each of our three factors are fairly constant across each of our six sample populations.

2 The term bi-polar is commonly used in factor analysis and refers to the presence of both positive and negative coefficient loadings which collectively may be expressed as a continuum (Child, 1970).

3 This view is also supported by the fact that four of the items within this continuum relate directly to the degree to which the patient should be held responsible and blamed for their condition and resulting behaviour.

4 To some extent this latter distinction between types of antisocial behaviour was highlighted by the verdicts of two trials in the early 1980s. In the cases of both Peter Sutcliffe and Dennis Nilsen the juries rejected expert psychiatric testimony as to their state of mind, preferring instead to find them guilty of malice aforethought and murder respectively.

5 It will be observed from Table A14a that the grand mean for the 'sick' role factor is 4.25. This figure is above the continuum's midpoint of 3.00 and, therefore, represents a sympathetic rather than moralistic approach.

6 At a statistical level the items of this factor inter-relate to form a complete indice, and, of course, we will treat them as such at both a theoretical and practical level. However, purely for the purpose of explaining the nature of this factor, we will describe the items in terms of two submodels.

7 This point was recently reflected in the Home Secretaries Ten Point Plan directed at ensuring the safe discharge of potentially violent patients into the community (National Heath Service Executive, 1994).

8 The independence of each factor is shown by the following correlation matrix:

Correlat'n	'Sick' role	Med-control	Soc-treatment
'Sick' role	1.0000		
Med-control	-.1263*	1.0000	
Soc-treatm't	.0966	-.0964	1.0000
1-Tailed Signif: * - .01 ** - .001			

9 The code at the end of each quote identifies the respodent:
   LAY   = Member of a lay samples (students or politician)
   POL   = Police
   SW   = Social Worker
   PROB   = Probation Officer
   MHP   = Mental Health Practitioner
   d1/s1   = Depressive offender/Schizophrenic offender
   d2/s2   = Depression/Schizophrenia

   The figure at the end of each code is the respondents' sample number.
10 In recognition of this fact researchers are frequently advised to use a third
   person referent such as 'some people' in the construction of questions designed
   to elicit sensitive information (Kidder et al, 1981; Moser and Kalton, 1971).
11 The fact that the age variable does not show a significantly higher level of
   support for the social-treatment model amongst the younger respondents adds
   further support to the argument that the adoption of a more liberal approach
   does not fully explain the difference.
12 This author was recently presented with a petition signed by over 200
   residents demanding that a former psychiatric patient who was now living in
   their area be re-housed by the City Council. The resident actually drew
   attention to himself via an environmental health issue, however, the petitioners
   were primarily concerned at the committee stage with the fact that he was, as
   their representing solicitor put it 'a madman'. The petition was rejected.

Conclusions

The need to understand attitudes and beliefs towards the mentally ill has been recognised for some time (Royal Commission, 1957). More recently, it has been suggested that the way in which society thinks about the mentally ill could, to some degree, impact on the success of certain policies and procedures associated with the care and management of this minority, such as attempts to promote patient rehabilitation and social integration (Wolff et al, 1996a). Furthermore, several reports have suggested that not only is the practice of multi-agency co-operation desirable when caring for the mentally ill in general and the mentally ill offender in particular (Department of Health/Home Office, 1992), but that the success of such schemes must to some extent be based upon the existence of a common ideological approach towards such individuals (Department of Health/Home Office Circular, 66/90).

The central concern of the present study was to explore the nature of popular beliefs in a way which may be considered as more ambitions than previous research attempts. In total, six sample populations were included in the survey spanning not only the general public, but also the Criminal Justice, Mental Health and Social Services. Furthermore, the respondents from each agency sample were experimentally manipulated in order for us to be able to test their implicit beliefs across a variety of treatment conditions, designed to represent various psychopathological (depression/schizophrenia) and criminal offence conditions (presence/absence of an offence). The use of specific multivariate techniques also enabled us to measure perceptions as they related to a number of important socio-demographic variables, including the respondents': age, gender, multi-agency group status and previous experience of dealing with the mentally ill.

The findings are numerous and diverse. Overall, they show that respondents have their own way of thinking about the mentally ill and that this is very different to the three formal scientific paradigms against which implicit theories were measured. Across each of the study's key independent variables a number of diverse findings were identified. In particular, perceptions of both the schizophrenic and depressive patient were fundamentally different, in terms of both their main and interaction effects with the type of offence. Numerous differences were also found between several of the study's socio-demographic variables, the most prominent of these relating to the ideological conflicts existing between several of the multi-agency populations.

From these findings it should, however, not be implied that our respondents' implicit views were unorganised and chaotic. On the contrary, it would appear that at both a substantive and structural level the nature of their beliefs was coherent, meaningful and clearly well organised with regard to the purpose of trying to make sense of the mental illness phenomena around them.

Despite this degree of stability and coherence broadly underlying implicit multi-agency theories, the differences that were identified in terms of both the treatment and socio-demographic factors tended to be significant and, as we have shown throughout our discussion, could well have a profound impact on the way in which the mentally ill are managed, treated and cared for in the future.

Ultimately, this research has shown that the existence of certain implicit beliefs may, to some extent, be acting as a catalyst on the way in which specific programme objectives, methods of management and general processes involving interaction with the mentally ill, are approached and implemented in practice. Our own inability to gain a clear understanding of the implicit beliefs we hold both as individuals as well as within the context of specific groups, could in fact be one of the biggest challenges we face in the task of ultimately developing a sound and workable approach towards the better care and management of the mentally ill.

This research represents a comprehensive attempt to gain a detailed understanding of how a series of multi-agency populations implicitly thinks about a range of mentally ill offender-patients. In the final analysis, both the study's results and the implications drawn from these findings demonstrate that research directed towards a consideration of implicit theories is not only worthwhile, but should become a fundamental and integral part of the debate surrounding how we should go about caring for and managing those individuals who society defines as psychopathologically and criminally deviant.

Bibliography

Ahmed, S. and Vishwanathan, P. (1984). 'Factor-Analytical Study of Nunnally's Scale of Popular Concepts of Mental Health'. *Psychological Reports*, 54, 455-461.

Alder, Leta, et al. (1952). *Mental Illness in Washington County Arkansas*. University of Arkansas: Institute of Science and Technology, Research Series.

Allen, L. (1943). 'A Study of Community Attitudes Toward Mental Hygiene'. *Mental Hygiene*, 27, 248-254.

American Psychiatric Association. (1994). *Diagnostic and Statistical Manual of Mental Disorders (4th Edn.) (DSM IV)*. Washington: American Psychiatric Association.

Angermayer, M.C., Link, B. and Majchev, A. (1987). 'Stigma Perceived by Patients Attending Modern Treatment Settings'. *Journal of Nervous and Mental Disease*, 175, 4-10.

Anon. (1974). Editorial. S*chizophrenia Bulletin*, 10, 6-8.

Appleby, L., Ellis, N.C., Rogers, G.W. and Zimmerman, W.A. (1961). 'A Psychological Contribution to the Study of Hospital Structure'. *Journal of Clinical Psychology*, 17, 390-393.

Appleby, L. and Wessely, S. (1988). 'Public Attitudes to Mental Illness: The Influence of the Hungerford Massacre'. *Medicine Science and the Law*, 28, 291-295.

Arkar, H. and Eker, D. (1994). 'Effect of Psychiatric Labels on Attitudes Toward Mental Illness in a Turkish Sample'. *The International Journal of Social Psychiatry*, 40, 205-213.

Aronson, E. and Carlsmith, J.M. (1968). *Experimentation in Social Psychology*. In Lindzey, G. and Aronson, E. (Eds.). *Handbook of Social Psychology*, Vol.II. Reading, Mass.: Addison-Wesley.

Babbie, E.R. (1973). *Survey Research Methods*. Belmont, Calif.: Wadsworth Publishing Co.

Babbie, E.R. (1989). *The Practice of Social Research*. Belmont, Calif.: Wadsworth Publishing Co.

Baker, J.E. (1966). 'Preparing Prisoners for Their Return to the Community'. *Federal Probation*, 30, 43-50.

Baker, F. and Schulberg, H.C. (1967). 'The Development of a Community Mental Health Ideology Scale' *Community Mental Health Journal*, 3, 216-225.

Bean, P. (1980). *Compulsory Admissions to Mental Hospitals*. Chichester: John Wiley & Sons.

Bean, P. (1985) (Ed.). *Mental Illness: Changes and Trends*. Chichester: Wiley & Sons.

Bean, P. (1986). *Mental Disorder and Legal Control*. Cambridge: Cambridge University Press.

Beck, A.T. (1989). *Cognitive Therapy and the Emotional Disorders*. New York: International Universities Press.

Becker, H.S. (1963). *Outsiders: Studies in the Sociology of Deviance*. New York: Free Press.

Bentz, W.K. and Edgerton, J.W. (1970). 'Consensus on Attitudes Towards Mental Illness'. *Archives of General Psychiatry*, 22, 468-473.

Bentz, W.K. and Edgerton, J.W. (1971). 'The Consequences of Labelling a Person Mentally Ill'. *Social Psychiatry,* 6, 29-33.

Bentz, W.K., Edgerton, J.W. and Kherlopian, M. (1969). 'Perceptions of Mental Illness Among People in a Rural Area'. *Mental Hygiene*, 53, 459-465.

Berelson, B. (1952). *Content Analysis in Communication Research*. Glencoe, Ill.: Free Press.

Bergin, A. and Lambert, M. (1978). *The Evaluation of Therapeutic Outcomes*. In Garfield, S. and Bergin, A. (Eds.). *Handbook of Psychotherapy and Behaviour Change*. Chichester: Wiley.

Bhugra, D. (1989). 'Attitudes Towards Mental Illness'. *Acta Psychiatrica Scandinavica*, 80, 1-12.

Bingham, J. (1951). 'What the Public Thinks of Psychiatry' *American Journal of Psychiatry*. 107, 599-601.

Blalock, H.M., Jr. and Blalock, A.B. (Eds.). (1968). *Methodology in Social Research*. New York: McGraw-Hill.

Blalock, H.M., Jr. (1972). *Social Statistics*. New York: McGraw-Hill.

Blau, P.M. (1964). *Exchange and Power in Social Life*. New York: Wiley.

Bluglass, R. and Bowden, P. (1990). *Principles and Practice of Forensic Psychiatry*. Edinburgh: Churchill Livingstone.

Bogardus, E. (1925). 'Measuring Social Distance'. *Journal of Applied Sociology*, 9, 299-308.

Bogardus, E. (1933). 'A Social Distance Scale'. *Sociology and Social Research*, 17, 265-271.

Bohrnstedt, G.W. (1983). 'Measurement'. In Rossi, P.H., Wright, J.D. and Anderson, A.B. *Handbook of Survey Research*. London: Academic Press.

Bord, R.J. (1971). 'Rejection of the Mentally Ill: Continuities and Further Developments' *Social Problems*, 18, 496-509.

Box, S., Hale, C. and Andrews, J. (1988). 'Crime News in Colorado Newspapers'. *American Journal of Sociology*, 57, 325-330.

British Crime Survey (1992). London: Home Office.

Brockington, I.F., Hall, P.H., Levings, J. et al. (1993). 'The Community's Tolerance of the Mentally Ill'. *British Journal of Psychiatry*, 162, 93-99.

Brockman, J., D'Arcy, C. and Edmonds, L. (1979). 'Facts or Artifacts? Changing Public Attitudes Towards the Mentally Ill'. *Social Science and Medicine*, 13A, 673-682.

Bryman, A. and Cramer, D. (1990). *Quantitative Data Analysis for Social Scientists*. London: Routledge.

Buchanan, A. and Bhugra, D. (1992). 'Attitudes of the Medical Profession to Psychiatry'. *Acta Psychiatrica Scandinavica*, 85, 1-5.

Caplan, G. (1981). 'Mastery of Stress: Psychosocial Aspects'. *American Journal of Psychiatry*, 138, 413-420.

Caro, I., Miralles, A. and Rippere, V. (1983). 'What's the Thing to Do When You're Feeling Depressed? A Cross Cultural Replication'. *Behaviour Research and Therapy*, 21, 477-483.

Carstairs, G.M. and Wing, J.K. (1958). 'Attitudes of the General Public to Mental Illness'. *British Medical Journal*, 4, 594-597.

Chalmers, A. (1986). *What Is This Thing Called Science?* Milton Keynes: Open University Press.

Child, D. (1970). *The Essentials of Factor Analysis*. London: Holt, Rinehart and Winston.

Chinsky, J. and Rappaport, J. (1970). 'Attitude Change in College Students and Chronic Patients: A Dual Perspective'. *Journal of Consulting and Clinical Psychology*, 35, 388-394.

Clare, A.W. (1980). *Psychiatry in Dissent*. London: Tavistock.

Clark, A.W. and Binks, N.M. (1966). 'Relation of Age and Education to Attitudes Toward Mental Illness'. *Psychological Reports*, 19, 649-650.

Cohen, N. and Rivkin, D. (1971). 'Civil Disabilities: The Forgotten Punishment'. *Federal Probation*, 35, 19-25.

Cohen, J. and Struening, E.L. (1962). 'Opinions about Mental Illness in the Personnel of Two Large Mental Hospitals'. *Journal of Abnormal and Social Psychology*, 64, 349-360.

Cohen, J. and Struening, E.L. (1963). 'Opinions about Mental Illness: Mental Hospital Occupational Profiles and Profile Clusters'. *Psychological Reports*, 12, 111-124.

Cohen, J. and Struening, E.L. (1964). 'Opinions about Mental Illness: Hospital Social Atmosphere Profiles and their Relevance to Effectiveness'. *Journal of Consulting Psychology*, 28, 291-298.

Cohen, J. and Struening, E.L. (1965). 'Opinions about Mental Illness: Hospital Differences in Attitude for Eight Occupational Groups'. *Psychological Reports*, 17, 25-26.

Cohn, S.F., Barkan, S.E. and Holteman, W.A. (1991). 'Punitive Attitudes Toward Criminals: Racial Consensus or Racial Conflict?' *Social Problems*, 38, 287-296.

Colson, C.E. (1970). 'Effects of Different Explanations of Disordered Behaviour on Treatment Referrals'. *Journal of Consulting and Clinical Psychology*, 34, 432-435.

Cook, F.L. (1979). *Who Should Be Helped?* Beverly Hills, Calif.: Sage Publications, 1979.

Creswell, J.W. (1994). *Research Design: Qualitative and Quantitative Approaches*. Thousand Oaks, Calif: Sage Publications.

Crocetti, G. and Lemkau, P. (1963). 'Public Opinion of Psychiatric Home Care in an Urban Area'. *American Journal of Public Health*, 53, 409-417.

Crocetti, G., Spiro, H., Lemkau, P. and Siassi, I. (1972). 'Multiple Models and Mental Illness: A Rejoinder to 'Failure of a Moral Enterprise: Attitudes of the Public Toward Mental Illness' By Sarbin, T. and Mancuso, J'. *Journal of Consulting and Clinical Psychology*, 39, 1-5.

Crocetti, G., Spiro, H. and Siassi, I. (1971). 'Are the Ranks Closed? Attitudinal Social Distance and Mental Illness'. *American Journal of Psychiatry*, 127, 1121-1127.

Crocetti, G., Spiro, H. and Siassi, I. (1974). *Contemporary Attitudes towards Mental Illness*. Pittsburgh: University of Pittsburgh Press.

Cumming, E. and Cumming, J. (1957). *Closed Ranks: An Experiment in Mental Health Education*. Cambridge Mass: Harvard University Press.

Cumming, E. and Cumming, J. (1965). 'On the Stigma of Mental Illness'. *Community Mental Health Journal*, 1, 135-143.

Daily Telegraph, August 5, 1993.

Daniel, B. (1962). 'Discussion'. *American Journal of Psychiatry*, 118, 699-700. A response to: Lemkau, P.O. and Crocetti, G.M. (1962). 'An Urban Population's Opinion and Knowledge About Mental Illness'. *American Journal of Psychiatry*, 118, 692-700.

D'Arcy, C. and Brockman, J. (1976). 'Changing Public Recognition of Psychiatric Symptoms? Blackfoot Revisited'. *Journal of Health and Social Behaviour*, 17, 302-310.

D'Arcy, C. and Brockman, J. (1977). 'Public Rejection of the Ex-Mental Patient: Are Attitudes Changing?' *Canadian Review of Sociology and Anthropology*, 14, 68-80.

Davies, N. (1993). *Murder on Ward Four: The Story of Bev Allitt, and the Most Terrifying Crime since the Moors Murders.* London: Chatto & Windus.

Dayson, D. (1993). 'The TAPS Project. 12: Crime, Vagrancy, Death and Readmission of the Long-Term Mentally Ill During Their First Year of Local Reprovision'. *British Journal of Psychiatry*, 162, 40-44.

Department of Health and Social Services/Home Office. (1957). *Report of the Royal Commission on the Law Relating to Mental Illness and Mental Deficiency 1954-1957.* Cmnd. 169. London.

Department of Health and Social Services/Home Office (1975). *Report of the Committee on Mentally Abnormal Offenders (The Butler Report).* Cmnd. 6244. London: HSMO.

Department of Health/Home Office (1992). *Review of Health and Social Services for Mentally Disordered Offenders and Others Requiring Similar Services: Final Summary Report.* (Cmnd. 2088). London: HMSO.

Deutcher, I. (1966). 'Words and Deeds: Social Science and Social Policy'. *Social Problems*, 13, 235-254.

Diener, E. and Crandall, R. (1978). *Ethics in Social and Behavioural Research.* Chicago: University of Chicago Press.

Dillman, D.A. (1978). *Mail and Telephone Surveys: The Total Design Method.* New York: Wiley-Interscience.

Dillman, D.A. (1983). 'Mail and Other Self-Administered Questionnaires'. In Rossi, P.H., Wright, J.D. and Anderson, A.B. *Handbook of Survey Research.* London: Academic Press.

Dohrenwend, B.P., Bernard, V. and Kolb, L. (1962). 'The Orientations of Leaders in an Urban Area Toward Problems of Mental Illness'. *American Journal of Psychiatry*, 118, 683-691.

Dohrenwend, B.P. and Chin-Shong E. (1967). 'Social Status and Attitudes Towards Psychological Disorder: The Problem of Tolerance of Deviance'. *American Sociological Review*, 32, 417-433.

Dohrenwend, B.P. (1975). 'Socio-Cultural and Social-Psychological Factors in the Genesis of Mental Disorders'. *Journal of Health and Social Behaviour*, 16, 365-392.

Doll, W., Thompson, E.H. and Lefton, M. (1976). 'Beneath Acceptance: Dimensions of Family Affect Towards Former Mental Patients'. *Social Science and Medicine*, 10, 312.

Drolen, C.S. (1993). 'The Effect of Educational Setting on Student Opinions of Mental Illness'. *Community Mental Health Journal*, 29, 223-234.

Edgerton, R.B. and Karno, M. (1971). 'Mexican American Bilingualism and the Perception of Mental Illness'. *Archives of General Psychiatry*, 24, 286-290.

Edwards, A.L. (1969). *Experimental Design in Psychological Research.* London: Holt, Rinehart and Winston.

Ehrlich, D. and Sabshin, M. (1964). 'A Study of Socio-Therapeutically Orientated Psychiatrists'. *American Journal of Othropsychiatry*, 34, 469-486.

Eker, D. (1985). 'Effect of Type of Cause on Attitudes Towards Mental Illness and Relationships between the Attitudes'. *International Journal of Social Psychiatry*, 31, 24.

Elinson, J., Padella, E. and Perkins, M. (1967). *Public Image of Mental Health Services.* New York: Mental Health Materials Center.

Ellsworth, R.B. (1965). 'A Behavioural Study of Staff Attitudes Toward Mental Illness'. *Journal of Abnormal Psychology*, 70, 194-200.

Ennis, B. and Emery, R. (1978). *The Rights of Mental Patients - An American Civil Liberties Union Handbook.* New York: Avon.

Erskine, H. (1974). 'The Poles: Causes of Crime'. *Public Opinion Quarterly*, 38, 288-295.

Eysenck, H.J. (1975). *The Future of Psychiatry.* London: Methuen.

Eysenck, H.J. (1981) (Ed.). *A Model for Personality.* Berlin: Springer.

Farina, A. (1983). *The Stigma of Mental Disorders.* In Miller, A.G. (Ed.). *In the Eye of the Beholder.* New York: Holt, Rinehart and Winston.

Farina, A., Holland, C. and Ring, K. (1971). 'Role of Stigma and Set in Interpersonal Reaction'. *Journal of Abnormal Psychology*, 76, 421-429.

Farina, A. and Fischer, J. (1982). *Beliefs About Mental Disorders. Findings and Implications.* In Weary, C. and Mirels, A. (Eds.). *Integration of Clinical and Social Psychology.* London: Oxford University Press.

Finlay-Jones, R. and Eckhardt, B. (1981). 'Psychiatric Disorder Among the Young Unemployed'. *Australian and New Zealand Journal of Psychiatry*, 15, 265-270.

Fischer, E. (1971). 'Altruistic Attitudes, Beliefs About Psychiatric Patients, and Volunteering for Companionship with Mental Hospital Patients'. *Proceedings of the 79th Annual Convention of the American Psychological Association,* 6, 343-344.

Fitzpatrick, R. (1984). 'Lay Concepts of Illness'. In Fitzpatrick, R., Hinton, J., Newman, S., Scambler, G. and Thompson, J. (Eds.). *The Experience of Illness.* London: Tavistock.

Flew, A. (1985). 'Mental Health, Mental Illness, Mental Disease: The Medical Model'. In Bean, P. (Ed.). *Mental Illness: Changes and Trends.* Chichester: Wiley & Sons.

Fournet, G. (1967). 'Cultural Correlates with Attitudes, Perception, Knowledge and Reported Incidence of Mental Disorders'. *Dissertation Abstracts*, 28, 339.

Fracchia, J., Canale, D., Cambria, E., et al. (1976). 'Public Views of Ex-Mental Patients: A Note on Perceived Dangerousness and Unpredictability'. *Psychological Reports*, 38, 495-498.

Freeman, H.E. (1961). 'Attitudes Towards Mental Illness Among Relatives of Former Patients'. *American Sociological Review*, 26 59-66.

Friedson, E. (1975). *Profession of Medicine*. New York: Dodd and Mead.

Furnham, A. (1988). *Lay Theories*. Oxford: Pergamon.

Furnham, A. and Bower, P. (1992). 'A Comparison of Academic and Lay Theories of Schizophrenia'. *British Journal of Psychiatry*, 161, 201-210.

Furnham, A. and Henderson, M. (1983). 'Lay Theories of Delinquency'. *European Journal of Social Psychology*, 13, 107-120.

Furnham, A. and Rees, J. (1988). 'Lay Theories of Schizophrenia'. The *International Journal of Social Psychiatry*, 34, 212-220.

Gatherer, A. and Reid, J.J. (1963). *Public Attitudes and Mental Health Education*. Northamptonshire Mental Health Project.

Gans, H. (1972). 'The Positive Functions of Poverty'. *American Journal of Sociology*, 78, 275-289.

Gelder, M. (1986). 'Cognitive Therapy'. In Granville-Grossman, K. (Ed.). *Recent Advances in Clinical Psychiatry 5*. Edinburgh: Churchill Livingstone.

Gibbons, D.C. (1975). 'Some Notes On Treatment, Theory in Corrections'. In Peterson, D.M. and Thomas, C.W. (Eds.). *Corrections: Problems and Prospects*. Anglewood Cliffs, N.J.: Prentice-Hall.

Giddens, A. (1975). *Positivism and Sociology*. London: Heinemann.

Gilbert, D.C. and Levinson, D.J. (1957). "Custodialism' and 'Humanism' in Staff Ideology'. In Levinson, D.J. and Williams, R.H. (Eds.). *The Patient and the Mental Hospital*. Glencoe,Ill.: Free Press, 1957.

Goffman, E. (1961). *Asylums*. Harmondsworth: Penguin.

Goffman, E. (1963). *Stigma: Notes of the Management of Spoiled Identity*. New York: Prentice Hall.

Goldie, N., Pilgrim, D. and Roger, A. (1989). *Community Mental Health Centres: Policy and Practice*. London: Good Practices and Mental Health.

Gostin, L.O. (1975). *A Human Condition: The Mental Health Act from 1959-1975: Observations, Analysis and Proposals for Reform - Volume 1*. London: Special Report MIND.

Gostin, L.O. (1975 Ed.). *Secure Provision: Special Services for the Mentally Ill and Mentally Handicapped in England and Wales*. London: Tavictock.

Gottesman, I.I. and Shields, J. (1972). *Schizophrenia: The Epigenetic Puzzle*. New York: Academic Press.

Gove, W.R. (1970). Societal Reaction as an Explanation of Mental Illness: An Evaluation'. *American Sociological Review*, 35 873-884.

Gove, W.R. (1975). 'The Labelling Theory of Mental Illness: A Reply to Scheff'. *American Sociological Review*, 40, 242-248.

Granville-Grossman, K. (1985 Ed.). *Recent Advances in Clinical Psychiatry 5.* Edinburgh: Churchill Livingstone.

Guttman, L. (1945). 'A Basis for Analysing Test-Retest Reliability'. *Psychometrika*, 10, 255-282.

Guttman, L. (1959). 'A Structural Theory for Intergroup Beliefs and Action'. *American Sociological Review*, 24, 318-328.

Hagan, F.E. (1989). *Research Methods in Criminal Justice and Criminology.* New York: Macmillan.

Haldipur, C. (1984). 'Madness in Ancient India, Concept of Insanity' in Charaka Samhita. *Comprehensive Psychiatry*, 25, 335-344.

Hall et al (1979). Cited in Rabkin, J.G., Muhlin, G. and Cohen, P. W. (1984). 'What the Neighbours Think: Community Attitudes Toward Local Psychiatric Facilities'. *Community Mental Health Journal*, 20, 304-312.

Hall, L. and Tucker, C. (1985). 'Relationships Between Ethnicity, Conceptions of Mental Illness, and Attitudes Associated with Seeking Psychological Help'. *Psychological Report*, 57, 907-916.

Hall, P., Brockington, I.F., Levings, J. and Murphy, C. (1993). 'A Comparison of Responses to the Mentally Ill in Two Communities'. *British Journal of Psychiatry*, 162, 99-101.

Halpert, H.P. (1969). 'Public Acceptance of the Mentally Ill'. *Public Health Reports*, 84, 59-64.

Hawton, K. et al (1989). *Cognitive Behaviour Therapy for Psychiatric Problems: A Practical Guide.* Oxford: Oxford University Press.

Hays, W.L. (1994). *Statistics.* Austin, Texas: Harcout Brace College Publishers.

Herbert, M. (1985). 'Psychological Treatment of Psychopathology'. In Bean, P. (Ed.). *Mental Illness: Changes and Trends.* Chichester: Wiley & Sons.

Heston, L. (1972). 'Genes and Psychiatry'. In Mendels, J. (Ed.). *Biological Psychiatry.* New York: Wiley.

Hill, D. (1982). 'Public Attitudes to Mentally Abnormal Offender'. In Gun, J. and Fafington, D.P. (Eds.). *Abnormal Offenders, Delinquency and the Criminal Justice System.* Chichester: Wiley.

Hindelang, M. (1974). 'Public Opinion Regarding Crime, Criminal Justice and Related Topics'. *Journal of Research in Crime and Delinquency*, 11, 101-116.

Hodgins, S. (1993). 'The Criminality of Mentally Disordered Persons'. In Hodgins, S. *Mental Disorder and Crime.* London: Sage.

Hoggett, B. (1990). *Mental Health Law.* London: Sweet & Maxwell.

Hollingshead, A. and Redlich, F. (1958). *Social Class and Mental Illness.* New York: John Wiley & Sons.

Holmes, D. (1968). *Changes in Attitudes about Mental Illness.* Center for Community Research, New York (Mimeo.).

Holsti, O. le (1969). *Content Analysis for the Social Sciences and Humanities.* Reading, Mass: Addison-Wesley.

Homans, G. (1969). *Social Behaviour. Its Elementary Forms.* New York: Harcourt.

Homant, R. and Kennedy, D. (1982). 'Attitudes Towards Ex-Offenders: A Comparison of Social Stigmas'. *Journal of Criminal Justice*, 10, 383-391.

Home Office (1990). Circular No.66/90: *Provision for Mentally Disordered Offenders.* London: Home Office.

Hough, M. and Mayhew, P. (1985). *Taking Account of Crime.* London: HMSO.

Howells, K. (1984). 'Public Perceptions of Mentally Ill Offenders'. In Muller, D.J., Blackman, D.E. and Chapman, A.J. (Eds.). *Psychology and Law.* Chichester: Wiley.

Hull, C. (1943). *Principles of Behaviour.* New York: Appleton-Century-Crofts.

Hunter, R. (1973). 'Psychiatry and Neurology: Psychosyndrome or Brain Disease'. *Proceedings of the Royal Society of Medicine*, 66, 17-22.

Ingleby, D. (1980. Ed). *Critical Psychiatry - The Politics of Mental Health.* New York: Pantheon Books.

Iversen, G.R. and Norpoth, H. (1976). *Analysis of Variance: Quantitative Applications in the Social Sciences.* Beverly Hills, Calif.: Sage Publications.

Jackson, M.W. (1988). 'Lay and Professional Perceptions of Dangerousness and Other Forensic Issues'. *Canadian Journal of Criminology*, 30, 215-228.

Jaspars, J. (1983). 'Attribution Theory and Research: The State of Art'. In Jaspars, J., Fincham, F. and Hewstone, M. (Eds.). *Attribution Theory and Research.* London: Academic Press.

Jegede, R.O. (1976). 'A Scale for the Measurement of Attitudes to Mental Illness'. *The Journal of Psychology*, 93, 269-272.

Jehu, D. (1985). 'Contemporary Behaviour Therapy'. In Bean, P. (Ed.). *Mental Illness: Changes and Trends.* Chichester: Wiley & Sons.

Johannsen, W. (1969). 'Attitudes Toward Mental Patients'. *Mental Hygene*, 53, 218-228.

Joint Commission on Mental Illness and Health (1961 Eds.). *Action for Mental Health.* New York: Basic Books Inc.

Jones, K. (1972). *A History of the Mental Health Services.* London: Routledge.

Jones, E.E., Farina, A., Hastorf, A.H., Markus, H., Miller, D.T. and Scott, R.A. (1984). *Social Stigma: The Psychology of Marked Relationships.* New York: Freeman and Company.

Kaiser, H.F. (1974). 'An Index of Factorial Simplicity'. *Psychometrika*, 39, 31-36.

Kallmann, F.J. (1959). 'The Genetics of Mental Illness'. In Arieti, S. (Ed.). *American Handbook of Psychiatry (Vol.1).* New York: Basic Books.

Karasu, T.B. (1990). 'Psychotherapy for Depression'. *American Journal of Psychiatry*, 147, 2-3.

Kazdin, A.E. (1978). *History of Behaviour Modification: Experimental Foundations of Contemporary Research.* Baltimore: University Park Press.

Kelleher, M.J. and Copeland, J.R. (1972). 'Compulsory Psychiatric Admissions by the Police'. *Medicine, Science and Law*, 12, 220-224.

Kendall, P.L. and Lazarsfeld, P.F. (1974). 'Problems of Survey Analysis'. In Merton, R.K. and Lazarsfeld, P.F. (Eds.). *Continuities in Social Research.* New York: Arno Press.

Kendell, R.E. (1975). *The Role of Diagnosis in Psychiatry.* Oxford: Blackwell Scientific Publications.

Kennedy, L. and Silverman, R. (1985). 'Significant Others and Fear of Crime Among the Elderly'. *International Journal of Aging and Human Development*, 20, 241-256.

Kidder, L.H. (1981). *Research Methods in Social Relations.* Japan: Holt-Saunerds, Ltd.

Kidder, L. and Cohen, E. (1979). 'Public Views of Crime and Crime Protection'. In Frieze, I., Baral, D. and Carrol, J. (Eds.). *New Approaches to Social Problems.* San Francisco: Jossey-Bass.

Kirk, S.A. (1974). 'The Impact of Labelling on Rejection of the Mentally Ill: An Experimental Study'. *Journal of Health and Social Behaviour*, 15, 108-117.

Kish, L. (1965). *Survey Sampling.* New York: John Wiley.

Kroll, J. and Backrach, B. (1982). 'Visions and Psychopathology in the Middle Ages'. *Journal of Nervous and Mental Disease*, 170, 41-49.

Kuhn, T.S. (1970). *The Structure of Scientific Revolutions.* Chicago, Ill.: The University of Chicago Press.

La Piere, R.T. (1934). 'Attitudes vs Actions'. *Social Forces*, 13, 230-237.

Laing, R.D. (1961). *The Self and Others.* London: Tavistock.

Laing, R.D. (1967). *The Politics of Experience.* Harmondsworth: Penguin.

Lamy, R.E. (1966). 'Generalizability and Specificity of the Stigma Associated with the Mental Illness Label'. *Journal of Consulting Psychology*, 30, 450.

Last, P. and Jackson, S. (1989). *The Bristol Fear and Risk of Crime Project (A Preliminary Report on Fear of Crime).* Bristol: Avon and Somerset Constabulary.

Lawson, W.K. (1984). 'Depression and Crime: A Discursive Approach'. In Craft and Craft (Eds.). *Mentally Abnormal Offenders.* London: Bailliere Tindall.

Lawton, M.P. (1964). 'Correlates of the Opinion about Mental Illness Scale'. *Journal of Consulting Psychology*, 28, 94.

Lawton, M.P. (1965). 'Personality and Attitudinal Correlates of Psychiatric-Aid Performance'. *Journal of Social Psychology*, 66, 215-226.

Leff, J.P. and Vaughn, C.E. (1985). *Expressed Emotion in Families.* New York: Guilford Press.

Lemert, E.M. (1951). *Social Pathology.* New York: McGraw Hill.

Lemkau, M. (1962). *Professional and Public Attitudes Regarding the Care of Mental Patients in Carroll County, Maryland.* Department of Sociology, Western Maryland College. Mimeographed (Unpublished).

Lemkau, P.O. and Crocetti, G.M. (1962). 'An Urban Population's Opinion and Knowledge About Mental Illness'. *American Journal of Psychiatry*, 118, 692-700.

Lerner, M. (1980). *The Belief in a Just World: A Fundamental Delusion.* New York: Plenum Press.

Levey, S., Howells, K. and Cowden, E. (1995). 'Dangerousness, Unpredictability and the Fear of People with Schizophrenia'. *Journal of Forensic Psychiatry*, 6, 19-39.

Lindqvist, P. and Allebeck, P. (1990). 'Schizophrenia and Crime: A Longitudinal Follow-up of 644 Schizophrenics in Stockholm'. *British Journal of Psychiatry*, 157, 345-350.

Link, B. (1982). 'Mental Patient Status, Work and Income: An Examination of the Effects of a Psychiatric Label'. *American Sociological Review*, 47, 202-215.

Link, B.G. and Cullen, F.T. (1986). 'Contact with the Mentally Ill and Perceptions of How Dangerous They Are'. *Journal of Health and Social Behaviour*, 27, 289-302.

Lord, F.M. and Novick, M.R. (1968). *Statistical Theories of Mental Test Scores.* Reading, Mass.: Addison-Wesley.

Mackay, R.D. (1991). 'Insanity and Fitness to Stand Trial in Canada and England: A Comparative Study'. *Journal of Forensic Psychiatry*, 1, 277-301.

McKenna, P.J. (1987). 'Pathology, Phenomenology and the Dopamine Hypothesis of Schizophrenia'. *British Journal of Psychiatry*, 151, 288-301.

McKeon, P. and Carrick, S. (1991). 'Public Attitudes to Depression - A National Survey'. *Irish Journal of Psychological Medicine*, 8, 116-121.

MacLean, U. (1969). 'Community Attitudes to Mental Illness in Edinburgh'. *British Journal of Preventative Social Medicine*, 23, 45-52.

MacMillan, J.F. and Johnson A.L. (1987). 'Contact with the Police in Early Schizophrenia: Its Nature, Frequency and Relevance to the Outcome of Treatment'. *Medicine, Science and the Law*, 27, 15-24.

Malla, A. and Shaw, T. (1987). 'Attitudes Towards Mental Illness: The Influence of Education and Experience'. *International Journal of Social Psychiatry*, 33, 33-41.

Martin, J.P. (1985). *Hospitals in Trouble.* Oxford: Blackwell.

Matas, M., El-Guebaly, N., Peterkin, A., Green, M. and Harper D. (1985). 'Mental Illness and the Media Assessment of Attitudes and Communication'. *Canadian Journal of Psychiatry*, 30, 12-19.

Meyer, J.K. (1964). 'Attitudes Towards Mental Illness in a Maryland Community'. *Public Health Reports*, 79, 769-772.

Middleton, J. (1953). 'The Prejudices and Opinions of Mental Hospital Employees Regarding Mental Illness'. *American Journal of Psychiatry*, 110, 133-138.

Miller, D.C. (1977). *Handbook of Research Design and Social Measurement*. Newbury Park, Calif.: Sage Publications, Inc.

Miller, D.C. (1991). *Handbook of Research Design and Social Measurement*. Newbury Park, Calif.: Sage Publications, Inc.

Miller, E. and Cooper, P.J. (1988 Eds.). *Adult Abnormal Psychology*. Edinburgh: Churchill Livingstone.

Miles, A. (1987). *The Mentally Ill in Contemporary Society*. Oxford: Basil Blackwell.

Minto, A. (1985). 'Changing Clinical Practice, 1950-1980'. In Bean, P. (Ed.). *Mental Illness: Changes and Trends*. Chichester: Wiley & Sons.

Miralles, A., Caro, I. and Rippere, V. (1983). 'What Makes Depressed People Feel Worse? A Cross Cultural replication'. *Behaviour Research and Therapy*, 21, 485-490.

Monahan, J. (1981). *The Clinical Prediction of Violent Behaviour*. Crime and Delinquency Issues Monograph, US Department of Health, Meryland, DHHS No. (ADM) 81-921.

Monahan, J. (1992). 'Mental Disorder and Violent Behaviour: Perceptions and Evidence'. *American Psychologist*, 47, 511-521.

Moore, E. and Kuipers, L. (1992). 'Behavioural Correlates of Expressed Emotion in Staff-Patient Interactions'. *Social Psychiatry and Psychiatric Epidemiology*, 27, 298-303.

Morrison, J.K., Bushell, J.D., Hanson, G.D., Fentiman, J.R. and Holdridge-Crane, S. (1977). 'Relationship Between Psychiatric Patients' Attitudes Toward Mental Illness and Attitudes of Dependence'. *Psychological Reports*, 41, 1194.

Moser, C.A. and Kalton, G. (1971). *Survey Methods in Social Investigation*. London: Heinemann Educational Books, Ltd.

Murphy, B.M., Black, P., Duffy, M., Kieran, J. and Mallon, J. (1993). 'Attitudes Toward the Mentally Ill in Ireland'. *Irish Journal of Psychological Medicine*, 10, 75-79.

Myers, J.K. and Bean, L.L. (1968). *A Decade Later: A Follow-up Study of Social Class and Mental Illness*. New York: Wiley.

National Health Service Executive (1994). *Guidance on the Discharge of Mentally Disordered People and Their Continuing Care in the Community*. (HSG(94)27)ondon: Department of Health.

Naylor, B. and Wincup, E. (1994). *Survey of Women's Safety in Cambridge: A Report to the Safer Cambridge Steering Group*. Cambridge: Cambridge City Council.

Nettle, G. (1970). *Explanations*. New York: McGraw-Hill.

Nieradzik, K. and Cochrane, R. (1985). 'Public Attitudes Towards Mental Illness - The Effects of Behaviour, Role and Psychiatric Labels'. *International Journal of Social Psychiatry*, 31, 23-33.

Norman, D. (1980). 'Twelve Issues for Cognitive Science'. *Cognitive Science*, 4, 1-32.

Norman, R.M. and Malla, A.K. (1983). 'Adolescences' Attitudes Towards Mental Illness: Relationship Between Components and Sex Differences'. *Social Psychiatry*, 18, 45-50.

North East Thames and South East Thames Regional Health Authorities, (1994). *The Report of the Enquiry into the Care and Treatment of Christopher Clunis*. London: HMSO.

Norusis, M. J. (1990). *SPSS/PC+ Advanced Statistics*. Chicago: SPSS, Inc.

Norusis, M.J. (1992). *SPSS/PC+ Base System User's Guide, Version 5.0*. Chicago: SPSS, Inc.

Nunnally, J.C. (1961). *Popular Conceptions of Mental Health: Their Development and Change*. New York: Holt Rinehart and Winston.

Nuehring, E.M. and Raybin, L. (1986). 'Mentally Ill Offenders in Community Based Program: Attitudes of Service Providers'. *Journal of Offender Counselling, Services and Rehabilitation*, 11, 19-37.

Olmstead, D.W. and Durham, K. (1976). 'Stability of Mental Health Attitudes: A Semantic Differential Study'. *Journal of Health and Social Behaviour*, 17, 35-44.

Osgood, C., Suci, G. and Tannenbaum, P. (1957). *The Measurement of Meaning*. Urbana, Ill.: University of Illinois Press.

Osmond, H. (1961). *Models of Madness*. New Scientist, 12, 777-780.

Parsons, T. (1951). *The Social System*. New York: Free Press.

Parsons, T. (1958). 'Definitions of Health and Illness in the Light of American Values and Social Structure'. In Jaco, E.G. (Ed.). *Parents, Physicians and Illness*. New York: Free Press.

Peay, J. (1989). *Tribunals on Trial: A Study of Decision-making Under the Mental Health Act 1983*. Oxford: Oxford University Press.

Percy, Lord (1957). *Report of the Royal Commission on the Law Relating to Mental Illness and Mental Deficiency 1954-1957*. London: H.M.S.O.

Phillips, D.L. (1963). 'Rejection: A Possible Consequence of Seeking Help for Mental Disorders'. *American Sociological Review*, 18, 963-972.

Phillips, D.L. (1964). 'Rejection of the Mentally Ill: The Influence of Behaviour and Sex'. *American Sociological Review*, 19, 679-686.

Phillips, D.L. (1966). 'Public Identification and Acceptance of the Mentally Ill'. *American Journal of Public Health*, 56, 755-763.

Phillips, D.L. (1967). 'Identification of Mental Illness: Its Consequences for Rejection'. *Community Mental Health Journal*, 3, 262-266.

Pilgrim, D. and Rogers, A. (1993). *A Sociology of Mental Health and Illness.* Buckingham: Open University Press.

Porter, R. (1987). *A Social History of Madness.* London: Weidenfeld and Nicholson.

Prins, H. A. (1984). 'Attitudes Towards the Mentally Disordered'. *Medicine, Science and the Law*, 24, 181-191.

Rabkin, J. (1972). 'Opinions about Mental Illness: A Review of the Literature'. *Psychological Bulletin*, 77, 152-171.

Rabkin, J. (1974). 'Public Attitudes Towards Mental Illness: A Review of the Literature'. *Schizophrenia Bulletin*, 10, 8-33.

Rabkin, J. (1980a). 'Determinants of Public Attitudes About Mental Illness: Summary of the Research Literature'. In Rabkin, J., Lazar J. (Eds.). *Attitudes Towards the Mentally Ill: Research Perspectives.* Washington: DHHS Publications.

Rabkin, J. (1980b). 'Stressful Life Events and Schizophrenia: A Review'. *Psychological Bulletin*, 87, 408-425.

Rabkin, J. (1981). 'Public Attitudes: New Research Directions'. *Hospital and Community Psychiatry*, 32, 157-159.

Rack, P.H. (1982). *Race, Culture and Mental Disorder.* London: Tavistock.

Ramsey, G.V. and Siepp, M. (1948a). 'Attitudes and Opinions Concerning Mental Illness'. *Psychiatric Quarterly*, 22, 428-444.

Ramsey, C.V. and Siepp, M. (1948b). 'Public Opinions and Information Concerning Mental Health'. *Journal of Clinical Psychology*, 4, 397-406.

Reber, A.S. (1987). *Dictionary of Psychology.* London: Penguin.

Reed, J. and Nance, D. (1972). 'Society Perpetuates the Stigma of a Conviction'. *Federal Probation Journal*, 36, 27-31.

Reed, J. (1979). 'Civil Disabilities, Attitudes and Re-Entry: Or How Can the Offender Re-Acquire a Conventional Status?' *Offender Rehabilitation*, 3, 219-228.

Reynolds, P.D. (1982). *Ethics and Social Science Research.* Anglewood Cliffs, N.J.: Prentice-Hall.

Ring, S. and Schein, L. (1970). 'Attitudes Toward Mental Illness and the Use of Caretakers in a Black Community'. *American Journal of Orthopsychiatry*, 40, 710-716.

Rippere, V. (1977). 'Common-Sense Beliefs About Depression and Antidepressive Behaviour. A Study of Social Consensus'. *Behaviour Research and Therapy*, 15, 465-473.

Rippere, V. (1981). "How Depressing': Another Cognitive Dimension of Common-Sense Knowledge'. *Behaviour Research and Therapy*, 19, 169-181.

Rix, K.J.B. (1987). *A Handbook for Trainee Psychiatrists.* London: Balliere Tindall.

Rogers, A. (1993). 'Deconstructing Schizophrenia'. In Wright, P. and Treacher, A. (Eds.). *The Problem of Medical Knowledge*. Edinburgh: Edinburgh University Press.

Rootman, I. and Lafave, H. (1969). 'Are Popular Attitudes Towards the Mentally Ill Changing?' *American Journal of Psychiatry*, 126, 261-265.

Rosenberg, M. (1968). *The Logic of Survey Analysis*. New York: Basic Books.

Rosenthal, R. (1966). *Experimental Effects in Behavioural Research*. New York: Appleton - Century Crofts.

Roskin, G., Carsen, M.L., Rabiner, C.J. and Marell, S.K. (1988). 'Attitudes Toward Patients Among Different Mental Health Professional Groups'. *Comprehensive Psychiatry*, 29, 188-194.

Rossi, P.H., Wright, J.D. and Anderson, A.B. (1983). *Handbook of Survey Research*. London: Academic Press, Inc.

Roth, M. (1976). 'Schizophrenia and the Theories of Thomas Szasz'. *British Journal of Psychiatry*, 129, 317-326.

Rubin, S. (1958). *Crime and Juvenile Delinquency*. New York: Oceana.

Samson, C. (1992). *Confusing Symbolic Events With Realities: The Case of Community Mental Health in the USA*. Paper presented at the BSA Medical Sociology Group and European Society of Medical Sociology, Edinburgh.

Sanders, A. (1988). 'The Limits of Diversion from Prosecution'. *British Journal of Criminology*, 28, 513-532.

Sarbin, T.R. and Mancuso, J.C. (1970). 'Failure of a Moral Enterprise: Attitudes of the Public Towards Mental Illness'. *Journal of Consulting and Clinical Psychology*, 35, 159-172.

Sarbin, T.R. and Mancuso, J.C. (1972). 'Paradigms and Moral Judgment: Improper Conduct is not Disease'. *Journal of Consulting and Clinical Psychology*, 39, 1-5.

Sarbin, T., Taft, R. and Bailey, D. (1960). *Clinical Inference and Cognitive Theory*. New York: Holt, Rinehart & Winston.

Sayce, L. (1989). 'Community Health Centres - Rhetoric or Reality?' In Bracks, A. and Grimshaw, C. (Eds.). *Mental Health Care in Crisis*. London: Pluto.

Scheff, T.J. (1966). *Being Mentally Ill: A Sociological Theory*. London: Weidenfeld and Nicolson.

Schoenberg, E. (1972). *The Anti-Therapeutic Team in Psychiatry*. In Schoenberg, E. (Ed.). *A Hospital Looks at Itself: Essays from Claybury*.

Schroder, D. and Erlich, D. (1968). 'Rejection by Mental Health Professionals: A Possible Consequence of Not Seeking Appropriate Help for Emotional Disorders'. *Journal of Health and Social Behaviour*, 9, 222-232.

Schwartz, R. and Skolnick, J. (1962). 'Two Studies of Legal Stigma'. *Social Problems*, 10, 133-142.

Scott, J., Mark, J., Williams, G. and Beck A.T. (1989). *Cognitive Therapy in Clinical Practice: An Illustrative Casebook*. London: Routledge.

Sedlack, G. and Stanley, J. (1992). *Social Research: Theory and Methods.* Boston: Allyn and Bacon.

Segal, S.P. and Aviram, U. (1978). *The Mentally Ill in Community Based Sheltered Care.* New York: Wiley.

Segal, S., Baumohl, J. and Mayles, E. (1980). 'Neighbourhood Types and Community Reaction to the Mentally Ill'. *Journal of Health and Social Behaviour,* 21, 343-359.

Senna, J. and Siegel, L. (1978). *Introduction to Criminal Justice.* St. Paul: West Publishing Co.

Seyd, P. and Whiteley, P. (1992). *Labour's Grass Roots: The Politics of Party Membership.* Oxford: Clarendon.

Sheatsley. P.D. (1983). 'Questionnaire Construction and Item Writing'. Rossi, P.H., Wright, J.D. and Anderson, A.B. (1983). *Handbook of Survey Research.* London: Academic Press, Inc.

Siassi, I., Spiro, H.R. and Crocetti, G. (1973). 'The Social Acceptance of the Ex-Mental Hospital Patient'. *Community Mental Health,* 9, 233-243.

Siegler, M. and Osmond, H. (1966). 'Models of Madness'. *British Journal of Psychiatry,* 112, 1193-1203.

Siegler, M. and Osmond, H. (1974). *Models of Madness, Models of Medicine.* London: Macmillan Publishing Inc.

Silverman, R. and Kennedy, L. (1985). 'Loneliness, Satisfaction and Fear of Crime: A Test for Non-Recursive Effects'. *Canadian Journal of Criminology,* 27, 1-13.

Sims, A. and Symonds, R.L. (1975). 'Psychiatric Referrals from the Police'. *British Journal of Psychiatry,* 127, 171-178.

Skinner, L.J., Berry, K.K. and Griffith, S.E. (1995). 'Generalizability and Specificity of the Stigma Associated with the Mental Illness Label: A Reconsideration 25 Years Later'. *Journal of Community Psychology,* 23, 3-17.

Smith, C.J. (1981). 'Residential Proximity and Community Acceptance of the Mentally Ill'. *Journal of Operational Psychiatry,* 12, 2-12.

Smith, H. W. (1975). *Strategies of Social Research: The Methodological Imagination.* London: Prentice/Hall International, Inc.

Smith, J.J. (1969). 'Psychiatric Hospital Experience and Attitudes Toward 'Mental Illness'. *Journal of Consulting and Clinical Psychology,* 33, 302-306.

Socall, D.W. and Holtgraves, T. (1992). 'Attitudes Towards the Mentally Ill: The Effects of Label and Beliefs'. *Sociological Quarterly,* 33, 435-445.

Spitzer, A. and Cameron, C. (1995). 'School-Age Children's Perceptions of Mental Illness'. *Western Journal of Nursing Research,* 17, 398-415.

Spry, W.B. (1984). 'Schizophrenia and Crime'. In Craft and Craft (Eds.). *Mentally Abnormal Offenders.* London: Bailliere Tindall.

Stacey, B. (1978). *Political Socialization in Western Society.* London: Edward Arnold.

Stacey, B. (1985). 'Economic Socialization'. *Annual Review of Political Science,* 2, 114-128.

Star, S. (1952). *What the Public Thinks About Mental Health and Mental Illness.* Paper presented at the annual meeting of the National Association for Mental Health, November 19. Chicago: University of Chicago Microfilms.

Star, S. (1955). *The Public's Idea About Mental Illness.* Paper presented at the annual meeting of the National Association for Mental Health, November 5. Chicago: National Opinion Research Centre (NORC) Library.

Steadman, H.J. and Cocozza, J. (1978). 'Selective Reporting and the Public's Misconceptions of the Criminally Insane'. *Public Opinion Quarterly,* 41, 523-533.

Struening, E.L. and Cohen, J. (1963). 'Factorial Invariance and Other Psychometric Characteristics of Five Opinions About Mental Illness Factors'. *Educational and Psychological Measurement,* 23, 289-298.

Sudman, S. (1983). 'Applied Sampling'. Rossi, P.H., Wright, J.D. and Anderson, A.B. (1983). *Handbook of Survey Research.* London: Academic Press, Inc.

Sudman, S. and Bradburn, N.M. (1983). *Asking Questions: A Practical Guide to Questionnaire Design.* San Francisco: Jossey-Bass.

Swarte, J.H. (1969). 'Stereotypes and Attitudes About the Mentally Ill'. In Freeman, H. (Ed.). *Progress in Mental Health.* London: Churchill.

Swingle, P.G. (1965). 'Relatives' Concepts of Mental Patients'. *Mental Hygiene,* 49, 461-465.

Sydiaha, D. (1971). 'An Idiographic Perspective in Mission-Oriented Research'. *The Canadian Psychologist,* 12, 287-293.

Szasz, T. (1960). 'The Myth of Mental Illness'. *American Psychologist,* 15, 113-118.

Szasz, T. (1961). *The Myth of Mental Illness.* New York: Harper.

Szasz, T. (1985). In Bean, P. (Ed.). *Mental Illness: Changes and Trends.* Chichester: Wiley & Sons.

Szasz, T. (1987). *The Myth of Mental Illness: The Foundations of a Theory of Personal Contact.* London: Grafton Books.

Taylor, M.S. and Dear, M.J. (1981). 'Scaling Community Attitudes Toward the Mentally Ill'. *Schizophrenia Bulletin,* 7, 225-248.

Taylor, J. and Taylor, D. (1989). *Mental Health in the 1990s: From Custody to Care?* London: Office of Health Economics.

Thibout, J. and Kelly, H. (1959). *The Social Psychology of Groups.* New York: Wiley.

Thompson, J.W. (1994). 'Trends in the Development of Psychiatric Services, 1844-1994'. *Hospital and Community Psychiatry,* 45, 987-992.

Townsend, J.M. (1975). 'Cultural Conceptions and Mental Illness: A Controlled Comparison of Germany and America'. *Journal of Nervous and Mental Diseases*, 160, 409-421.

Tringo, J.L. (1970). 'The Hierarchy of Preference Towards Disability Groups'. *Journal of Special Education*, 4, 295-306.

Trute, B., Tefft, B. and Segall, A. (1989). 'Social Rejection of the Mentally Ill: A Replication Study of Public Attitude'. *Social Psychiatry and Psychiatric Epidemiology*, 24, 69-76.

Tucker, C. (1979). 'Underutilization of Mental Health Services by Blacks: Strategies for Change'. *University of Florida Psychological and Vocational Counselling Centre Monograph Series*, 3, 1-5.

Tyrer, P. (1987). 'Benefits and Risks of Benzodiazepines'. *Proceedings of the Royal Society of Medicine*, 114, 7-11.

Valentine, E. (1982). *Conceptual Issues in Psychology*. London: Allen & Unwin.

Varsity (Friday 10, December 1993). *Graduate Edition*. University of Cambridge.

Walker, N. and Hough, M. (1988). *Public Attitudes to Sentencing: Surveys in Five Countries*. Aldershot: Gower.

Walsh, A. (1990). *Statistics for the Social Sciences: With Computer Applications*. New York: Harper & Row.

Warr, P. (1982). 'Psychological Aspects of Employment and Unemployment'. *Psychological Medicine*, 12, 7-11.

Watson, W. and Grounds, A.T. (1993 Eds.). *The Mentally Disordered Offender in an Era of Community Care: New Directions in Provision*. Cambridge: Cambridge University Press.

Wehler, R. (1979). 'Attitudes Toward Mental Illness and Dependency Among Hospitalized Psychiatric Patients'. *Psychological Reports*, 44, 283-286.

Weiss, M. (1985). 'Children's Attitudes Towards Mental Illness as Assessed by the Opinions About Mental Illness Scale'. *Psychological Reports*, 57, 251.

Weiss, M. F. (1986). 'Children's Attitudes Towards Mental Illness: A Developmental Analysis'. *Psychological Reports*, 58, 11-20.

Weiss, M. (1994). 'Children's Attitudes Toward the Mentally Ill: An 8 Year Longitudinal Follow-up'. *Psychological Reports*, 74, 51-56.

Weissman, M.M. and Klerman, G.L. (1977). 'Sex Differences and the Epidemiology of Depression'. *Archives of General Psychiatry*, 34, 98-111.

Weissman, M.M. and Klerman, G.L. (1985). 'Gender and Depression'. *Trends in Neurosciences*, 8, 416-419.

Westbrook, M., Legge, V. and Pennay, M. (1993). 'Attitudes Towards Disabilities in a Multicultural Society'. *Social Science and Medicine*, 36, 615-623.

Whatley, C. (1959). 'Social Attitudes Towards Discharged Mental Patients'. *Social Problems*, 6, 313-320.

Whitman, J.R. and Duffey, R.F. (1961). 'The Relationship Between Type of Therapy Received and a Patient's Perception of His Illness'. *Journal of Nervous and Mental Disorders*, 113, 288-292.

Wicker, A. (1969). 'Attitudes Versus Actions: The Relationship of Verbal and Overt Behavioral Responses to Attitude Objects'. *Journal of Social Issues*, 25, 41-78.

Willcocks, A. (1968). Cited by: Anon. (1968). 'Public Attitudes to Mental Health Education'. (Editorial). *British Medical Journal*, 5584, 69-70.

Williams, E. (1971). *Models of Madness*. New Society.

Williams, P. and Dickinson, J. (1993). 'Fear of Crime: Read All About It? The Relationship Between Newspaper Crime Reporting and Fear of Crime'. *British Journal of Criminology*, 17, 398-415.

Williams, J. and Williams, H.M. (1961). 'Attitudes Towards Mental Illness, Anomia and Authoritarianism Among State Hospital Nursing Students and Attendance'. *Mental Hygiene*, 45, 418-424.

Wing, J.K. (1978). *Reasoning About Madness*. Oxford: Oxford University Press.

Wolff, G., Pathare, S., Craig, T. and Leff, J. (1996a). 'Who's In the Lion's Den? The Community's Perception of Community Care for the Mentally Ill'. *Psychiatric Bulletin of the Royal College of Psychiatrists*, 20, 68-71.

Wolff, G., Pathare, S., Craig, T. and Leff, J. (1996b). 'Community Attitudes to Mental Illness'. *British Journal of Psychiatry*, 168, 183-190.

Wolff, G., Pathare, S., Craig, T. and Leff, J. (1996c). 'Community Knowledge of Mental Illness and Reaction to Mentally Ill People'. *British Journal of Psychiatry*, 168, 191-198.

Appendix

Abbreviations

For presentation purposes several abbreviations have been used to represent specific variables. In designing these summary terms, every effort was made to ensure that they are as logical and comprehensible as possible.

ANOVA	Analysis of variance
Col%	Column percentage
Depr'n/Schiz'a	Depression or Schizophrenia
Dts-pat	Duties of the patient
Dts-soc	Duties of society
F-hosp	Function of the hospital
Grpsvd	Groups surveyed
KnownMDP	Known a mentally disordered person
Mental H Staff	Mental health staff
Polit'l Party	Political party
Prob'n Offic's	Probation officers
Social Work's	Social workers
RelatMDP	Relationship to a mentally disodered offender
Rts-pat	Rights of the patient
Rts-soc	Rights of society
Std-dev	Standard deviation
Treat	Treatment

The measuring instrument: dimensions and statements relating to each model

MEDICAL (ORGANIC) MODEL

Dimension	Statement
Aetiology	Tom's depr'n/schiz'a was caused by medical problems such as brain damage.
Behaviour	Tom's behaviour clearly shows how mentally ill he really is.
Treatment:1	Tom's depr'n/schiz'a should be treated through the use of surgery.
Treatment:2	Tom's depr'n/schiz'a should be treated with medical drugs.
F-hosp	Tom should be sent to a mental hospital which provides care like a normal hospital.
Prognosis	A great deal can be done in order to significantly improve Tom's depr'n/schiz'a.
Rts-pat:1	Tom should NOT be blamed for his actions since he has little control over what he does.
Rts-pat:2	Tom should NOT be held responsible for his depr'n/schiz'a as he could not help becoming sick.
Dts-pat	Tom has a duty to accept medical treatment.
Rts-soc:1	Society has a right to restrain Tom against his will while he is a danger to the public.
Rts-soc:2	Society has a right to force Tom to take any medical treatment which might improve his depr'n/schiz'a, no matter what the side-effects may be.
Dts-soc	Society has a duty to show Tom sympathy and understanding.

MORAL (COGNITIVE-BEHAVIOURAL) MODEL

Dimension	Statement
Aetiology	Tom's depr'n/schiz'a was caused by learning from others with similarly strange and bizarre behaviour.
Behaviour	Tom's behaviour can only be described as bad and wrong.
Treatment:1	Tom's depr'n/schiz'a should be treated by punishing his bad and rewarding his good behaviour.

Treatment:2   Tom's depr'n/schiz'a should be treated by teaching him the proper way to act and think.
F-hosp:1   Tom should be sent to a mental hospital which teaches him how to behave more responsibly.
F-hosp:2   Tom should be sent to a mental hospital which acts like a prison.
Prognosis   A great deal can be done in order to significantly improve Tom's depr'n/schiz'a.
Rts-pat   Tom has the right to be released when his behaviour is acceptable to society.
Dts-pat   Tom has a duty to take responsibility for his own actions and their outcomes.
Rts-soc   Society has a right to punish and imprison Tom as his behaviour clearly breaks both moral and legal standards.
Dts-soc   Society has a duty to provide people and places in order to teach Tom how to behave properly.

PSYCHOSOCIAL MODEL

Dimension	Statement
Aetiology	Tom's depr'n/schiz'a was caused by a number of social stresses such as money worries.
Behaviour	Tom's behaviour is a clear example of how out of control society really is.
Treatment:1	Tom's depr'n/schiz'a should be treated by improving the particular environment in which he lives.
Treatment:2	Tom's depr'n/schiz'a should be treated by producing a more comfortable and less stressful society.
F-hosp	Mental hospitals often end up as no more than shelters for people like Tom.
Prognosis	A great deal can be done in order to significantly improve Tom's depr'n/schiz'a.
Rts-pat	Tom has the right to be cared for as a victim of a stressful society.
Dts-pat	Tom has a duty to co-operate with any social help offered which is likely to improve the environment in which he lives.
Rts-soc	Society has NO rights over Tom as society in general was responsible for causing Tom's depr'n/schiz'a in the first place.
Dts-soc	Society has a duty to change so as to reduce the social stresses and disadvantages that Tom may be suffering.

Table A1
Frequency distribution of the six groups surveyed

Group Surveyed	Frequency	Percent	Valid Percent	Cum Percent
Students	335	34.9	34.9	34.9
Political Members	145	15.1	15.1	49.9
Police	148	15.4	15.4	65.3
Social Workers	81	8.4	8.4	73.8
Probation Officers	107	11.1	11.1	84.9
Mental Health Staff	145	15.1	15.1	100.0
Total	961	100	100	

Table A2
Cross-tab of gender by levels of group surveyed

Count Col % Gender	Group Surveyed						Row Total
	Stud-ents	Polit'l Party	Police	Social Work's	Prob'n Offic's	Mental H.Staff	
Male	234	97	125	23	65	50	594
	69.9	66.9	84.5	28.4	60.7	34.5	61.8
Female	101	48	23	58	42	95	367
	30.1	33.1	15.5	71.6	39.3	65.5	38.2
Column Totals	335	145	148	81	107	145	961
	34.9	15.1	15.4	8.4	11.1	15.1	100.0

Table A3a
Summary of age by levels of group surveyed

Group Surveyed	Mean	Std Dev	Min-Max	Cases
For Entire Population	34.47	11.43	18-80	953
Students	26.36	6.14	20-67	335
Political Members	44.24	15.32	18-80	145
Police	34.21	8.52	21-58	146
Social Workers	40.36	8.19	25-58	80
Probation Officers	39.34	10.06	23-65	105
Mental Health Staff	36.94	8.24	22-63	142

Table A3b
Cross-tab of age by levels of group surveyed

Count Col % / Age	Group Surveyed						Row Total
	Stud-ents	Polit'l Party	Police	Social Work's	Prob'n Offic's	Mental H. Staff	
18 - 35	316	42	93	23	42	66	582
	94.3	29.0	63.7	28.8	40.0	46.5	61.1
=> 36	19	103	53	57	63	76	371
	5.7	71.0	36.3	71.3	60.0	53.5	38.9
Column Totals	335	145	146	80	105	142	953
	34.9	15.1	15.4	8.4	11.1	15.1	100.0

Table A4a
Cross-tab of knowing a mentally ill person by levels of group surveyed

Count Col %	Group Surveyed						Row Total
Known MDP	Stud-ents	Polit'l Party	Police	Social Work's	Prob'n Offic's	Mental H.Staff	
Yes	137 40.9	73 50.3	69 47.3	51 63.0	72 68.6	106 74.1	508 53.2
No	198 59.1	72 49.7	77 52.7	30 37.0	33 31.4	37 25.9	447 46.8
Column Totals	335 35.1	145 15.2	146 15.3	81 8.5	105 11.0	142 15.0	955 100.0

Table A4b
Cross-tab of relationship with the mentally ill by levels of group surveyed

Count Col %	Group Surveyed						Row Total
Relat MDP	Stud-ents	Polit'l Party	Police	Social Work's	Prob'n Offic's	Mental H.Staff	
Friend	54 40.9	23 31.9	22 32.4	19 37.3	23 31.9	43 40.6	184 36.7
Yourself	2 1.5	4 5.6	1 1.5	3 5.9		1 0.9	11 2.2
Persn in Com'ity	34 25.8	20 27.8	32 47.1	19 37.3	31 43.1	37 34.9	173 34.5
Relative	42 31.8	25 34.7	13 19.1	10 19.6	18 25.0	25 23.6	133 26.5
Column Totals	132 26.3	72 14.4	68 13.6	51 10.2	72 14.4	106 21.2	501 100.0

Table A5
Cross-tab of offered further information by levels of group surveyed

Count Col %	Group Surveyed						Row Total
Offered Inform'n	Stud-ents	Polit'l Party	Police	Social Work's	Prob'n Offic's	Mental H.Staff	
Yes	128 38.2	45 31.0	39 26.4	22 27.2	30 28.0	30 20.7	294 30.6
No	207 61.8	100 69.0	109 73.6	59 72.8	77 72.0	115 79.3	667 69.4
Column Totals	335 34.9	145 15.1	148 15.4	81 8.4	107 11.1	146 15.1	961 100.0

Table A6
Summary of years of service by levels of group surveyed

Group Surveyed	Mean	Std Dev	Cases
For Entire Population	11.54	7.99	328
Police	11.36	8.66	145
Social Workers	12.42	6.61	79
Probation Officers	11.14	8.03	104

Table A7
Frequency distribution: course being studied

Course Studied	Frequency	Percent	Valid Percent	Cum Percent
Doctoral	260	77.6	78.3	78.3
Masters	51	15.2	15.4	93.7
Other	21	6.3	6.3	100.0
Total	335	100.0	100.0	

Table A8
Frequency distribution: year of completing FT/education

Year of Completing FT/Education	Frequency	Percent	Valid Percent	Cum Percent
< 15	9	6.2	6.2	6.2
15	6	4.1	4.1	10.3
16	16	11.0	11.0	21.4
17	9	6.2	6.2	27.6
18	20	13.8	13.8	41.0
19	15	10.3	10.3	51.7
=> 20	70	48.3	48.3	100.0
Total	145	100.0	100.0	

Table A9
Frequency distribution: police officers' rank

Course Studied	Frequency	Percent	Valid Percent	Cum Percent
Constable	109	73.6	74.1	74.1
Sergeant	29	19.6	19.7	93.9
Inspector or above	9	6.2	6.1	100.0
Total	148	100.0	100.0	

Table A10
Summary of Person's chi square values and significance levels

Independent Variables	Chi-Square Value	Expected Frequency	Signif'ce Level
Group Surveyed	6.48382	19.049	.97043
Gender	2.94513	86.308	.40016
Age	1.82085	86.813	.61041
Known a Mentally Ill Person	.51812	104.378	.91489
Type of Disorder	5.67261	230.835	.45134
Type of Offence	5.67262	230.835	.45134

Table A11
Mean and percentage agreement scores for the nine dimensions for the three models across the whole sample

(N = 961) Dimensions	Theoretical Models		
	Medical	Moral	Social
Aetiology	3.48 (55.5)	0.90 (3.4)	3.03 (44.0)
Behaviour	4.20 (71.1)	1.30 (17.3)	1.68 (18.2)
Treatment:1	1.06 (6.3)	1.40 (13.8)	4.16 (77.2)
Treatment:2	3.88 (67.0)	2.80 (43.2)	3.28 (55.2)
Prognosis	4.19 (67.7)	4.19 (67.7)	4.19 (67.7)
Function of the Hospital:1	3.76 (65.7)	2.28 (35.5)	3.39 (57.4)
Function of the Hospital:2	-- (--)	1.54 (22.7)	-- (--)
Rights of the Patient:1	4.03 (68.1)	4.63 (79.8)	4.18 (75.0)
Rights of the Patient:2	4.54 (78.7)	-- (--)	-- (--)
Duties of the Patient	3.84 (69.1)	3.54 (65.6)	3.85 (70.0)
Rights of Society:1	2.01 (28.9)	1.49 (21.6)	1.17 (9.0)
Rights of Society:2	4.82 (88.9)	-- (--)	-- (--)
Duties of Society	4.79 (86.4)	3.51 (62.8)	2.93 (47.6)

Scale = Strongly Agree 6 5 4 3 2 1 0 Strongly Disagree

Table A12a
Correlation matrix for the various dimensions of the medical (organic) model

Correlat'n Matrix	Aetiology	Behaviour	Treat:1	Treat:2	F-Hosp	Prognosis
Aetiology	1.0000					
Behaviour	.3819**	1.0000				
Treat:1	.1144**	-.0582	1.0000			
Treat:2	.4229**	.4062**	.0412	1.0000		
F-Hosp	.0812*	.1997**	.0614	.1704**	1.0000	
Prognosis	-.1857**	-.0102	-.1874**	.0338	.0215	1.0000
Rts-Soc:1	.2596**	.2479**	.0854*	.2545**	.0181	-.1259**
Rts-Soc:2	.2099**	.3060**	.0417	.2895**	.1191**	-.0377
Rts-Pat:1	.0578	.1350**	-.0992*	.1115**	.1671**	.0472
Rts-Pat:2	.0472	.1021**	-.1029**	.1352**	.1430**	.0794*
Dts-Pat	.2194**	.2655**	.1263**	.2050**	.0793*	-.0980*
Dts-Soc	.0535	.0460	-.0645	.1215**	.0865*	.0913*

Continued	Rts-Soc:1	Rts-Soc:2	Rts-Pat:1	Rts-Pat:2	Dts-Pat	Dts-
Rts-Soc:1	1.0000					
Rts-Soc:2	.2408**	1.0000				
Rtpt:1	-.0827*	-.0867*	1.0000			
Rtpt:2	-.1466**	-.0084	.5190**	1.0000		
Dtpt	.3439**	.3258**	-.1263**	-.0775*	1.0000	
Dtsoc	-.1409**	.0013	.4189**	.3984**	-.0303	1.0000

Minimum Pairwise N of Cases: 952
1-Tailed Signif: * - .01 ** - .001

Table A12b
Correlation matrix for the various dimensions of the moral (cognitive-behavioural) model

Correlat'n Matrix	Aetiology	Behaviour	Treat:1	Treat:2	F-hosp:1	F-hosp:2
Aetiology	1.0000					
Behaviour	.1864**	1.0000				
Treat:1	.1865**	.3951**	1.0000			
Treat:2	.1957**	.1525**	.2565**	1.0000		
F-Hosp:1	.1627**	.3862**	.4900	.3420**	1.0000	
F-Hosp:2	.1229**	.4708**	.3575**	.0976*	.3941**	1.0000
Prognosis	-.1220**	-.1761**	-.2116**	-.1419**	-.1729**	-.1108**
Rts-Soc	.1619**	.5489**	.4023**	.1537**	.4201**	.5898**
Rts-Pat	-.1484**	-.3058**	-.2578**	.1720*	-.1599**	-.3403**
Dts-Pat	.0552	.2691**	.2465**	.0455	.2825**	.2988**
Dts-Soc	.1804**	.1686**	.2869**	.4648**	.4149**	.1518**

Continued	Prognosis	Rts-Soc	Rts-Pat	Dts-Pat	Dts-Soc
Prognosis	1.0000				
Rts-Soc	-.1773**	1.0000			
Rts-pat	-.0967*	-.3309**	1.0000		
Dts-pat	.0080	.3329**	-.2022**	1.0000	
Dts-soc	-.1722**	.2469**	.0429	.0945*	1.0000

Minimum Pairwise N of Cases: 949
1-Tailed Signif: * - .01 ** - .001

Table A12c
Correlation matrix for the various dimensions of the
psychosocial model

Correlat'n Matrix	Aetiology	Behaviour	Treat:1	Treat:2	F-hosp	Prognosis
Aetiology	1.0000					
Behaviour	.2822**	1.0000				
Treat:1	.3782**	.1747**	1.0000			
Treat:2	.4362**	.3090**	.3647**	1.0000		
F-Hosp	.0523	.1199**	.0737	.1207**	1.0000	
Prognosis	-.0311	-.1090**	.0828*	-.0785*	-.1187**	1.0000
Rts-Soc	.2054**	.2094**	.1569**	.2167**	.0596	-.0693
Rts-Pat	.2511**	.1657**	.3369**	.2825**	.0701	.0314
Dts-Pat	.0685	.1331**	.0577	.1537**	.1559**	-.1078**
Dts-Soc	.1850**	.3041**	.3027**	.4413**	.0751	-.0424

Continued	Rts-Soc	Rts-Pat	Dts-Pat	Dts-Soc
Rts-Soc	1.0000			
Rts-pat	.1468**	1.0000		
Dts-pat	-.1441**	.0075	1.0000	
Dts-soc	.2277**	.3366**	.1039**	1.0000

Minimum Pairwise N of Cases: 950
1-Tailed Signif: * - .01 ** - .001

Table A13

Coefficient values and questionnaire items associated with each factor

Factor one: 'sick' role

Factor Coeff	Item Number	Model	Dimen-sion
0.74626	21	Medical	Rts-pat:1
0.61802	4	Medical	Rts-pat:2
0.64182	28	Medical	Dts-soc
0.55810	25	Moral	Rts-pat
-0.66898	13	Moral	Behaviour
-0.61567	6	Moral	Treat:1
-0.74626	10	Moral	Rts-soc
-0.55423	3	Moral	F-hops:1
-0.67405	17	Moral	F-hosp:2
-0.50606	31	Moral	Dts-pat

Total variance accounted for = 21.4%
Alpha coefficient value = 0.8408

Factor two: medical-control

Factor Coeff	Item Number	Model	Dimen-sion
0.55671	9	Medical	Aetiology
0.62740	19	Medical	Behaviour
0.63543	26	Medical	Treat:2
0.61407	15	Medical	Rts-soc:1
0.52291	12	Medical	Rts-soc:2
0.62704	23	Medical	Dts-pat
0.47961	18	Social	Dts-pat
-0.48262	27	Social	Rts-soc

Total variance accounted for = 12.5%
Alpha coefficient value = 0.7796

Factor three: social-treatment

Factor Coeff	Item Number	Model	Dimen-sion
0.52328	24	Social	Aetiology
0.70620	16	Social	Treat:1
0.58748	30	Social	Treat:2
0.58196	2	Social	Rts-pat
0.62105	14	Social	Dts-soc
0.57183	8	Moral	Dts-soc

Total variance accounted for = 11.4%
Alpha coefficient value = 0.6924

Table A14a

Summary of ANOVA main and interaction effect mean scores for factor one - 'sick' role

Independent variables		Main effects	Two-way interaction effects Depression	Schizophrenia	Two-way interaction effects No-offence	Offence
Grand mean		4.25				
Disorder	Depression	4.15				
	Schizophrenia	4.35				
Offence	Absence	4.71	4.60	4.81		
	Presence	3.80	3.67	3.93		
Grpsvd	Students	4.04	3.92	4.15	4.62	3.50
	Polit'l Party	4.15	4.00	4.32	4.59	3.66
	Police	3.76	3.78	3.73	4.38	3.15
	Social Workers	4.62	4.51	4.74	4.96	4.23
	Probation	4.78	4.69	4.87	5.07	4.46
	Mental H. Staff	4.74	4.60	4.91	4.88	4.63
Gender	Male	4.17	4.13	4.22	4.67	3.67
	Female	4.36	4.17	4.55	4.74	4.00
Age	18 - 35	4.16	4.06	4.25	4.67	3.62
	=> 36	4.39	4.28	4.50	4.75	4,06
Known	Yes	4.46	4.31	4.62	4.82	4.10
MDP	No	3.99	3.95	4.05	4.55	3.47

Table A14b

Summary of ANOVA main and interaction effect mean scores for factor two - medical-control

Independent variables		Main effects	Two-way interaction effects		Two-way interaction effects	
			Depression	Schizophrenia	No-offence	Offence
Grand mean		3.87				
Disorder	Depression	3.73				
	Schizophrenia	4.00				
offence	Absence	3.49	3.31	3.69		
	Presence	4.22	4.18	4.26		
Grpsvd	Students	3.62	3.65	4.00	3.43	4.18
	Polit'l Party	4.11	3.98	4.25	3.76	4.52
	Police	3.98	4.02	3.94	3.72	4.23
	Social Workers	3.41	3.16	3.69	3.20	3.68
	Probation	3.44	3.15	3.72	3.03	3.91
	Mental H Staff	4.09	4.07	4.13	3.64	4.48
Gender	Male	3.88	3.76	4.00	3.49	4.26
	Female	3.82	3.68	3.97	3.48	4.16
Age	18 - 35	3.79	3.66	3.93	3.43	4.17
	=> 36	3.96	3.85	4.08	3.59	4.30
Known	Yes	3.84	3.77	3.92	3.46	4.24
MDP	No	3.87	3.69	4.06	3.52	4.20

Table A14c

Summary of ANOVA main and interaction effect mean scores for factor three - social-treatment

Independent variables		Main effects	Two-way interaction effects		Two-way interaction effects	
			Depression	Schizophrenia	No-offence	Offence
Grand mean		3.50				
Disorder	Depression	3.60				
	Schizophrenia	3.40				
offence	Absence	3.64	3.71	3.56		
	Presence	3.37	3.49	3.26		
Grpsvd	Students	3.56	3.64	3.47	3.64	3.49
	Polit'l Party	3.55	3.75	3.34	3.79	3.29
	Police	3.52	3.54	3.49	3.57	3.47
	Social Workers	3.74	3.78	3.70	3.80	3.66
	Probation	3.77	3.81	3.73	4.11	3.39
	Mental H Staff	2.99	3.20	2.75	3.04	2.95
Gender	Male	3.62	3.73	3.49	3.79	3.44
	Female	3.32	3.38	3.27	3.39	3.26
Age	18 - 35	3.53	3.65	3.40	3.63	3.42
	=> 36	3.47	3.54	3.40	3.66	3.30
Known	Yes	3.51	3.59	3.42	3.69	3.32
MDP	No	3.51	3.62	3.38	3.59	3.43

Table A15
Summary of ANOVA main and interaction effect results for each of the three factors

Independent variables main and interaction effects	'Sick' role factor		Medical-control factor		Social-treatment factor	
	F-ratio	Signif of F	F-ratio	Signif of F	F-ratio	Signif of F
MAIN EFFECTS						
Disorder	14.884	0.000	17.663	0.000	8.212	0.004
Offence	215.521	0.000	150.788	0.000	11.782	0.001
Group surveyed	18.523	0.000	12.683	0.000	7.943	0.000
Gender	0.297	0.586	0.232	0.630	11.116	0.001
Age	0.735	0.392	6.421	0.010	0.618	0.432
KnownMDP	22.133	0.000	0.000	0.997	0.639	0.424
2-WAY INTERACTIONS						
Disorder Offence	0.223	0.637	7.620	0.006	0.476	0.490
Disorder Group Surveyed	0.602	0.699	2.756	0.008	2.908	0.011
Disorder Gender	1.992	0.159	0.697	0.404	1.838	0.176
Disorder Age	0.022	0.881	0.653	0.419	5.702	0.027
Disorder KnownMDP	0.979	0.323	2.662	0.103	0.918	0.338
Offence Group Surveyed	3.912	0.002	0.880	0.494	0.776	0.567
Offence Gender	0.007	0.933	0.482	0.488	0.985	0.321
Offence Age	2.351	0.126	0.452	0.502	0.329	0.566
Offence KnownMDP	3.941	0.047	0.302	0.583	0.540	0.463

Table A16

Thematic content analysis for each group surveyed

Model	Theme	Two Lay Groups	Police	Social/ Prob'n	Mental H.Staff	Two Lay Groups	Police	Social/ Prob'n	Mental H.Staff	Two Lay Groups	Police	Social/ Prob'n	Mental H.Staff
'Sick' role	Sympathy	21	5	13	8	7	3	5	5	14	2	8	3
	Responsibility	27	11	16	14	19	8	10	9	8	3	6	5
Medical-control	Individual Disorder	11	2	1	3	8		1	1	3	2		2
	Previous Experience	6	4	6	3	4	4	5	1	2		1	2
	Aetiology&treat	29		4	5	8		1	3	21		3	3
	Labels	12	4		1	12	4		1		4		
	Stigma	17	4	9	5	2		1	2	15	8	8	3
	Control	35	10	13	11	9	2	5	5	26	5	8	6
Social-treat	Aetiology	13	1	9	2	7	1	6	2	6	2	3	2
	Care in Comun'ty	16	13	17	7	10	8	8	5	6	5	9	3
	Environmental-treatment												
General comments	Education	29	16	11	7	18	14	5	4	11	4	6	3
	Multi-agency	14	7	4	3	8	2	2	2	6	1	2	1
	working	3	5	15	6					3	4	6	4
	Religion	5		1		4		9	2	1		1	
		Data for all respondents =511				For 2 depression cases = 262				For 2 schizophr'c cases = 249			

218

Table A16a
Overview of the substantive content of each theme

Model	Theme	Description
'Sick' Role	Sympathy	The mentally ill should be treated with care, respect, compassion, understanding and as human beings. They are sick just like the physically ill.
	Responsibility	The mentally ill can control their behaviour some of the time. They should be held accountable for their behaviour. They deserve some form of punishment. They should learn to manage their problems. They should have some control over their treatment.
	Individual-Disorder	There is more than one type of mental illness. There are various stages of mental illness. Mental disorder can exist with other problems such as drug addiction.
	Previous Experience	Respondents discussed personal involvement with depressive and schizophrenic sufferers.
Medical-control	Aetiology/treatment	Mental illness is caused by internal physical/bio-chemical problems. It is inherited, genetic or congenital. It should be treated with medication.
	Labels	The way in which the respondents referred to the depressive patient ie, sad, very unhappy, etc but not as mentally ill.
	Stigma	The mentally ill are dangerous, unpredictable, unusual, different from 'normal' people. Such negative evaluations were expressed at both a latent and manifest level.
	Control	Expresses the need to manage the mental patient within a secure environment or through the use of medication.
Social-treatment	Aetiology	Refers to social factors such as work and family stress, bereavement, lack of community, having no friends, etc as primary causes of mental illness.
	Care in the Community	Relates primarily to concerns that care in the community has failed/is failing in practice
	Environmental-Treatment	Refers to the need to improve community based care programmes. Provide help to families who look after the mentally ill. The general need for a more comprehensive system of care.
General	Comments on	The need for more mental health education, the role of religion and issues in inter-agency co-operation.

Abbreviations used in the Bar Charts and Line Graphs:

Stud   Students
MPP   Members of a political party
Pol   Police
SW   Social workers
Prob   Probation officers
MHP   Mental health practitioners

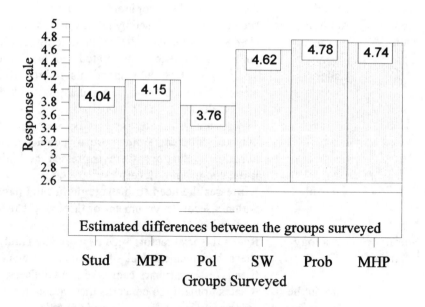

Figure A1 Bar chart of group surveyed data for factor one - 'sick' role

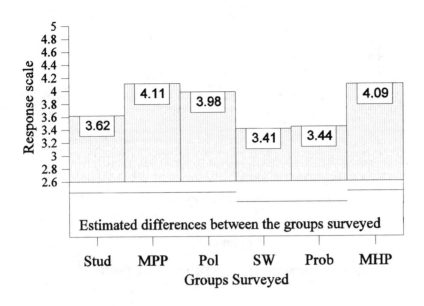

Figure A2 Bar chart of group surveyed data for factor two - medical-control

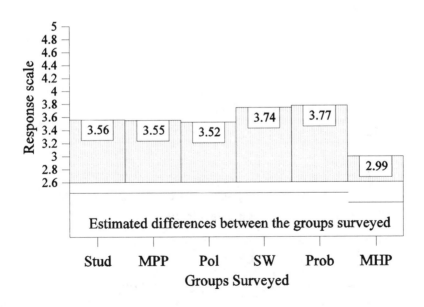

**Figure A3   Bar chart of group surveyed data for factor three - social-
treatment**

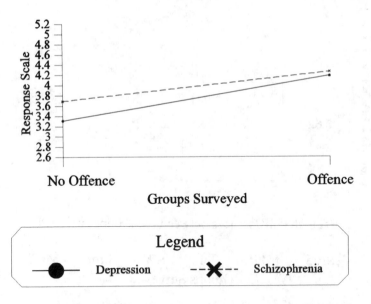

Figure A4 Line graph of the two way interaction effect (disorder by offence) for factor two - medical-control

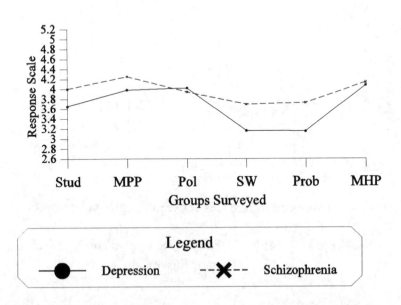

Figure A5 Line graph of the two way interaction effect (disorder by group surveyed) for factor two - medical-control

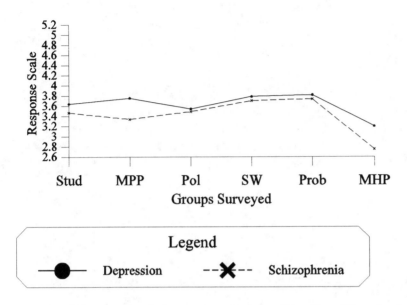

Figure A6   Line graph of the two way interaction effect (disorder by group surveyed) for factor three - social-treatment

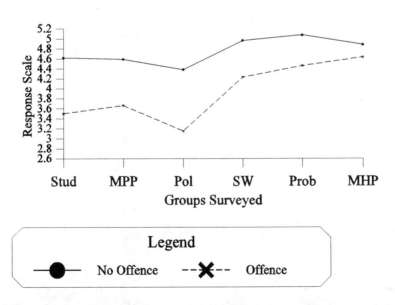

Figure A7   Line graph of the two way interaction effect (offence by group surveyed) for factor one - 'sick' role

Index